THREE-LEGGED FRIENDS

THREE-LEGGED FRIENDS

and other animals in a vet's life

CATLIN BARBER

SOUVENIR PRESS

ISBN 0 285 62962 X

Photoset in Great Britain by
Rowland Phototypesetting Ltd,
Bury St Edmunds, Suffolk
Printed in Great Britain by
Mackays of Chatham plc, Chatham, Kent

AUTHOR'S NOTE

Many years ago, I had a small poodle called Psyche. People who saw her name written down called her Persitchy, Pikey, Sicky or Pish. Those who heard me talking about her generally spelt her name 'Sikey'.

Remembering this trouble, I should explain that my lurcher's name is spelt 'Ceilidh' and pronounced 'Caley'.

1

His prison was small and smelly and very dark. He hated it, and at the top of his voice begged somebody to come and let him out. He shouted and yelled all day, but no one heard. He howled and cried all night, but nobody heeded.

The next day, it rained. At first, he licked thirstily at the water oozing under the door, but the oily puddle rapidly spread until it covered the floor. His frantic efforts to escape churned it into a thick, soupy mud which filled his eyes and ears and plastered itself all over his skinny body. He dug at the floor under the doorsill, biting at the wood in desperation, and the glutinous mess filled his mouth and made him choke and retch miserably.

His pleas that night were hoarse and despairing and, as a cold dawn light filled the sky outside, he gave up. Sprawled in the mud, he pressed his face against the door and closed his bleary eyes. The weary day wore on, and the breath lifting his meagre chest became ever more faint. An occasional shudder shook him. Remorselessly, quietly, death drew near.

*   *   *

The old tramp pounded angrily on the counter of the police station.

'I tell you, there IS somebody in there,' he insisted.

'I 'eard 'em, night afore last--fair made my blood run cold, it did.'

Sergeant Hudson leaned towards him, realised suddenly why the old man was called 'Dirty Harry', and hastily stepped back.

'And I tell you I personally checked the place after we ejected those squatters last week. There's nobody there.'

'Well, will you come with me and have another look? Just to make sure, like?'

'As a matter of fact, one of my officers is in that area now. I'll call him up, and get him to meet you there.'

Harry hurried away, muttering darkly to himself about people who thought they knew it all, just because they wore a uniform. Behind him, the sergeant sprayed air freshener all round the office, muttering darkly to himself about dirty old men who heard strange noises when they were drunk, and—phew! When did the old boy last have a bath?

*   *   *

Constable Jefferies pushed at the front door and stepped into the derelict old house, wrinkling his nose in disgust. The squatters had gone, but they had left filth behind them. He peered into each echoing room in turn, but found nothing but dirt and debris.

'What's out the back?' he asked Harry. 'You've kipped here a few times, so don't pretend you don't know.'

'There's the kazi,' Harry replied. 'Outside lav. We didn't use it much.'

The young policeman was ready to believe this. Judging by the smell, they had mostly used the corners of the rooms.

'Might as well check the back yard,' he said, and emerged thankfully into the relatively fresh air.

'Hello!' he exclaimed. 'Why has that old shed got bricks against the door?'

'That's the kazi,' declared the tramp. 'Probably trying to stop the stink getting out.' He chuckled wheezily as he kicked the bricks away and hauled the door open. He peered inside.

'Nothin' in 'ere,' he announced, "cept a lot of mud on the—oh, my Gawd!' He stopped in dismay and gasped. 'Pore little bleeder! Must 'ave bin 'ere for days. Too late now, it's dead as a flippin' doornail.'

The policeman pushed him aside and looked into the malodorous shed. He winced at the prostrate corpse.

'The squatters must have left it behind,' he said.

Harry scratched his head in amazement. 'Never 'ave thought such a tiddly liddle runt could 'ave made all that row.'

'There's a pile of old newspapers in the kitchen, Harry. Fetch us a few, there's a good chap. I can at least see he gets a decent burial.'

He spread papers on the ground, gingerly picked up the dirty little body, and almost dropped it again when a small eye suddenly opened, regarding him fixedly, and a long stringy tail began to twitch frantically.

As he left the house, a small newspaper-wrapped bundle tucked carefully under his arm, Constable Jefferies felt unmanly tears prickling his eyelids as the puppy, trying to lick his rescuer's hand with a cracked and dirty tongue, croaked his incoherent, heartfelt thanks.

*   *   *

I was in general veterinary practice in Marshton at the time, and used to call regularly at the local animal shelter. This was an ordinary boarding kennels, part of which was maintained by a local charity, to house homeless animals until new homes could be found for them. Zoë, the manageress, did not look the part. A former beautician, her elegant hairstyle and beautifully manicured hands gave no hint of her arduous and often mucky job. She had a brisk, no-nonsense approach to her temporary guests, which sometimes antagonised the sentimental ladies who held their coffee mornings and flag days to help support the animals. They did not realise that her highly enamelled exterior hid a heart of purest marshmallow, and that her little bungalow was bursting at the seams with animals no one else would adopt.

It was a lovely day. 'Morning, Zoë,' I carolled happily. 'Anything new?'

She was in a cheerful mood, too.

'Only two,' she replied. 'And I've got good homes for both of them.'

Silky, the first customer, was a pretty golden bitch with a

long plumed tail. Her owners had moved to a new housing estate where they were not allowed to keep dogs. She had been adopted by a family with two young children.

'They are sensible kids, and I've given them my usual lecture, about it being a live animal and not a teddy bear,' Zoë grinned. 'She's a kind, friendly soul. They should get on well.'

I gave Silky a clean bill of health, and Zoë put her back in the kennels to wait for her new family to collect her.

'Now, then,' she said, 'the other chap's a bit different.' She fetched what looked like a small brown velvet cushion, with a leg at each corner. A small pointed head was stuck on the end of an almost non-existent neck.

'This is Humphrey,' she announced. 'Part dachshund, part question mark. And I've got the perfect home for him.'

'Past his first youth, isn't he?' I was doubtful.

'That's the point. Miss Williams' beloved Peke died last week, and she's desolate without a dog, but she didn't want to take on a young one in case she died herself and left it homeless—she's nearly ninety, you know. Anyway, providing she doesn't overfeed this sluggish little lump,' she stroked the cushion affectionately, 'they should suit each other very well.'

All the time we were talking, I had been aware of an extraordinary noise in the background. A wailing child? An angry cat? A lost soul? I asked Zoë. She put on a hunted expression.

'It's a little lurcher the police found abandoned last week in an empty house. He can't stand or walk properly, his legs are all wobbly. I thought it was just starvation at first, but he's eating well, and still can't stay up on his feet. I was going to ask you to put him to sleep.'

I followed her into the yard, and she opened the door of the isolation kennel in the corner. A small projectile hurtled through the door and fell in a heap at my feet. Gathering his wobbly limbs beneath him, he propelled himself in-elegantly across the grass. His legs seemed to be made of india-rubber, and collapsed when he put weight on them. Seizing a small twig, he lolloped back to me, and placed it carefully on my shoe.

10

'For you,' he said, and rolled over onto his back, large ungainly paws dangling.

'Tickle me,' he demanded, laughing up at me.

I obliged, and he panted, open-mouthed, and lashed his remarkably long tail ecstatically. Pushing himself more or less upright again, he grabbed the twig and staggered off. I bent to pick him up and he thought it was a great game and tried to escape.

'Can't have it,' he declared, throwing the twig in the air and snapping at it. 'Mine!' He tripped over his front feet and fell in an untidy heap, yelping in dismay. I picked him up and carried him into the office, putting him on the table where he grinned with delight and wagged his incredible tail while I felt his limbs and joints.

'He's got rickets,' I diagnosed. 'He'll never be much of a dog. Always have big joints and crooked bones.'

He washed my hands energetically as I opened my case and took out a bottle and a syringe. He rolled on his back, almost falling off the table.

'Go on,' he demanded, 'tickle me again.'

I swallowed unhappily, carefully measured a dose into the syringe, then pushed the needle into the scruff of his neck and injected it.

'Ouch!' he yelled. 'That hurt!' Indignantly, he seized my hand with needle teeth, then apologetically licked it. I picked him up again and he put his head on my shoulder and was immediately and trustfully asleep. Zoë looked away.

'You usually inject into a vein, and they go straight off. How long will this take to—?' she stopped miserably.

I stroked the head on my shoulder. The puppy half woke, nipped the lobe of my ear absentmindedly, and went contentedly back to sleep again. I gazed out of the window.

'That was a dose of calcium and vitamin D,' I said casually. 'I'll leave some stuff to put on his food.'

Zoë gasped furiously. 'But—'

'But nothing,' I replied. 'I can't possibly kill this dog. He has tried so hard to live and enjoys it so much, and he trusts me.'

'Poppycock,' Zoë cried. 'They all trust you. They all enjoy

11

life. What's so special about this rather horrible little lurcher?'

I didn't know the answer to this.

'And what am I going to do with him?' Zoë clutched her head and groaned. 'I can't stand the noise much longer.'

The puppy woke up, yawning loudly, and demanded to be put down. He squirmed his way to the ground and gambolled ungracefully out onto the grass. He looked just like a large grey hairy spider. He found his twig again and growled happily to himself.

'Put him where he can see other dogs, and let him out on the grass whenever you can. I'll look in again in a week or so and see how he's getting on.'

Zoë followed me out to the car.

'I can't find homes for nice ordinary lurchers, with nice ordinary straight legs. What I am going to do with—?'

'Goodbye, Zoë, see you next week.' I made my escape, but true to my word, visited again about a week later. The puppy, looking more like a spider than ever, was having a battle with a bone slightly larger and heavier than himself.

'Hello, Ugly,' I greeted him.

He disentangled his teeth from the bone and walked fairly steadily to my feet. Untying my shoelaces, he beamed up at me, then fell over and waved his large paws.

'Tickle me,' he commanded. He was a dog of limited ideas.

Zoë came out of the office.

'He's much better,' she admitted. 'But I ask you, who, in their right mind, would ever adopt him?'

As in a dream, I heard myself saying, 'I'll have him.' I stopped. What had I said? I already had five dogs.

'But you've already got five dogs,' objected Zoë.

'You've got at least seven. I expect we're both a little mad,' I returned.

He settled on the back seat of the car as if he knew all about it, and dozed all the way home, where I took him out into the garden to meet his new family.

He thought the garden was a delightful place, full of lovely smells and exciting things. My daughters had taken our Scottie bitch, Jeannie, and the Pups for a walk, Nina the terrier was fast asleep in the kitchen, and Zeeta was the only dog on the reception committee. She was fascinated and horrified, and sat shivering on my feet until the puppy suddenly saw her and hurtled across the lawn to invite her to play. She screamed a high poodle scream, snapped angrily, and begged me to pick her up and take her away. All things considered, it seemed the wisest course, so I carried her to the car and deposited her on the driving seat, where she curled up contentedly. Like all my dogs, she loved the car.

She had come into my life sixteen years previously, brought into morning surgery by a near-hysterical middle-aged couple. They had bought a dear little poodle puppy, imagining it would grow into a dear, fluffy little lapdog. Unfortunately, Zeeta had grown instead into a gawky, long-legged, hyperactive adolescent. Her owners took her for a ten-minute walk on a lead, three times a day, during which she screamed incessantly. The rest of the time she was tied to the kitchen table, because if they let her loose she rushed about and damaged the furniture. They put a shivering, nervous wreck on the surgery table, and begged me with tears in their eyes to put it out of its misery. My advice and suggestions about management fell on deaf ears. They were adamant that they were not taking the Poodle home again. The only way out was to offer to adopt her myself.

Fortunately it was my half-day off, so that afternoon I took Zeeta, and the two tiny white toy Poodles I had at the time, to the local park. I put on their leads and walked them, Zeeta screeching like a banshee, to the wild part at the far end. There I sat down under a tree and took off all three leads. Frolic and Psyche, the two toy bitches, wandered off together, chatting amicably. Zeeta spun round three times like a whirligig, then shot off and disappeared over the horizon. Within seconds she was back, running as hard as she possibly could, then circled round and round the tree until she collapsed, panting and exhausted. Casually I called all three Poodles and suggested they might like to come and sit with me. Frolic and Psyche came at once, and sat side by side on my lap, like two little old ladies at a garden party. Zeeta approached hesitantly, and stopped just out of reach. I ignored her, stroking the Poodles on my knee. She crept a bit closer, and pushed her head under my hand. I resisted the temptation to grab her collar, and caressed her head gently. She backed off, did her spinning round trick again, and shot off. Circling round at top speed, she ran straight back again and sat close by me. I clipped leads on all three collars and led three calm, happy Poodles back to the car, and we went home. From that time, Zeeta walked happily on the lead, and always came at once whenever I called her.

She was a particularly intelligent Poodle, but always remained nervous and highly suspicious of strangers or unusual happenings. I left her resting in the car and returned to my new responsibility. He had cheerfully invited Fanny to join in his game. Fanny, a part-bred Siamese, was always short-tempered, and above all else liked a quiet life. She did not approve of this ill-mannered hairy yob and, unsheathing the claws on her right paw, tapped him smartly on the nose. He yipped in surprise, then sat and wept, licking the spots of blood off the end of his nose. Suddenly, he saw Arfer, and forgot his sore nose. In his distant youth, Arfer had met a stud buck older, heavier, and more experienced than himself. When rabbits fight, they have the curious habit of trying to emasculate each other. Arfer's opponent had partly succeeded, before he was rescued and brought to me for repair. Sewing him up, I commented to my daughter Liz, who was helping, that in future he would be only half a rabbit. He was immediately dubbed Arfer, and when his breeder did not want him back, we kept him. He had outlived several mates and many descendants and now lived a life of great comfort. The door of his hutch was permanently propped open, and he came and went as he pleased. He was not pleased by this bouncing newcomer, and advanced menacingly, ears tipped forward over his face. With Fanny's reception still fresh in his memory, the lurcher backed off, and collided with a large coloured ball behind him. His first yelp of dismay became a song of delight when he found that not only was it harmless, it was fun, too. He pushed it with his nose, shouldered it aside in a thundering charge, and pursued it all round the garden.

My daughters returned with the other three dogs and watched his antics.

'Mad party, isn't he?' grinned Liz.

'Very mad party,' I agreed. 'We'll call him Ceilidh.'

Liz unlatched the garden gate.

'Come on, musketeers,' she said. 'Tell everybody what you did.'

'What happened?' I enquired apprehensively.

'We went to the beach,' replied Liz, 'and there was a yellow Labrador.'

There was no need for her to continue. Normally sunny-natured and placid, the sight of a yellow Labrador had a Jekyll and Hyde effect on Jeannie, and she attacked them on sight. The Pups didn't know what the fuss was about, but if Mum wanted a fight, they were game to join in. Their short, fat hairy legs could propel their clumsy-looking bodies at an astonishing speed, and shouted commands to 'Come Back', and 'Stay', had no effect on them.

'Did they catch it?' I asked.

'Oh, yes,' replied Liz. 'They bit it.' I groaned.

'I hope nobody recognised you. It'll probably come into the surgery tomorrow, and I'll have to patch it up.' I smacked the Scottie lightly on her rump. 'Jeannie, you're a rotten dog.'

It was her favourite endearment, and she gazed up at me, beaming with pleasure. Her tail waved in erratic circles. She never wagged it back and forth like other dogs but always in circles. The happier she felt, the wider the circles.

Ceilidh approached, bouncing stiff-legged. Jeannie's tail stopped, and she held it stiffly over her back, her head up, ears pricked forward, lips slightly raised to show her dagger-like fangs. The pups watched and waited. Very carefully, the lurcher pup approached, sniffed at Jeannie's tatty trousers and presented himself for her inspection. She pushed at him, and he fell submissively, whimpering.

She decided he was harmless and continued on her way up the garden path. She needed a drink after all that exercise, and you never knew, those blasted cats might

15

have left some of that white stuff in the dish by the fridge. She quickened her pace. The Pups, in their turn, investigated the newcomer and allowed him to accompany them to their favourite spot behind the compost heap. Jeannie, full of stolen milk, disappeared under the settee for a snooze.

She had joined our family about ten years previously, when we were living on the Isle of Wight. One of my clients at the time bred Scotties, but her particular strain were bad whelpers. When the time came to deliver their pups, they gave a half-hearted heave and decided the effort was too much. Most of them had had at least one Caesarean, generally in the middle of the night, or at teatime on Sunday.

I visited one day to remove the stitches from the latest patient. The girls were with me, but I decided not to take them into the house with me.

'It would be more tactful,' I said, 'if you two stayed in the car. Mrs Scott-Moncrieff is a bit fussy about people bringing germs into the house.'

'That's all right,' they agreed cheerfully. 'We'll look at that pony over there.'

I glanced across the road. A damp and dismal pony drooped over a broken gate, sunk in gloomy introspection. As I got out of the car, the two Poodles, Frolic and Psyche, moved across to the driving seat and curled up together. I made no objection. It was nice to come back to a warm seat.

'Shan't be long,' I said. 'Only some stitches to take out of a Caesarean.'

Mrs Scott-Moncrieff let me into the house, glaring suspiciously at my perfectly clean shoes.

'You'll want to wash your hands first. I expect you've been to all those nasty farms,' she suggested.

We went to the kitchen, where a clean sheet had been spread on the table, and she fetched the patient from the kennel block in the garden. The wound had healed well. I stroked the Scottie's head approvingly.

'Good girl. How are the puppies?'

'Och, they're fine. All four doing well. As soon as they're

16

weaned, Heather will have to go. That's the second Caesarean she's had.'

'She'll make somebody a nice pet,' I agreed. 'She's got a lovely temperament.' I decided not to add that she would be better off as a family pet than a puppy machine. Mrs Scott-Moncrieff treated her dogs well, but expected them to make her a good living from puppy sales.

'Oh, while you're here,' she said, 'there's a six-week-old pup I wish you would look at. Its eyes are all wrong.'

She took Heather back to her family outside, and returned carrying a wriggling black infant. I inspected it closely. The right eye returned my stare unblinkingly. The left was a mere glint of reflection sunk between contracted eyelids.

'It's a developmental fault,' I explained. 'Probably best to leave it alone at this stage. We could refer you to a specialist later. It might be possible to—'

'Put it to sleep,' commanded the owner. 'I can never sell an imperfect puppy. I have my reputation to consider.'

I was horrified.

'She's not in pain or in any way distressed. I agree, she ought not to breed, but she would make an acceptable pet for somebody.' I snapped my bag shut decisively. 'I am not going to kill a perfectly healthy puppy. Good afternoon, Mrs Scott-Moncrieff.'

I returned crossly to the car. The girls were still discussing the pony.

'He needs worming,' declared Liz. 'And a lot more food.'

'If he were mine,' sighed Louise, 'I'd call him Tornado.'

'Looks more like a faint breeze to me,' I said sourly.

Mrs Scott-Moncrieff appeared at the car window, and thrust the little puppy at me. 'You can have her for half price,' she said. 'Take it off my bill.'

There was a gasp from behind me, and Liz leaned forward and carefully took the pup.

'It's Jeannie,' she breathed. 'Oh, Mummy, we've got Jeannie.'

She had been reading *Thurber's Dogs*, and had been greatly taken by the tales of his Scottie bitch. Louise added her plea.

'You've got the Poodles,' she pointed out. 'It's only fair for us to have our own dog, too.'

Ecstatic at so much unaccustomed attention, Jeannie rolled over on Liz's lap, waving stumpy black legs. Sighing, I realised there was nothing else to do but accept the situation and the puppy.

The next day, Sunday, I had a few calls to make. The girls decided to stay at home and play with Jeannie. The Poodles, of course, came with me. We had an arrangement with the next-door neighbour.

'If you need anything—' I began.

'We shout, or bang on the wall, and Mrs Robinson will come,' they chorused. 'If you're not back by eleven, we'll make some cocoa and have a biscuit, and we might clean the hamsters out or even do our homework.'

I returned at half-past eleven. As I came in the front door, the girls called out from the bedroom upstairs.

'We're doing our homework up here, because Jeannie went to sleep and we didn't want to disturb her.'

'I shall have to wake her up now,' I replied. 'It's time to start cooking the lunch.'

I pushed open the kitchen door, and cried out in dismay. Jeannie sat in the middle of the floor, looking very pleased with herself. Behind her, the open larder door revealed ransacked lower shelves. On the floor around her, packets of rice, flour, sugar, washing powder and cocoa lay chewed and ripped, their contents all mixed together. Jeannie's carrot-shaped tail wagged furiously, clearing a fan of clear floor behind her.

'Oh, Jeannie,' I wailed.

I shouted up the stairs. 'Your puppy has made a mess in the kitchen.'

'Oh, no,' protested Louise. 'We've already cleared up two puddles and a pooh. There can't be much left inside her.'

'This is a different kind of mess,' I assured them. 'Come and see.'

As she grew, Jeannie chewed up several slippers, my best shoes, and an ancient and deeply mourned Teddy Bear. She cut her teeth on the dining-room chair legs, and

18

they bear the marks to this day. She was offhandedly polite to the Poodles and generally ignored other dogs. If their friendly overtures became too persistent she lifted her lip to show alarmingly large fangs. Her jaws were incredibly strong, and we could lift her off the ground, teeth clamped on a rope or stick. The only love of her life was Teddy, a crossbred Retriever who lived on a farm a short distance away. He would sometimes come and call for her, pushing at the kitchen door until it opened, and together they would disappear, looking like Laurel and Hardy.

After her first season she had a false pregnancy, and dragged toys, slippers, a glass ashtray and a live kitten into her basket. She let me return the kitten to its rightful parent, but became hysterical with rage when Liz tried to take her slippers. At about the time her next season was due, her breeder rang one day and inquired about her eye.

'It's much better,' I said. 'Still a bit smaller than the other eye, but she can see out of it, and there's so much eyebrow that it doesn't really notice.'

It transpired that Jeannie came from illustrious ancestors, and Mrs Scott-Moncrieff was anxious to continue the line. Remembering her false pregnancy, I agreed it might do her good, and at the appointed time took the Scottie back to her breeder. The encounter with the intended father of her litter was a fiasco. She disliked him on sight, refused to have anything to do with him, and sat determinedly, ignoring his blandishments.

Mrs Scott-Moncrieff became impatient.

'We'll have to muzzle her and hold her up,' she declared. 'Perhaps you could give her an injection to quieten her?'

I was quite prepared for Jeannie to have an arranged marriage if she did not object, but the idea of rape was repugnant.

The breeder followed us out.

'We could try again tomorrow,' she said. 'Now that she's met the dog, she might be keener next time.'

Watching Jeannie's stiff-necked indignation as she clambered laboriously back into the car, I had my doubts.

Teddy sat outside our house, and Jeannie wriggled from my arms and dashed over to him. She told him all about her ordeal, but he had discovered she was delightfully interesting, and had obvious ungentlemanly aspirations. I hastily picked her up, commanded him to 'Go Home' and, pushing Jeannie into the house, went back to the surgery.

When I returned later that afternoon, the two girls were eating their tea. 'We had bacon and egg and fried bread and we finished the apple crumble and Teddy called for Jeannie and they've gone for a walk,' they informed me.

Horrified, I rushed out to search for them. The guilty pair were at the bottom of the garden. I shall never know how they managed it, but they had mated. They were tied, and Jeannie was suspended several inches off the ground in a ludicrous and unladylike predicament. They separated as I approached, and Teddy fled unheroically. Jeannie shook herself vigorously, and preceded me up the garden path with an air of great self-satisfaction.

I contemplated injecting her with hormones to prevent pregnancy, but decided against it. Time passed, her pregnancy became obvious, and she ballooned impossibly. As the time for the puppies' birth approached, she selected and rejected several nest sites, settling eventually on a large cardboard box at the foot of Liz's bed.

On the appointed day, she huffed and puffed restlessly all over the house. The girls were very worried, but I assured them this first stage of labour might go on all day.

'Watch her,' I commanded, 'and let me know if she actually goes into her bed and really strains. I've got the evening surgery. I'll leave her in your care.'

I returned home at about seven o'clock. Two round-eyed and solemn young ladies whispered to me that Jeannie was trying very hard. I rather doubted it, but inspection showed they were right. Sitting upright in her box, Jeannie panted hard. Suddenly, she raised her head, clenched her teeth and PUSHED.

'How long has she been doing this?' I was alarmed.

'About an hour,' they replied, 'but nothing seems to have happened.'

She heaved and puffed and strained, but achieved nothing. I examined her, and decided she would have to admit defeat and accept our help. Both my daughters had helped with Caesareans since they were very small, and I knew I could rely on them.

'I'll do the anaesthetic,' asserted Liz, 'because I'm the oldest. Louise can scrub up and help you and deal with the babies.'

They would have been very upset if I had suggested calling out one of the surgery nurses, so we carried the patient reverently out to the car and I drove back to the surgery. There, Liz held the Scottie on the table, and murmured endearments while I clipped her hairy arm, slipped a needle into the vein, and injected carefully. As she sighed and relaxed, we connected her to the gas machine and wheeled the trolley into the operating theatre.

Half an hour later, I had removed two very large pups from her distended womb, and she was groggily licking them. Liz had laid claim to the first-born, and Louise to the second. I sighed to myself, and supposed that six dogs was not really very many.

'Good job they're both bitches,' said Liz. 'I shall call mine Boadicea.'

'What a weird idea,' shuddered Louise. 'Mine will be plain Penny.'

So Penny Plain and Boadicea came home with us. Separately, they soon became Pen and Bo, but to the end of their lives were known mostly as 'the Pups'. Their legs remained short and stumpy like their mother's, but their bodies grew as disproportionately large as retrievers'. They went everywhere and did everything together, sitting on the parcel shelf at the back of the car like hairy bookends. Wherever Jeannie went, they went, following their little mother like a double black shadow.

2

'Bo!' I cried. 'Drop it! Put that down at once!' She obediently deposited the long-dead, rotting dogfish on the sand. I scraped a hole with the heel of my welly boot, kicked the smelly object into it, and covered it with loose sand. Bo immediately exhumed it, obligingly joining in this new game I had invented. Ceilidh barked at a gull and, losing interest in the rotten fish, Bo lolloped off to the edge of the sea.

Until we returned to the mainland, I had not realised how slow was the pace of life on the Isle of Wight, and how my own life had decelerated in rhythm. Of course, we had accidents and emergencies and could move fast if we had to, but on the whole, people spoke slowly, weighing words carefully before dropping them like pearls. Nothing was urgent, there was always tomorrow, and their favourite word was 'presently', which could mean sooner or later.

When the stresses of my new job became too much, I found that walking the length of Marshton beach with the dogs, very early in the morning, helped to restore my equilibrium. I find autumn a melancholy time, and on one particular Sunday morning, I was in a deep black hole of depression. Having no wish to inflict my misery on my horse—he always picks up my moods—I got up early and drove with the dogs to the deserted, shining wet beach.

Both girls were enjoying their new schools and had made friends. We had moved out of the claustrophobic flat over the surgery and settled in our pleasant little house. I had found grazing for my horse and the pony within reasonable cycling distance of home, and the various cats and dogs had adapted well to a more restricted life. I was getting on well with the local farmers, some of whom actually asked for 'the new woman', and very few pet owners were disappointed when they found I was taking the surgery. Why, then, was I so unhappy? I looked out to sea as I splashed along. Far out, almost on the horizon, a white sail glittered in the early morning sun, and then I knew why I was sad. Thinking of Sundays on the island, I allowed myself to wallow in the luxury of remembrance and regret. Almost sleep-walking through the wavelets, I thought back to one particular Sunday . . .

*   *   *

'Three ham rolls, three cheese, two cans of coke and a half of shandy, please.' Jed put the shandy and cokes on the bar and slapped my change beside them.

'Missus is making more rolls,' he said, 'they'll be out presently.' On the Isle of Wight, 'presently' can mean anything from two minutes to two years, and I looked around for somebody to talk to. We often had Sunday lunch at the village pub on my weekends off. The menu was short and simple in the extreme—cheese rolls, ham rolls, pickled eggs and crisps—but the rolls were crusty and delicious, the cheddar imported from Somerset and the ham cooked on the premises and carved in succulent pink wedges.

There was a sudden shout of laughter at the other end of the bar, and a great deal of backslapping and goodnatured guffaws.

'What's the joke?' I asked Jed. Delighted with a fresh audience, he leaned confidentially over the bar.

'Haven't you heard about Ted and Amos?' he grinned. 'In 'ere last night they was, and both pretty well tanked up. About ten o'clock, young Ted decided he'd better go home and make sure their old mum was all right.' (Ted and Amos lived in a tumbledown cottage in the village with their old widowed mother. Liz called them Bill and Ben.) 'Well, he took a short cut through the churchyard, not quite sure which way up he was, and fell arse over tit—beg pardon, ma'am—straight into the new grave dug for old Mrs Ellis, her as they're burying tomorrow. He picked himself up, but could he get out again? He could not!'

23

I could well believe it. Young Ted was sixty years old if he was a day, barely five feet tall and doubled up with arthritis.

'Anyway,' continued Jed, ''e gave up arter a bit and curled up in a corner and went fast asleep.' I saw that this situation would be regarded by the locals as hilarious, but there was more.

'Later on,' went on the landlord, 'old Amos decided 'e'd best go and look for his brother since 'e 'adn't returned, so off 'e goes, full of ale, takes the same short cut and falls slap bang in the same grave. 'E didn't notice Ted asleep there, and sets up a right 'ollering and tries to climb out. Ted ups and groans, waking up, like, and says, ''Tain't no use you going on like that, I've been trying to get out for ages!' Well, old Amos thought it was someone in a coffin speaking to 'im, and 'e gives one yell, pops out of that grave like a jack-in-the-box, and legs it home so fast 'e leaves smoke be'ind 'im.'

I laughed aloud, and Ted and Amos lifted hands in greeting and grinned sheepishly.

'Yes. Reckon they'll be able to drink on that story for a day or two.' The landlord paused significantly. I put the change back on the bar.

'Of course. Whatever they're drinking.' Jed selected a couple of coins and pushed the rest back.

'Two boilers,' he said and carried two brimming glasses to the brothers. His wife appeared with a huge tray of fresh rolls, and put my order and the drinks on a little tray. I carried it out to the girls waiting outside in the sunshine. Tables and chairs were provided but we usually perched on a low mossy wall on the other side of the lane, where the dogs who accompanied us would not be fed by other customers on crisps and bits of bread. Nina never came with us on these occasions and Jeannie had uncharacteristically decided to stay at home, so we just had Zeeta and the Pups with us, Frolic and Psyche having long since died of old age. I was surprised and uneasy to see a strange man sitting on the wall between Liz and Louise, apparently deep in conversation. They looked up as I approached.

'Gosh, you were ages,' Liz complained. 'We're starving.'

24

They fell on the food like ravening wolves, then Louise remembered her manners.

'This is Sam,' she said, indicating the stranger. 'He rescued Zeeta.'

'Rescued her from what?' I demanded. Louise looked shamefaced.

'She slipped her collar when you went in the pub and we didn't notice. Sam found her walking up the road and thought she must belong to us because of the other dogs.' He stood up and held out his hand.

'Sam Gascoigne,' he said, 'from London. I've got a little boat down in the creek.' I shook his hand.

'Kate Barber,' I replied, 'we live over there.' I waved in the general direction of the village. We sat on the wall, eating, drinking and chatting. A sudden shout of laughter from the bar intrigued Sam.

'What's the joke?' he demanded. 'Do you know?' I told them about Amos and Ted's graveyard capers. Louise was delighted.

'I'll put that in the local news bulletin in school tomorrow. If you drink too much you go to an early grave!' Both girls found this excruciatingly funny. Sam grinned at me over his glass of bitter.

'Fine pair of comedians you've got there,' he observed.

Liz picked herself up off the grass, where she had fallen in her paroxysm of mirth.

'Can I finish your shandy? My coke's all gone.'

'Certainly not!' I answered. 'I want it. I'm thirsty.' I drained the glass and picked up my second roll.

'That food looks really good,' said Sam. 'I think I'll join you.' He picked up his empty glass and strolled across the lane into the bar. I turned to the girls. They anticipated my disapproval.

'We know! We know!' they protested. 'Never speak to strangers. He was only talking to us, and we were safe enough here with all these people about. He seemed really interested in the village, and the Pups liked him.' This was the final accolade, and I dismissed the subject. We finished our rolls.

'Sam's a long time,' said Louise.

25

'Probably not coming back,' sighed Liz. 'I expect he's found a buxom wench in the bar.' Was that a twinge of jealousy I felt? I was about to suggest a walk down to the creek when Sam reappeared, carrying a large tray with plates and glasses.

'Sorry to be so long,' he cried. 'I had to hear the tale of Ted and Amos again. What is this "boiler" they drink?'

'Mild and brown,' I replied. 'Half of mild with a bottle of brown ale added. It's quite good.'

'Well, I've got you shandy,' he said, 'and coke for the lasses. And do you think they might help eat some of these rolls and crisps and stuff?' They thought they might, and we sat in companionable silence, dozing in the sun. Sam stood up suddenly.

'What are you doing this afternoon?' he demanded.

'Too hot to go for a ride,' decided Liz. 'We could walk the dogs to the quay.'

'How about sailing?' he suggested. Liz's face fell.

'We can't,' she explained. 'Mummy took our scow home to paint it and left it in the yard and Jack—that's our pony—jumped over it and landed in it and he's kicked in the gunwale and the top strake.' She paused for breath. 'And we can't afford to have it mended. Not at the moment.'

'We could all go out in my boat,' offered Sam. The girls looked doubtful.

'All of us?' asked Louise. 'Would there be room?'

He appeared to consider, then nodded.

'Room enough, if we squeeze up a bit.' They looked at me beseechingly. On a warm Sunday afternoon, the Solent is about as lonely as Victoria Station in the rush hour. I reflected we should be perfectly safe in such a crowd, and he would hardly abduct all three of us. I nodded, and everybody cheered.

'I'll take the dogs home and catch you up,' Liz suggested.

Sam waved this aside. 'Bring them,' he commanded. 'We'll squash them in somewhere.'

We walked down to the quay, the Pups sniffing happily in the brambles for rabbits, Zeeta close by my side.

'Those are very odd looking dogs,' he said. I scowled.

'Not odd. Different. Their mother is our Scottie, and dad is a sort of Retriever.'

'Mummy calls them her scotch egg retrievers,' chimed in Liz. 'Some of our hens leave eggs all over the place and up in the bales in the barn, and they fetch them.' He looked incredulous.

'Without breaking them?'

'They break some, on purpose,' I admitted. 'They like eggs. But I get most of them.' He was very impressed.

'Does this little black curly job do anything special?'

'Oh, yes,' said Louise cheerfully. 'Zeeta has fits.'

'Only when she's really upset,' I added hastily. 'Not very often.'

He promised not to upset her, and we arrived at the quay. Sam untied a rubber dinghy and we all stepped in carefully. The floor undulated with the waves as he began to row out into the creek. Zeeta was quite happy on my lap, but the Pups, sitting at the girls' feet, were uneasy.

'Not much room for everybody,' whispered Liz, 'and where's the sail? Surely he's not going to row us out to sea?' We approached a line of sleek yachts, and Sam eased the dinghy behind the third one, stood up carefully and, reaching over the transom, found a short ladder and hooked it on.

'There we are,' he smiled. 'Easier than climbing over the side.'

Wide-eyed, Liz and Louise climbed aboard, and I handed Zeeta up to them while Sam held the dinghy steady. The bow wave of a passing motor boat surged under us and the Pups yelped in dismay, hurled themselves overboard and began to swim back to shore. Sam threw himself full length in the dinghy, reached over the bow, and just caught their collars. With some difficulty, he hauled them inboard.

We all got ourselves on board the yacht, and Sam produced a towel to dry them.

'The dogs had all better stay below,' he said. 'They'll be safer there than on deck. You'll find lifebelts in the forrard locker. I'll get the sails up.' Liz and Louise explored the cabin.

'Look,' they cried, 'there's a cooker on gimbals so you can

27

still cook as the boat heels over, and a fridge, and a shower and even a proper lavatory.'

'Heads,' I corrected. 'Yachty people call the loo the heads.'

'Silly name,' said Louise squashingly.

We had a magical afternoon. There was a good breeze out on the water. Liz retired to the cabin when the boat leaned over, saying she would make sure the dogs did not need comforting, although the boot was really on the other foot. Louise sat right up at the sharp end, as she insisted on calling it, legs hanging over the side, and above the slap and surge of the waves and the shrilling of the wind in the rigging, I heard her singing a wild, wordless song. I stayed in the cockpit and learned how to steer a yacht, which handled very differently from my little scow.

We returned to the quay in the late afternoon, the girls yawning mightily and declaring they were going to bed straight after supper. I helped take down the sails.

'Come back when they're in bed and have dinner with me,' said Sam. 'Please?' I considered.

'If Richard is staying in tonight, I can come,' I promised.

'Richard?' he frowned.

'Agricultural student,' I explained. 'Local farmer employs students on sandwich courses. They lodge with me. Richard is the current one.' His brow cleared.

'That's all right, then,' he conceded.

Arrived home, I did the evening feeding and milking, while the girls cooked their very favourite supper of fish fingers, fried eggs and baked beans. They offered to cook some for me, but I explained I was having supper with Sam. They sighed.

'He's a lovely man,' said Liz. 'I'd like to marry him when I'm bigger.' She dug some ice-cream out of the freezer while Louise opened a tin of peaches.

'That's out!' I said flatly. 'He's already married. He told me this afternoon. May the Lord have mercy on your stomachs, the pair of you. All that junk food!'

'What a shame,' murmured Louise. 'You could have . . .'

'No, I couldn't,' I interrupted. 'We're all right as we are.

I'm not going to be dependent on anyone, ever again, in any way.'

Richard had no plans to go out, and agreed happily to keep watch over the family. I walked back to the creek. Sam was waiting on the quay.

'I see you've brought your mad dog with you,' he said.

'She's no bother,' I assured him. 'She just likes to be near me.'

'I can understand that,' he agreed. He rowed us out to the boat. We had avocado and steak with all the trimmings and a bottle of wine, then washed up in the tiny sink and stacked the plates tidily in the locker.

'We could take your mad Poodle for a walk along the beach,' he suggested, 'then come back for brandy and coffee.' It sounded very civilised, and we walked the length of the beach in the last of the evening light, then rowed back to the boat.

'Mustn't be too long having coffee,' I said. 'The tide's going out fast. There'll be just mud here soon, and I'd be stuck on the boat all night.'

'Suits me,' he grinned cheerfully, but I was not so sure. I went below to make the coffee while Sam tidied the deck and checked the anchor. Suddenly, there was a shout from Sam. A small splash was followed by a curse, then a much bigger splash. Puzzled, I climbed the short ladder to the deck. Sam appeared over the transom and deposited a half-drowned Poodle on the deck.

'Daft bitch!' he spluttered. 'She didn't know where you were and jumped overboard to find you. You can dry her on that towel hanging over there. It's the one we used on the other Herberts this afternoon.'

I wrapped Zeeta in the towel and gently rubbed her dry, talking to her reassuringly. She seemed none the worse for her impromptu swim. Carrying her down below, I wrapped her in somebody's jersey I found, and settled her on the bunk.

'There,' I said. 'Go to sleep now. You're quite safe.' I turned. Sam had followed me and was standing at the foot of the ladder. A piece of seaweed hung over one ear, and water flattened his black hair, dripped off his nose and chin and overflowed from his shoes into a rapidly widening puddle on the floor.

'My!' I marvelled. 'You certainly are wet!'

Totally unselfconscious, he stripped off his wet clothes and tossed them through the hatch onto the deck above. He reached into the locker beside him, pulled out a fresh towel and handed it to me.

'Dry me, too!' he said.

I was woken by the sound and smell of frying bacon, and sat up, yawning and stretching. Sam handed me a mug of tea.

'You sleep sound, lady,' he said admiringly. 'I took your potty dog ashore for a walk. She did what was expected and she's had breakfast.'

'Breakfast?' I squeaked. 'Zeeta never has breakfast!'

He looked nonplussed. 'Well, she definitely wanted something, and I didn't want to upset her in case she had a fit, so I gave her a tin of corned beef.' I looked at my poodle sitting on the end of the bed, her ridiculous stump of tail tick-tocking happily. She licked her chops and looked smug.

'What about breakfast for people?' asked Sam. 'I've got to get back to London and you must return to the bosom of your family.' He peered at his watch. 'On the other hand,' he said thoughtfully, 'it's only five o'clock . . .'

Later, walking back up the path from the creek, I admitted to myself that I was probably in love, but with reservations.

'Come on, Zeeta,' I called, 'leave that rabbit hole alone. I don't want to be late for work!'

*   *   *

. . . A large wave splashed into my boots, oozing coldly into my socks. The Isle of Wight, the quay, Sam, all vanished. The little sail had disappeared over the horizon. The dogs were still happily investigating crabs, chasing gulls, getting themselves soaked and covered in sand. Except Zeeta, who minced along trying to stay close to me and keep her feet dry at the same time. The walk had given me a splendid appetite.

'Come on, then,' I called. 'Let's go home to breakfast.'

*   *   *

We gave Ceilidh a couple of weeks to settle in his new home, then one morning I took him to the surgery for his first vaccinations. He followed me happily through the main door, gave Carol, the receptionist, a friendly smile and a rapid swish of the tail, and trotted importantly into the empty waiting room. Well, it should have been empty, but there was a smartly dressed elderly lady sitting by the window, with her hands folded in her lap over what appeared to be a fur muff.

'Sorry, Mrs Barber,' said Carol. 'I know there's no surgery this morning, but Mrs Sheperd particularly wanted you to look at her Poodle puppy.'

Ceilidh was sitting at the old lady's feet, holding an excited conversation with the fur muff, which had come to life and was peering out over her clasped hands, its small black bewhiskered face yipping shrilly. Wriggling frantically, the tiny black Poodle pup reached out and licked Ceilidh's face. He yawned widely, and the Poodle put his head between the gaping crocodile jaws, apparently inspecting his tonsil. Ceilidh rolled his eyes beseechingly.

I hastened to his side, propped his jaws open, and extricated the miniature liontamer. The lurcher's jaws snapped shut, and he shook himself with relief. Mrs Sheperd took a firmer hold of the squirming pup on her lap.

'Oh, Mrs Barber, I'm so worried,' she declared.

'Looks very healthy to me,' I replied.

'He is indeed very healthy,' she agreed, 'too healthy, really, for me to cope with, but it's not that. I was checking his pedigree yesterday, and it described him as silver, but, well, see for yourself.' The inky black visage gazed up at me solemnly.

'Silver poodles are born black,' I reassured her, 'and change colour gradually. You'll see a bit of silver on his face and feet when he has his first puppy clip, but it will probably be months before he is silver all over.'

'Oh, what a relief,' she said. 'You see, he was a present from my grandchildren, and of course I love him, but he's constantly under my feet and if he stayed black I wouldn't be able to see him. Thank you, Mrs Barber. We'll see you next week when he comes for his injections.'

The old lady gathered up her pet and walked carefully out to her waiting taxi. I took Ceilidh into the surgery and administered the first dose of vaccine, a procedure which he quite ignored. He was growing out of ugly puppyhood and into awkward adolescence. In spite of adequate vitamins and minerals, his joints were knobbly and his legs crooked, especially the left front. He was an active, energetic dog, friendly, but not effusive towards people, and always ready to play with other dogs. My cats were perfectly safe with him, but any animal which ran away —other cats, rabbits in the fields—he pursued with evil intent. So far, they all outran him. The only part of him which caused damage was his tail. It was a good idea to stand well back when Ceilidh was feeling happy. When not inflicting GBH on unsuspecting shins, he carried his tail in a permanent question mark over his back. For a lurcher, he was very obedient, but as he grew up he sometimes showed a streak of independence and dislike of authority, common to males of any species as they approach young manhood.

We were arranging at that time to keep our horses on a piece of land about three or four miles away. It was mostly derelict orchard and rough grazing, surrounded by a chain-link fence, except where a short row of houses and gardens backed on to it.

I drove there one Sunday afternoon, with all the dogs in the car, to meet Mr and Mrs Bellman, the owners, and discuss details. We walked around the ten acres or so, with their two Alsatian guard-dogs gambolling harmlessly about us. My dogs were shut in the car. I did not feel quite happy about Bandit and Robber, the guard-dogs; in fact they were perfectly safe with people who walked with confidence, but woe betide anybody or anything running away from them. We came to an amicable arrangement about rent, and the Bellmans said they intended to visit one of the tenants, and suggested my dogs might like to explore the land.

They ordered Bandit and Robber into their van and slid the door closed. With the two guards out of the way, I let the gang out of my car, and they had a wonderful time, chasing rabbits, leaping at pheasants, digging holes, racing between the old trees, generally enjoying themselves. As teatime approached, we returned to the car, I opened the back of it, and all the dogs jumped in. All, that is, except Ceilidh. He had noticed the van parked a few yards away, and went to investigate. Bandit and Robber hurled themselves at the window, yelling with fury. Ceilidh beamed at them, waving his tail gently. The door of the van moved back a fraction of an inch.

'Ceilidh!' I called sharply. 'Come here.' He glanced back at me placatingly before returning his attention to the van. Balancing precariously on three legs, he lifted the fourth and pee'd on the van wheel. It was a trick he had just learned and he scratched the ground vigorously, kicking back proudly with his hind legs. Bandit and Robber redoubled their attack on the door and it began to slide back.

'Ceilidh,' I called urgently, 'in the car, quickly.'

He began to saunter towards me. The van door slid open and the Alsatians launched themselves at his retreating figure. He turned, and for a fraction of a second faced them bravely, then they seized him. One grabbed his shoulders and the other his hips, and a horrendous tug of war began.

Screaming even louder than the terrified lurcher, I searched frantically for a weapon, grabbed and uprooted a post from the fence, and belaboured the two snarling dogs. Either my screeching unnerved them or I was hitting them harder than I thought, but they let go and fled back to the van. Following them, I slammed the door shut and ran back to poor Ceilidh stretched out on the blood stained grass. He tried to lift his head as I approached, but it hurt him, and he fell back with a sad cry. Tears streaming down my face, I comforted him and gently explored his mauled body. To my great relief there were no broken bones and no symptoms of internal bleeding, but he was savagely torn. Several larger bites were bleeding freely, and his skin hung in tatters. With infinite care, I wrapped him in my anorak, which was cleaner than the old blankets in the car, and we went straight to the surgery.

Carol came down to help, and I spent the rest of the afternoon doing some very fancy needlework. Forty-one stitches and several injections later, I put him gently into a heated recovery kennel, and took the rest of my dogs home to a belated tea.

It seemed strange to go to bed without a grey friend on the rug beside the bed, thumping the floor with his tail every time I moved.

At three o'clock in the morning, a despairing Carol rang.

'I can't stop him yelling,' she complained. 'He's round from the anaesthetic and is making a frightful noise. I've tried sitting and talking to him, but it's no use. I've switched the baby-alarm off now and shut the door, but I can still hear him.'

I threw on some clothes, backed the car out of the garage and went to fetch him. It was my weekend off duty, and I had been looking forward to a proper night's sleep, uninterrupted by animals in distress. Yawning prodigiously, I carried him, his tail beating ecstatically, out to the car and took him home. I made him a bed on the sitting-room floor, but he tried to follow me upstairs, squeaking at every step. Resignedly, I carried my bedclothes downstairs and made up an uncomfortable bed on the settee.

The next day I put up a camp bed, and slept downstairs for a week until the bruising had subsided enough for Ceilidh to crawl upstairs to his usual bed beside mine.

Perhaps he thought the beating-up was a punishment for his disobedience, but from that time, if ever I called him sharply, he came at once, at a gallop. He also, from that time, had a morbid fear of Alsatians.

His wounds healed well, and he rapidly recovered his former high spirits. His left fore leg remained crooked, and sometimes seemed to cause discomfort. He was cantering unsteadily across the garden one day when I was sitting there with a friend, having tea.

34

'I see why you call him Lurcher,' he laughed. 'Describes him exactly.'

'No, no.' I was distressed. 'He is A Lurcher. Not exactly a breed, but a definite type. A cross between a working dog and a running dog. Usually a greyhound collie cross, but Ceilidh is three-quarters deerhound and a quarter collie.'

'How do you know?' my friend enquired.

'Because I know the local gypsies, and they have several lurchers just like him. In fact, he probably came from them in the first place.'

'Do you think it's fair to keep him, lame as he is?'

'He's not really lame,' I objected, 'just a bit unsteady, and he'll get better as he grows.'

Ceilidh came and threw himself at my feet, laughing up at me. I stroked his smooth head.

'Lovely lurcher,' I assured him, 'I think you're beautiful.'

3

She was totally invisible, a wet black cat crouched, immobile, on a wet black road. Christmas shoppers swelled the early evening traffic, the wheels swishing by within an inch of her face. Terrified, unable to move, she lifted her head and mewed piteously. The driver of the van approaching her saw the sudden flash of her white chin and snowy chest, and slammed his foot on the brake with a startled curse. The car behind him slowed to a stop, the young man in the driving seat shouting angrily, then muttering apologetically as he saw the van driver stoop and pick something up from the road, and carry it carefully through the rain back to the van; something whose protesting wail cut through the noise of the traffic and the canned carols from the brightly-lit shops.

The surgery had been fairly quiet that evening, and Lynne, the nurse on duty, had made me a cup of tea while I brought the record cards up to date. I reached gratefully for the steaming mug, lifted it halfway to my mouth, and froze as a car was driven fast into the car park outside. With a great screeching of brakes, slamming of car doors and pounding of feet outside, an apparition burst into the waiting room. I put the mug down again.

'It's hurt real bad,' said the apparition, blood mixing with the rain running off his hands onto the floor. More rain cascaded from the purple hair hanging lankly from under a battered bowler hat, and dripped sadly from the hem of a floor-length Army greatcoat.

'Come straight into the consulting room, and put her on the table,' I said. 'You can clean yourself up at the sink over there.'

'The blood is mostly mine, I think.' He winced as he put

his hands into the water. 'It cried real loud on the way here. It must be badly hurt.'

He dried his hands, and wiped his face on the surgery towel. Two safety pins stuck through his earlobe glittered briefly in the light. He dropped the towel on the floor. Lynne picked it up and, carrying it ostentatiously by one corner, threw it into the bin.

'It's not my cat,' he assured me. 'I don't want no bills or nothing.'

I had been gently sponging blood and dirt from the little cat, and estimating the damage.

'Superficial wounds. No broken legs. Face and jaw OK.' I felt along her body. Her tail hung limply and there was no response when I stretched out her hind leg and nipped the web between her toes with my finger nails.

'Her spine seems intact, but she's probably broken her pelvis,' I decided. She sat quietly, and when I rubbed her head, produced a throaty purr. A newly healed scar on her flank indicated that she had recently been spayed—not by our practice. We all recognise our own work.

'We'll deal with the shock and give her a painkiller, and then X-ray her in the morning. If you would give Lynne here your name and address, and take our phone number, you could ring us tomorrow after ten and we'll tell you how she is.'

'I told you. It's not my bloody cat. Don't go sending me the bill. And why do you want my name?'

'She's a friendly, well-cared-for cat, and she has recently been doctored. Somebody cares about her and will probably be very grateful to you,' I explained.

Realisation dawned. 'Oh well, that's different. If there's going to be a reward . . .' He slouched out into the reception room, patting the cat as he passed. 'Good luck, moggy.'

He never contacted us, and the address he gave was false.

'Right, Lynne,' I said, 'you know the drill. Let's have a bit of help here.'

X-ray the next day showed a cracked pelvis. Although wobbly, her hind limbs functioned fairly well, but her tail was still paralysed. She had used the dirt tray in the cage during the night, and there was no sign of blood.

Nobody claimed her. Nobody asked the police, the RSPCA, or any of the local cat protection societies if they had found a lost cat. The only treatment she needed was cage rest, good food, and somebody to care, and we provided these. She sat in the kennel and purred. She ate heartily, used her tray tidily, and was friendly and agreeable. The girls in the surgery all loved her. Her tail began to twitch after about a week, and by Christmas Eve, a few days later, she could hold it straight up over her back.

She was the only patient in the hospital. I was on duty over the holiday. Carol was going away for Christmas so the routine care and feeding of the hospitalised patients would fall on me.

'Why don't you take her home for the holiday?' suggested Lynne. 'It would save having to come all this way, just to feed one cat.'

I took her home that evening. The dogs and the other cats accepted her without comment. She ate her supper, selected a chair, tucked her paws tidily under her chest, and closed her eyes.

'She's very pretty,' said Liz. 'Little white gloves and slippers. Little white bib. What shall we call her?'

'She's only here for a couple of days,' I said fairly firmly.

'Well, we'll call her the Crimpy Cat, then,' decided Louise. So she became Crimpy, and she lives with us still.

On Christmas Day, there were two urgent calls to deal with. When I returned, I was occupied putting the turkey in the oven and the pudding on to steam, and it was some time before I noticed Crimpy was missing.

'It's all right,' declared Louise. 'She wanted to go out, but I told her not to be too long, because dinner would soon be ready. She'll be back soon.'

She turned up ten minutes before feeding time, appearing nonchalantly at the back door. For the next few days, she disappeared each morning, and came back at feeding time. Gradually, she spent more time at home. Whether she had been trying to find her old home, or whether she was a natural wanderer, I don't know.

38

She was very vocal and affectionate and preferred a human lap to any other seating accommodation. She would become almost mesmerised when we stroked her, and would roll over on her back as if helpless. Sometimes, she actually fell on the floor.

A dripping kitchen tap was a source of great amusement. She would aim a blow at each drop and bat it as it fell. She loved the garden pond and would sit for hours at a time, staring at the silent, gliding fish. She came in once with pondweed on her feet and a disgruntled expression on her face.

'Fishing,' I told her, 'is not allowed. Those Koi carp are very expensive and not intended for greedy cats.'

She flicked a green speck off her foot and washed between her toes. 'Nasty things,' she seemed to say. 'Don't want 'em anyway.'

I was asked to help with one of the local fun dog shows, where there are classes for the dog with the saddest eyes, or the waggiest tail, or most like its owner. Miss Francis, a gushy lady, came to tea one day to discuss it. The girls said they couldn't stand the silly lady, and they hated little cucumber sandwiches, so they went to play with the horses and left me to cope alone. Miss Francis cooed and squeaked over the cats and dogs.

'Little darlings,' she squealed. 'How I love all little creatures.'

Highly embarrassed, the little darlings crept under chairs or behind bookcases and pretended they weren't there. Miss Francis raised her teacup daintily to her lips, then stopped, eyes goggling, staring in horror over my shoulder.

I put my cup down and turned.

Crimpy was sitting just inside the door, looking nonplussed. She opened her mouth to make some sort of comment, and something fell, hopped squelchily, and sprawled on the carpet.

'Oh, Crimpy,' I protested. 'Cats can't eat frogs.'

'Frogs!' Miss Francis jumped to her feet, throwing teacup, plate, sandwich and sponge cake onto the rug. Two long black noses appeared from underneath the chair, and the Pups cleared up the tea before it could soak in, and neatly demolished the food. Waste not, want not, was ever their motto.

Ignoring my guest's shuddering whimpers, I picked up the frog and carried the poor slippery creature into the kitchen. There, I rinsed it gently under the cold tap. There were no obvious wounds, and the cold water washed off the dirt and fluff and revived it wonderfully. Closely followed by Crimpy, I took it into the garden and put it by the pond. Crimply glared incredulously.

'You're letting my frog go,' her look said. 'I caught it, it's mine.'

The creature goggled at us, its throat pulsing, then leaped mightly into the water, disappearing under a waterlily. Satisfied, I returned to the sitting-room, where Miss Francis was collecting her handbag and gloves. She had just remembered she had promised to call on the vicar's wife. Stepping over the wet patch on the carpet and averting her eyes from Crimpy, she fled.

I went out to the kitchen, carrying the ruins of our tea. Crimpy scowled at me. 'You pinched my frog,' she said.

'Oh, come on, Crimps,' I protested. 'You couldn't have eaten it.' She washed her mouth fastidiously with the side of her paw and glanced casually at the empty milk dish. I filled the dish and she sank her pretty chin over the edge. Her flickering tongue sent ripples over the surface.

I stopped to stroke her head. 'Dear cat,' I said with foolish fondness. She ducked away from my hand and backed away from the dish, shaking her front feet contemptuously, then stalked to the door.

'Crimpy?' I called, uncertainly.

She turned and stared at me with icy malevolence.

'You pinched my frog,' she said.

*   *   *

It is a commonly held belief that all vets have a sentimental regard for all animals, but this is not so. Like most of my professional colleagues, I admire and respect all animal life and do my utmost to uphold their rights and welfare. For some animals I feel affection, even love, and a few—a very few—I have heartily disliked.

A golden Cocker Spaniel called Dannyboy was one such. His owner was a gentle lady whose life was entirely ruled by her canine tyrant. He obeyed her commands if he felt like it, and if he disagreed he bit her—not severely, but enough to hurt. It was not meant playfully. Being in poor health, his owner, Miss Grayson, could not give him the exercise he needed. Helpful neighbours had tried taking him for walks, but all gave up after one experience. The postman left the mail next door and the milkman left the bottles at the gate.

I had to visit this charming character every two months or so, to clip his overgrown claws and give him a general health check. Miss Grayson would take him for a walk in the morning of my visit, and leave his lead attached to his collar when they returned.

'Oh, Mrs Barber, I do think you're brave,' she fluttered. 'I would never dare make him so cross.'

I felt anything but brave. Having tied the lead short to the kitchen table, I was dangling a loop of bandage in front of his snarling face. He was quite determined to bite my fingers off, and I was equally determined he would not. He lunged at my hands and, catching him off balance, I slid the noose over his nose, pulled it tight, crossed the ends under his chin, and tied a bow behind his ears, all in one second. Unable to use his teeth, he could still kick and scratch, and he banged his clenched jaws painfully on my arm as I picked him up.

I trimmed his nails and inspected his eyes, ears and all the other bits and pieces Miss Grayson was worried about. He was in the rudest health. Liberating him was decidedly risky. Miss Grayson opened the back door into the garden. I untied the bandage bow on the back of his neck, then pushed him outside and shut the door. Within seconds, he had torn the bandage from his face and attacked the door in fury. I was very glad to have the barrier between us.

'He'll calm down when you've gone, then I'll bring him in and give him his dinner,' said his owner.

We shared a pot of tea to soothe our shattered nerves,

and as usual, I had a few words with her other pet, who was hardly more lovable than Dannyboy. Hunched morosely in his cage, he ignored my overtures, and when I foolishly put my fingers close to the bars, he sidled along the perch with obvious evil intent.

'You like parrots, don't you?' observed Miss Grayson.

I offered him a piece of biscuit, which he scorned. 'I do,' I replied. 'But yours doesn't seem very friendly.'

'Well, I'm afraid the poor thing has a very dull life,' she said. 'I'm not very well, and they tire me so.' She sighed, and sipped her tea.

'Dannyboy must be a great trial to you,' I began delicately.

'I know what you're going to suggest,' she interrupted, 'but he needs me. I could never let him go to anyone else.'

I had intended suggesting euthanasia, but thought better of it. I stood up.

'Thank you for the tea. 'I'll see you again in a couple of months,' I said.

Alas, six weeks later, a gravefaced Carol told me that Miss Grayson's sister had telephoned to say the little lady had died, and please would I ring her about the animals. I telephoned at once.

'My sister left instructions that you were to put Danny-boy to sleep straight away,' she explained, 'and I wish you would come very soon. He's behaving very oddly.'

My spirits dropped through the soles of my shoes. Dannyboy normal was bad enough. Behaving oddly, he was unthinkable.

I went through to the surgical preparation room, where the three nurses were getting ready for the day's work.

'Would one of you come with me to put a difficult dog to sleep?' I asked. There was a short silence. Nurses don't like being bitten.

'I'll come, Mrs Barber,' offered Wendy, 'if you can't manage him alone.'

I was very grateful, and we set off for Miss Grayson's house. The sister let us in. 'He's upstairs in Emily's room, and I'm terribly worried about him.'

We followed her up the stairs. There was a loud hush.

The bedroom door creaked open, and I saw Dannyboy. He was lying on a blanket beside the bed, his nose on his outstretched paws. He ignored us.

'Have you given him anything?' I asked, thinking he must have had a massive dose of tranquilliser.

'Oh, no. He hasn't eaten or drunk or been out in the garden. He howled terribly when my sister passed away, then sat down where you see him now and hasn't moved.' She shuddered. 'I'll leave you now, if you don't mind.'

'Is this your nasty dog?' Wendy was incredulous. She bent and stroked his head. I waited for the explosion, but nothing happened. She slid a hand under his chin and lifted his head. He drooped miserably. Gently she encircled the top of his arm with her fingers, and I knelt in front of him and clipped away some of the hair so that I could see the distended vein under the skin. I slid the needle into the vein and pressed the plunger of the syringe. I look my patients in the eye when I am putting them to sleep. For an instant, a gleam of the old spirit shone in his eyes, then he sighed deeply, and was dead. We wrapped him in the blanket.

Miss Grayson's sister waited in the hall.

'We are to bury him in the garden,' she said, 'and my sister wanted you to have this.' She handed me the cage. 'There's a lot of food and stuff, too. I'll help carry it out.'

Wendy flatly refused to hold the parrot's cage on her lap, so it travelled back to the surgery in the back of the car with the dogs. All of them were intrigued. Ceilidh pushed his nose through the bars and sniffed deeply. The parrot shuffled along the perch, its beak clicking angrily, a beak which could slice through the shell of a Brazil nut with no effort. Glancing in the mirror to make sure there was nobody behind us, I stamped briefly on the brake, and immediately accelerated again. Everything in the car swayed forwards, then back, and Ceilidh's nose slid away from the cage and bumped Wendy's neck. The parrot hung upside down, screeching and filling the car with peanut shells as its wings struggled to regain its balance.

'Ugh,' shivered Wendy. 'I don't know how you can bear to have such a horrible creature in your house.'

The girls were hardly more enthusiastic when they came home from school.

'What is it?' demanded Liz. 'I thought all parrots were grey, and talked.'

'It's an Amazon Green,' I replied, 'and nobody has ever tried to teach it to talk, so it only speaks parrotish.'

'What's its name?' Louise wanted to know.

'I thought we might call her Persephone,' I suggested. 'It's a lovely name.'

'Too lovely for this bird,' replied Louise. 'Look at its mad yellow eyes. And how do you know it's a girl?'

'I don't know,' I admitted. 'I just wanted to call it Persephone.'

'It's so ugly, it's got to be a male,' declared Liz, who had just had a major quarrel with her latest boyfriend and held all men in deep contempt. 'If you're so keen on the name, we'll pronounce it Percy Phone.'

The newly christened bird made no comment. He maintained an unfriendly silence all evening, and ignored our overtures.

'Perhaps he doesn't like being in a cage,' I suggested, and daringly opened the door. Suspiciously, Percy Phone poked his head out, then, seizing the open door with his beak, pulled it shut again. He opened and closed the door several times, then with beak and claw laboriously climbed out of the cage and down the leg of the table onto the floor. We all backed away nervously. Leaning forward and with an odd, pigeon-toed gait, he strutted across the hearthrug, and before I could realise his intention, seized the end of a slumbering Crimpy's tail and tweaked it. The cat leaped vertically into the air, twisted round and landed facing her tormentor, her lips drawn back in a hissing snarl and her maltreated tail lashing angrily. Percy Phone arched his wings, stretched his neck and clicked his beak at her. Crimply gave way in astonishment.

Watched by human, canine and incredulous feline eyes, the audacious bird made a complete circuit of the room. Nobody moved to stop him. Arriving back at his table, he

44

climbed the leg again with beak and claw, clambered to the top of his cage and shrieked, 'Geroff! Oyez! Oyez! Oyez!' ending with a wild yell of triumph.

We applauded him warmly and, disconcerted, he got back inside his cage. The door was hooked back, and as he settled into his new environment, he evolved a routine. He spent most of his time sitting on top of his cage, returning inside only to feed or drink, or leave his inoffensive droppings. He was very clean, grooming himself constantly. Sunflower seeds were eaten inside the cage. Peanuts were picked up in his beak, and transferred to a claw. He would then climb awkwardly to the top of the cage using one unoccupied claw and his beak. Having shelled, skinned and devoured the nut, he went back to the cage for another and repeated the mountaineering to eat it.

Several times a day he went walkabout, and nothing was safe from that awful beak. The furniture, the wallpaper, the curtains, the side of the door, all bore signs of his ravages. We all kept out of his way. He developed a deep hatred of my favourite red slippers, but only when they were on my feet. I learned to keep a wary eye on him, and hastily abandoned my footwear on his pigeon-toed malevolent approach.

He never showed any sign of friendliness or affection and was a most unlovable character. After a grooming session he liked to be sprayed with warm water, and this was the only time I felt safe in offering him a grape, or a sultana, in my fingers. He always took it reluctantly, giving the impression he would much rather nip off the top of my finger. Visitors heartily disliked him, giving his cage a wide berth and exclaiming at the damage to our home. The dogs and cats tried to ignore him, moving out of his way with a growl or a hiss.

He was to fall in love, briefly, once.

4

'It's a very small kitten,' the young man said. 'It won't be much bother.'

'You've got so many cats already,' added his wife disparagingly, glancing around the feline-festooned sitting-room. 'You won't even notice one little kitten.'

I have always found kittens of all ages very noticeable indeed, and remained unconvinced.

'We're moving next week,' continued the man, 'and we could come and fetch it in a couple of days, after we've settled. Shall I drop the kitten in, during the next day or two?'

I said I would think about it, but they delivered a cardboard box to my door the next day, while I was at work. When I returned home, my two daughters were delightedly playing with a skinny tabby kitten.

'What's its name?' they asked.

'I don't know,' I said. 'The owners just called it "the kitten".'

'That'll do,' declared Liz. 'We'll call it Kitten.'

Needless to say, the original owners never came for her, so we perforce added an ordinary little brown tabby cat to our household.

With about half a dozen cats generally in residence, there is rarely ever a problem with new additions, but Kitten refused to be integrated. Except at feeding time, when all cats and dogs gathered in the kitchen, she walked by herself. Other cats lived in the sitting-room, spread over the windowsills, lolling about in the chairs, or roasting themselves before the fire. They shared cushions, washed each other's faces and, when I sat down, sat companionably on my shoulders, on the back of my chair, and on my feet.

Kitten lived in the bathroom. She loved human com-

46

pany, and greeted anyone who wished to spend a penny with loud, happy purrs. If possible she slept in the dirty linen basket—the lid didn't quite fit and she could creep inside, but found it quite difficult to get out again. Visitors would be puzzled by deafening purring noises, startled by tabby paws like grapnels at the top of the linen basket, then mortified by the appearance of a triangular face between the paws, peering like Chad with a question mark in the 'Prrp-prrp-?' she used as a greeting. She put people off what they were doing, especially when she laboriously heaved herself out of the basket and rubbed her head on the seated victim's ankles. As a mark of particular esteem, she would sometimes stand up on her hindlegs and pat her guest's knees with her forepaws. She did this to me one day, and caught her claws in the waistband of my jeans. Her indignant efforts to free herself dragged the trousers down to my ankles. Delighted with this new idea, she hopped into the little hammock they made between my feet, and was most indignant to be ejected when I stood up and wished to rearrange my clothes.

One chilly spring day, both my daughters had invited their current boyfriends to tea on the same Sunday. Liz's friend Derek I had already met. Louise was bringing a new boy she had met at the disco a few days before. She seemed worried as she helped bake the scones for tea. 'Roger doesn't like cats,' she said nervously.

I glanced through the door into the sitting-room. I had lit the fire, and five approving cats sat toasting themselves before it. 'He's coming to the wrong house, then,' I replied.

Ceilidh and the other dogs greeted the visitors politely, then returned to the rug by the fire and went back to sleep. Not so the cats, who can immediately recognise anyone who dislikes them, and make a beeline for him. Roger had hardly sat down when he had cats on his lap, on his feet, round his neck, and fondly washing his face. They were persuaded to leave him alone while he had his tea, and he enjoyed Louise's scones and drank several cups of the expensive tea I keep for special occasions.

Louise actually helped wash up. She must have been very anxious to impress Roger. I could understand why. He had the blond good looks she admired, and apart from his antipathy to cats, seemed a charming lad, if slightly stuffy. He disappeared in the direction of the bathroom while we were putting my best teacups back in the cupboard, and had not reappeared when we went back into the sitting-room. Liz and Derek were playing Scrabble and had invented some long and possibly rather rude words. Louise and I joined in, and it was some time before I noticed Roger was still missing.

'Do you think he's all right? I worried. 'Derek, perhaps you? He might be embarrassed if one of us . . .'

Derek obligingly went to investigate, and I heard a muffled exchange through the bathroom door. He returned, looking amused and mystified.

'One of us is mad,' he declared. 'I asked him to repeat it, and he definitely said there's a cat in his trousers, and he can't get it out.'

Shouts of laughter were hastily suppressed to avoid upsetting poor Roger even more. 'Tell him to take the trousers right off, and shake her out,' I suggested.

Roger eventually reappeared, his mouth pursed primly. 'I'm terribly sorry,' I lied, 'but she must have taken a fancy to you.'

'She?' he repeated, horrified. 'It was a she? In the bathroom with me while I . . . ?' He stopped, abashed.

He left early, and avoided Louise at the next disco. She didn't mind. Her new boyfriend loved cats.

*　　*　　*

It was Kitten who was responsible for bringing another waif into the house, a young bird, newly hatched, which she deposited proudly on the sitting-room floor. I hastily rescued it from her and inspected the bedraggled, naked creature sprawled on my hand.

'It's probably a rook,' I said, 'or possibly a jackdaw. Difficult to tell without feathers. I'll put it in a box in the airing cupboard to recover from the shock, then see if it will feed.' Liz addressed our unrepentant tabby cat.

'Kitten!' she said sternly. 'I know you can't help catching

little birds, because that's what cats do, but please, PLEASE, either kill them quickly, or let them go again outside, where they belong. Don't keep bringing them in for Mummy to play with.'

'I don't play with them!' I protested. I was very proud of my ability to rear birds rescued from the cats. Adult birds were generally dead when taken from feline jaws, or died very quickly from injuries and shock, but fledglings, lacking exciting fluttering feathers, were gripped less tightly, and often survived capture. Older babies, accustomed to their parents' feeding, sometimes suffered fatal indigestion when offered my diet of chopped hardboiled egg, scraped raw kidney and mealworms, but very young, newly hatched birds thrived on it.

I took the little birds as soon as possible to a rescue establishment just outside Marshton, not wishing my murderous cats to have another go at them. There, a band of dedicated, slightly dotty people reared them to maturity, then released them. I had misgivings about the whole procedure. Small birds generally have well-defined territories, and deeply resent strangers. I wondered how many of the released birds actually survived in the wild. After all, most birds produced far too many offspring each year, which were then decimated by natural disasters and enemies. If they all survived, as I pointed out to the girls, we should soon be knee-deep in blackbirds and thrushes. The few I saved each year could make no difference at all to the population, but I still could not ignore the pathetic gaping beaks and squeaking twitters. I flatly refused to catch flies or murder spiders to feed them, and shuddered when I gave them live wriggling mealworms, but they needed some natural live food to balance their diet.

The newest arrival was only too happy to feed when removed from the airing cupboard later, accepting everything I offered, and trying manfully to swallow my finger too. We were very busy at the time, and no opportunity arose to take him to the rescue centre. He travelled around with me on the front seat of the car, to the dogs' deep disgust. I carried his food in a jar, feeding him at frequent intervals through the day.

49

He grew and thrived. As I expected, his first feathers were glossy black, then white patches appeared, and I realised to my dismay that he was a magpie. He learned to fly and to pick up food for himself, so I was finally able to leave him at home. He refused to leave us. I tried putting him in the garden and closing all the doors and windows. He flew in through a neighbour's bedroom window and created chaos, upsetting all the bottles on the dressing table and leaving ample evidence of his visit on the counterpane. I went to fetch him, and he accompanied me into the garden, sitting happily on my head, and was delighted to return to his own abode.

He was the messiest creature I ever met. Percy Phone, admittedly raucous and destructive, was nevertheless naturally clean, invariably returning to his cage to leave his discreet droppings. The magpie was less fussy, and with his varied and omnivorous diet soon produced a frightful smell. We kept sheets of newspaper under his favourite perches—on the dog-room door, and on the sitting-room mantelpiece. There was a roll of kitchen paper permanently to hand, and a cloth soaked in disinfectant, known as the plop cloth, lived on the hearth to cope with disasters.

Our home began to smell like an aviary. I tried calling him Pica, his Latin name, but he was usually referred to as That Wretched Bird, or just Bird. He carefully avoided the cats, but they ignored him, except Fanny who was obviously determined to have him for tea. She managed to catch a few feathers as he swooped over her head, and killed them ferociously, because she was an irritable, bad-tempered cat.

She had been brought to my surgery one evening by a group of students. They had found a trio of small children playing with a tiny baby kitten. They had put a wire tightly around its neck and were trying to hang it from a tree. Rescued, the kitten was installed in a cupboard in the college basement, and fed mostly on raw liver. The resultant smell gave her away to one of the lecturers, who decreed she must be immediately removed and destroyed.

She sat on the surgery table, her matted tortoiseshell coat like a mixture of burnt toast and marmalade; her head was about the same size as her skinny body, and her lank tail hung down like a piece of wet, black string. I gently stroked her wedge-shaped head, and she spat irritably and batted my hand with a dirty paw. She was infested with fleas, and obviously had worms. She had absolutely nothing to recommend her. I kept her in a cage at the surgery until we had eliminated her parasites and cured her diarrhoea, then she joined our household.

She was obviously part Siamese. She had a Siamese face, a discordant Siamese voice, and a strong Siamese opinion of her own importance. Happy, she was affectionate and gentle. She retrieved pingpong balls and bits of screwed-up paper like a dog, and enjoyed a game. She would put her paws on my shoulders and lick my face with a small sandpaper tongue. In some ways, she seemed more like a monkey, than a cat. Liz could make her very cross by imitating angry cat noises, and they would have arguments across the room. It was easy to upset Fanny, and we left her alone when she felt unfriendly. Bird brought out all her worst instincts.

He stole objects from around the house and hid them in secret places. The girls lost innumerable pieces of junk jewellery. He took a bath several times a day in the dogs' drinking bowl, flooding the kitchen floor. All food had to be kept in closed cupboards or lidded containers. He dived on a bowl of stewed rhubarb as I put it on the table, energetically bathed in it, then shook himself vigorously over the custard. I cleared up the mess and we had ice-cream instead. It was the only time in his life the girls actually approved of him.

Louise could no longer leave her guinea pig loose in the sitting-room because Bird attacked it, pecking viciously at the little creature's eyes. The local department store put purchases in distinctive black and white striped bags, and we had to remember not to bring these bags into the house where Bird could see them, because he attacked them furiously, screaming his staccato machine gun 'Kak-kak-kak-kak-kak-kak'.

I found and replaced the plastic covers for the armchairs, designed originally to stop Percy Phone destroying the upholstery, but now used for reasons of hygiene. Bird's favourite perch was on my shoulder, and I took to wearing an old waterproof jacket in the evenings to save my clothes. He would nibble my ear affectionately, making endearing croaking sounds, then suddenly aim a spiteful peck at my eye.

He lived with us for more than a year, and as the second spring approached, took to spending more time each day in the garden. Small birds mobbed him, and he always fled indoors to avoid them. When I worked in the garden, he accompanied me, flying short distances, then returning to perch on my head, much to the amazement of passers-by.

One bright May morning, he swooped across the sitting-room immediately above Fanny's head, apparently deliberately taunting her. She leaped at him and caught a tail feather. He flew on, out of the open window and into the rose bushes. Fanny got up, stretched, and hopped through the window. She sat in the middle of the lawn and washed her face. We never saw Bird again. Whether Fanny finally caught him, or whether he found a mate and returned to the wild, I didn't know. I didn't care much, either. He was probably the only guest in our house who definitely outstayed his welcome.

*   *   *

Carol put down the phone and called to me from the office.

'Another visit for this afternoon, I'm afraid, Mrs Barber.'

'That's all right,' I answered cheerfully. 'It only makes four, and I'm not doing the evening surgery.'

'Ah!' she continued, looking through the door of the consulting room, 'but I haven't told you who it is yet!'

I was tidying my case, changing empty bottles for full ones, throwing out used syringes and making sure I had plenty of new ones. I looked up, frowning.

'The three foolish virgins,' she grinned.

I sat down, clutching my head and groaning.

'What's the matter with the Misses Duckworth this time?' I asked. 'Has one of the Children got a scratch on its nose, or is the cruel farmer next door leaving his sheep out in the field when it's raining?' Perversely, I quite liked the dear ladies, but they tried my patience sorely and fully merited their nickname. Jointly left a large fortune by their father, they lived in a rambling old house on the outskirts of Marshton, which they shared at first with two very old aunts. When the aunts died, two more old ladies appeared, and were shortly joined by two more. The four were always referred to as the aunts, although in fact they were no relation to the Duckworths. They were constantly changing. Some were very near the end of their lives and were tended by a nurse, kept and paid for by the sisters. Others came for a few weeks' holiday, and one or two seemed to stay much longer. They had their own rooms on the ground floor, and a specially installed bathroom. The sisters fed them very well, took them on jaunts and outings, and were always ready to sit with them, talk to them and sympathise with their problems.

The old ladies paid a token amount for their keep, for, as the eldest Miss Duckworth explained, the old must keep their dignity and not be expected to accept charity. To absorb their overflowing goodwill, each sister had a dog, or rather a bitch. Males of any species were anathema to them, and they detested children. Their pets, known collectively as the Children, were outrageously spoiled, but remained charming characters. I had no objection to visiting them and coping with their (often imaginary) minor ailments, but nevertheless found that calls to the Duckworth ménage left me bad-tempered and exhausted.

'They've found a wild cat,' said Carol, 'and they want you to take it away before it kills the birds in their garden.'

'A wild cat?' I squeaked incredulously. 'There are no wild cats in Marshton!'

'Well,' said Carol, 'they claim they found it in a ditch and managed to get it home, and now it's under their sideboard.'

'All right,' I sighed resignedly, 'I'll go there last this afternoon.'

Miss Lily Duckworth came to the door.

'At last! We are so glad to see you.' She turned to the Corgi at her heels. 'Aren't we, Bronwen? You like your nice doctor, don't you, darling?'

I patted the Corgi and wished her a good afternoon, because I was expected to treat the Children as if they were people. Having had her tail, like all Pembroke Corgis, amputated in the name of fashion, the little bitch waggled her bottom instead. She really did seem pleased to see me. Miss Lily led the way to the sisters' sitting-room, announcing my arrival in ringing tones. Miss Babs fluttered into view, clutching her Poodle, Babette, who greeted me politely. Miss May's enormous hairy mongrel preceded her into the room and hurled herself at me with delighted abandon. Staggering under her weight, I involuntarily sat down on the floor, which pleased her even more.

'Mrs Barber, you are so clever,' cooed Miss May. 'Such good advice you gave us on your last visit.' I cast around in my memory.

'I told you I couldn't sleep properly because Maria is so restless,' she reminded me.' (All the dogs slept on their owners' beds.) 'You told me she should have her own bed. Well, come and see!'

I followed her upstairs, very conscious of the aunts peeking round the doors of their rooms to see the Children's famous doctor. Maria led the way into the bedroom, and bounced happily onto a brand new single divan, complete with pillows and duvet, drawn close to Miss May's chaste couch.

'There!' cried the dear lady. 'Her very own bed. And I can still reach out and touch her. We both sleep very well now.' I had meant, of course, that Maria ought to have a proper dog bed, but this would not have crossed the sisters' minds.

We descended to the sitting-room.

'Where's the cat?' I enquired, wondering if I was going to need the cat snare from my car. I opened the basket I had brought with me.

'It's still under the sideboard,' they said. Lying flat on the floor, I peered under the sideboard, but could see nothing. Miss Lily produced a flashlight, and, blinking and spitting in the beam, I saw a very small, very scraggy kitten. Incautiously, I reached to seize it, and had to withdraw my hand hastily, scratched and bleeding. Wiping the blood from my knuckles, I changed tactics and, taking the blanket from the basket, managed to entangle the kitten in it and then return the spitting, swearing bundle to the basket.

Refusing the sisters' offer of tea—it was my last call of the day and I was anxious to get home—I set off in the car. Had the 'wild' cat been an adult feral cat, I would have liberated it nearby, advising it to steer clear of the three foolish virgins, but this little kitten was too young to fend for itself. Ceilidh sniffed the basket, which almost exploded as the inmate attacked him through the wickerwork. Deeply offended, Ceilidh looked out of the window and pretended the basket did not exist.

The girls were markedly unenthusiastic.

'I like nice, playful kittens,' grumbled Louise, 'not spitting fireworks!'

'And I think kittens should be fluffy and pretty,' said Liz. 'This one is really very plain.' They could not understand at all why I should wish to keep the kitten, which I had dubbed 'Duckworth', but I regarded him as a challenge. We arranged accommodation for him. I found a large, lidded cardboard box, put a blanket inside it and cut a small hole in one side. We put it in a corner, behind the television. Next to it, I put a dirt tray, a dish of food and a saucer of water. Then I opened the basket and tipped Duckwroth out, as close to the box as possible. Swearing like a trooper, tail like a bottlebrush, he disappeared into his new home.

The other cats perfunctorily examined the box as they came in, but were told by the occupant in no uncertain terms to go away and leave him alone. They did so. For the next week or so, Duckworth remained invisible. Food and drink disappeared and he used the dirt tray. Then, one evening, when I put his dinner down, he crept out and began to eat before I had gone away. Gradually, he became bolder and began to investigate his immediate surroundings. The dogs and other cats took little notice, and he discovered the fire, and how delightfully warm it was on the hearthrug. Greatly daring, I tickled his hard little head, and he purred like a miniature steam engine. He found the Great Outdoors, and I thankfully threw out the dirt tray.

Inside the house he was calm and friendly, but if we met him in the garden, he cringed and slunk away.

The girls frequently invited friends to tea, who were introduced to the various animals.

'This is Fanny,' they said. 'She is part Siamese. And this is Lottie—she's a purebred Persian. And this is a Duckworth.'

'What is a Duckworth?' they asked, falling innocently into the trap.

'About two shillings a pound!' yelled Liz and Louise, hugging themselves with glee.

Although he had been cast out by the three foolish virgins as a potential bird killer, Duckworth never seemed to catch anything. The other cats brought in birds and small rodents, occasional baby rabbits, even a squirrel. They left feathers all over the place, or ate the mice except for the stomachs, which were always left like tiny black shoulder-bags just where I would be sure to tread on them barefoot. Duckworth never even chased a butterfly.

He grew from a plain, scraggy kitten into a plainer, scraggier cat. His rusty black coat stuck out in all directions and although he kept his white parts glittering white, he never looked really clean and tidy. He became effusively affectionate but was unpopular as a lapcat because in his ecstasy he unsheathed his claws and dug them painfully into people's knees.

One evening, Kitten appeared in the sitting-room and gave the strangled hunting call which meant she had caught something. I turned to see what it was, and if it was rescuable. She dropped a small creature, and immediately pounced on it, and missed. The little animal vanished under a chair. Furiously, Kitten poked a long arm underneath the chair, and a fieldmouse shot out of the other side, galloped across the hearthrug and collided with Duckworth, half asleep, paws tucked tidily under his chest. He turned, sniffed the mouse, shrugged his shoulders and went back to sleep. Frantically, the mouse burrowed into the fur behind his bony elbows and disappeared underneath him. Duckworth slept on. Kitten hunted for that mouse for nearly an hour, finally giving up and going into the kitchen for a drink. Quietly, I fished under the black and white cat's tummy, cupped the mouse in my hand and dropped him out of the window. He vanished across the lawn. What is a Duckworth, indeed? As a mouser, not very much!

*　　*　　*

Occasionally we were faced with more exotic patients than the usual cats and dogs.

'Keep away! Don't touch him! He doesn't like people, and could hurt you!' I heard Tom Ellis, curator of the Marshton Municipal Zoo giving agitated orders as I passed the door of the waiting room one morning. Peering in, I saw him standing guard over a tall crate. On the far side of the room, an embarrassed woman was trying to control an unruly dog and two unrulier children.

'For the sake of safety,' I said, 'perhaps we should move your crate into the prep room.' Tom thankfully agreed.

'What is it?' I asked.

'It's Old Harry, the cassowary,' he replied. 'The name suits him, he's a right devil. His feet could kill a man.' I looked at the enormous chicken-like feet visible at the bottom of the crate, armed with ferocious-looking talons.

'They could probably do quite a bit of damage to a woman, too,' I laughed.

However, getting the bird out of the crate was no laughing matter. Old Harry was exceptionally aggressive, even for a cassowary. Eventually, I blindfolded him with a towel, and as we hauled him out of the crate, Lynne rugby-tackled him and hobbled his lethal legs together with bandage. The bird collapsed in a shaggy grey heap on the floor. Alarmed, I took off the blindfold, thinking I had suffocated him, but a vicious peck in the general direction of my eye convinced me he felt quite well, thank you. There was no need to ask what the trouble was. About a foot of dirty pink sausage hung from his vent. I was mystified.

'I've dealt with a prolapsed oviduct in chickens and female budgies,' I said. 'They try to lay a big egg and turn themselves inside out. But I've never seen a prolapse in a

57

male bird before. I suppose this must be bowel.' As I spoke, I filled a bowl with warm water and began to sponge the prolapse clean.

'Can't you tell by seeing where it's coming from?' suggested Lynne. 'I mean, the bowel would come from his back passage, wouldn't it? And anything else from . . . whatever birds have,' she finished lamely.

I picked off some bits of grass and grit and continued washing.

'That's the difficulty with birds,' I lectured. 'All the systems open into the cloaca, which then opens to the outside through the vent. Males and females the same . . .'

I lubricated the prolapse with liquid paraffin and began to ease it back into the bird.

'So, how do you tell hes from shes?' demanded Lynne.

'Different colours, feathers, different behaviour. Robins have great trouble distinguishing the sex of other robins,' I said. 'Ah, that's better.' The bird's inside had returned to its proper place, inside.

'How do you know this is a male?' persisted Lynne.

'It was sold to us as a male,' replied Tom. 'And his name is Harry,' he added, as if that settled it.

We stood the bird up, and I took off the blindfold. He made a convulsive effort to attack me, and the whole lot fell out again. The second time round, it was easier to replace.

'Put your finger there,' I commanded Lynne, 'and hold it while I fetch the suture needles.'

'I don't like sitting here with my fingers up a cassowary's bum,' she complained. 'Be careful where you stick that needle.'

I put a stitch across the vent and pulled it tight enough to hold the prolapse in place.

'There!' I said proudly. 'Bring him back in a couple of weeks and I'll take the stitch out. Phew! It's going to take ages to get this smell off my hands.'

Two weeks later, as arranged, I took the stitch out. Old Harry aimed a kick at the side of the crate, the stubby talons splintering the wooden bars. And the prolapse fell out again.

I was getting quite good at putting back cassowary's

insides, and this time, I took a curved needle threaded with braided terylene, put a neat running stitch all round the vent, and pulled the ends of the suture to pucker the lips and make the hole smaller. Then I knotted the terylene tightly and cut off the ends.

'We'll leave that permanently,' I decided. 'If he has trouble passing his motions, let me know.'

'He won't have trouble,' Tom assured me. 'Messiest bird I've ever had.'

I saw Harry—from a distance—on my monthly visits of inspection to the zoo, and he seemed in rude health.

Louise's class at school were taken to the zoo one afternoon as part of a lesson in biology and conservation. She told her fascinated classmates about the stitch in the cassowary's nether region, holding his insides in. They made up a song about it, and chanted it all round the zoo, to the unfortunate teacher's great embarrassment.

Several weeks later, Tom and the crate reappeared in the surgery, I clutched my head in despair.

'Not again!' I begged.

'Oh, no,' said Tom. 'I don't know what the matter is. His back end is fine, but he's very sick. Off his food since yesterday, and his sits and mopes all the time.'

Blindfolded and hobbled, Old Harry was lifted onto the table. I inspected my handiwork, which seemed intact, and it was obviously not stopping him passing motions. Donning surgical gloves, I gently investigated further, and a beatific smile spread across my face.

'Well?' Tom asked anxiously. 'What is it?'

'The first thing to do,' I said, 'is to change his name. To Harriet. She's eggbound.'

5

Ceilidh had been accepted as part of my pack, but had no particular friend among the other dogs. Zeeta slept on my bed, and occupied my lap whenever I sat down, attacking any other animal that approached me. Jeannie and the Pups formed a self-sufficient trio who were very much a part of the family, but always went everywhere together and excluded outsiders. Nina was a stout Norwich Terrier whose owner had died, bequeathing her to a friend. Unfortunately, the friend's husband suffered from asthma, which was aggravated by the dog's hair, so they brought her to me, begging me tearfully to adopt her. They had promised her former owner that she would be allowed to live out her normal life, but nobody else could be found, willing to take in a fat, ten-year-old terrier.

She was grossly overweight and short of breath. I slimmed her down, and she lost enough weight to be able to walk and even run without stress. She had been used to a quiet and sedentary life, and found my exuberant household overpowering. She had been with us for five years, and although affectionate and good-tempered, had never really integrated into the family. She disliked exercise and rarely joined the others on their regular excursions to the beach or downs, much preferring a gentle potter along the road on a lead. Little old ladies would be greeted ecstatically, Nina sitting up on her fat behind and waving her paws beseechingly. The only other time she showed much animation was at feeding time. She had an internal clock which had its alarm set for five minutes before dinner. She would trot busily out to the kitchen and sit staring at the refrigerator, willing the door to open. Ceilidh never impinged on her thoughts at all, and he made no attempt to approach her.

Then Liz asked me if she could look after a friend's puppy, while they were away on holiday. Foolishly, I agreed, without asking for details. The puppy was a seven-month-old Irish Setter bitch, and the holiday was a three-month world cruise.

Ceilidh and Sasha, the Setter, immediately formed an unholy alliance. Separately, they were obedient, biddable dogs. Together, they were murder. They could jump any fence, open any gate, and if ever they found themselves in the garden or yard without supervision, they simply disappeared. There was a new housing estate about a mile away, which had a little shopping precinct and car park. Behind the parade of shops was a wide expanse of rough grass, where most of the local people walked their dogs. This was always the first place to look for them, but they would also go to the beach, or the farmland behind the house. This was very worrying, because although they had both been taught to ignore sheep and other livestock, two dogs make a pack, and without a restraining human presence they could not be trusted.

One day, when I had had to leave all the dogs behind, Ceilidh and Sasha shattered the living-room window, leaped out and, in an orgy of slaughter, killed all my neighbour's ornamental pheasants. I replaced the birds, at enormous expense, but it was a long time before he forgave me. It was an anxious time, and although Sasha was a charming bitch, we were all heartily glad when her owners returned from their holiday.

Ceilidh moped disconsolately. Any dog seen on the horizon which remotely resembled a Red Setter was immediately investigated, but he would always return, tail drooping, ears flattened. Talking to her friend on the telephone one day, Liz enquired after Sasha's health, and the mention of her name caused pandemonium as Ceilidh tried to look out of the window to see if his beloved was coming up the garden path.

I was too occupied with my own sorrows at the time to give him the attention he needed. In the space of a few short weeks, I had to part with first Nina, then Zeeta.

The old Norwich Terrier had had a tumour in her tummy

for years, but it had never caused any trouble. Now it suddenly began to grow. It was attached to her liver, was quite inoperable, and would have made her very ill. Before that could happen, I put her quietly to sleep one evening as she dozed before the fire. If dogs go to Heaven, she undoubtedly ran straight to her original owner, quivering with relief, and told her all about the madhouse she had been living in.

Zeeta was not so straightforward. There was no sudden distinct dividing line between happiness and distress for her. She had been very deaf for some time and her sight was failing, but she seemed well. Her appetite and digestion were good, and she loved going out in the car and walking with the other dogs. I had to keep a sharp eye on her, though. If we met people on the beach, she was quite likely to tag along behind them, then when I discovered she was missing and ran back to fetch her, she would be bewildered to find me behind her when she thought she was following me.

The only time she was perfectly relaxed and happy was sitting on my lap or curled close to me on the front seat of the car. If I disappeared, she wept. Gradually she became more and more senile. One evening, the girls took me to task, pointing out that it was not kind to keep her as a cabbage. They told me that if she were brought into surgery I would have only one course to advise, so I had to let her go. It was a heart-wrenching decision, and I missed her more than I can say.

At this critical time, Mrs Sheperd rang to ask if I would like to have her Poodle.

This idea needed careful consideration. Dogs are social animals, and any group will have a leader and a second in command. For domesticated dogs, the place of the pack leader is taken by the human owner and probably the owner's family. The dogs decide themselves, if necessary by quarrelling or even fighting, who is to be second in command. When Ceilidh first arrived, the resident group were all bitches. Zeeta regarded herself as special, but there was no real leader amongst them. As he grew up, Ceilidh assumed the role of second in command under me. If I spoke sharply to one of the other dogs, he would stand over her and growl, and I had to be tactful about correcting him in front of 'his' pack.

I have often noticed that in a group of dogs which includes a Poodle, the Poodle always takes command. Introducing a male Poodle to my current pack was therefore potentially hazardous. Ceilidh would either be aggressive or humiliated. Since both dogs were very young, I decided to take a chance, and agreed to take Oscar, the Poodle, on trial, to see how he and Ceilidh got along.

He was about five months old, and still very black except for his face and feet, and silvery streaks on his ears. I collected him in the car one evening, and he was very doubtful about coming with me. He had an inordinate amount of luggage—feeding bowls, coats, two beds, several blankets, collars, leads, and a little bag with brushes and combs. He had recently been bathed and clipped and was very elegant.

'He runs about in the garden, but he's not used to going on the lead, because I can't manage him.' Mrs Sheperd dabbed at her eyes with a tiny handkerchief. 'I really can't give him the sort of life he should have. He needs fun and other dogs to play with. It would not be fair for an old lady like me to keep such an active dog.'

She went back into her bungalow, pausing to wipe Oscar's muddy pawprints off the front step.

We only had a short way to go. Oscar climbed onto the front seat beside me and gazed out through the windscreen, his paws on the dashboard. Apart from his trips to my surgery, he had probably never seen the world outside the bungalow, and its little garden. He seemed to find it quite interesting.

Arrived at his new home, I carried him in and put him on the floor in the middle of the sitting-room. He sat down, and inspected the other animals. Jeannie and the Pups poked their noses out from under the settee, sniffed and decided he wasn't worth coming out for. Ceilidh stood up, waving his tail amiably. Oscar titupped over to him on his microscopic feet, stood up on his hind legs, and licked the lurcher's face. Ceilidh's tail waved faster, and he collapsed in a heap, rolling onto his back and kicking his legs in the air. The Poodle pounced on him, worrying the hair on his neck, growling a ridiculous falsetto growl. Ceilidh opened his mouth wide, and Oscar tried to grab his tongue, little needle teeth clicking on Ceilidh's fangs. From the very beginning, they were the best of friends, as if they remembered their first encounter all those months before. At feeding time, Oscar left his own daintily prepared dinner, and took a nice piece of meat off Ceilidh's plate. The big dog sat down and smiled benevolently, then pushed the plate towards his friend.

'Help yourself,' he said, and reached out a long tongue and demolished Oscar's dinner in one lick.

At bedtime, I put one poodle basket in the sitting-room, and the other, with a selection of blankets, by my bed, next to Ceilidh's old sheepskin rug. The new boy could take his pick. It caused no surprise when he followed his chum upstairs. He stepped daintily into his bed, and spent several minutes rearranging the blankets to his satisfaction. When they were all heaped up in the middle, he collapsed on them with a sigh, and closed his eyes. Ceilidh settled on his rug with his nose next to the basket, and composed himself for slumber. I climbed into bed, bade them goodnight, and switched off the light. There was a faint scrabbling, a grunt, and a small weight landed lightly on the end of my bed. I felt little feet walk up my legs, slide down the duvet and stagger up to the pillow, and Oscar sat on the back of my neck and went to sleep.

*   *   *

The Poodle showed no sign of pining for his old home. He followed Ceilidh everywhere and did everything he did. He accepted me as his new human and gave love and affection without reserve. He did everything wholeheartedly. When he chased gulls on the beach, he ran as fast as he could; at mealtimes he ate with singleminded concentration, and when he decided to misbehave, he did so with dedicated determination.

He was already properly housetrained when he arrived,

but as he grew up and learned to stand and cock his leg, he acquired the habit of marking every new thing he found, including new things in the house. A plastic shopping bag left in the middle of the kitchen, a pair of shoes dropped in a corner, a garden fork left in a flowerbed, all received close inspection and the regulation two yellow drops. Even people were not exempt. If I met a friend out walking, I had to be ready to pick Oscar up or distract his attention if I saw him sniff suspiciously at the person's shoes. He honestly never seemed to understand what he had done wrong when I chastised him. He would accept harsh words, even a smack, without rancour, then fetch a ball or a stick and offer to play to cheer me up. It was impossible to stay cross with him.

He loved dirty washing. Laundry day was a delight to him. Smelly socks, underwear, favourite jumpers, all would be taken from the heap in the kitchen and secreted behind a chair or tucked under the blankets in a dog-basket. They would be exhumed later and offered to visitors.

Like all the dogs, he loved riding in the car, and would balance himself on the back of the driving seat, where he often gradually slid down behind me. This did not make driving any easier.

On most days, I took all the dogs to work with me, and they used to sit in the car quite happily all day. Sometimes, I had to leave them behind, if I was collecting a patient for operation or spending all day on one farm, for instance, doing a tuberculin test. A neighbour's small daughter would let them out for me at lunch time, and they had the run of the whole house, but they hated being left behind. Especially Oscar.

He expressed his disapproval by attacking and rending the cushions in the armchairs. I often returned home to find yellow polyurethane foam scattered all over the house, and a yellow polyurethane foam-bedecked Poodle sitting exhausted and satisfied in the ruined chair.

Returning from school one day, Louise surveyed the mess on the floor, and raised her eyebrows disbelievingly.

'Gosh,' she said. 'Yellow snow.'

From that time, armchair cushions were known as Yellow Snow Kits.

The only other things which aroused Oscar's killer instincts were toilet rolls. New ones were removed from the cupboard in the bathroom and reduced to soggy confetti. With care, one toilet roll can be shredded to cover most of the rooms in a house.

For a change, he would seize the dangling end of the roll in use, and rush downstairs, the paper unrolling behind him. Short lengths would be woven through the legs of the table and chairs. Some would be ripped into little pieces. The drinking bowl in the kitchen would be buried under a mound of coloured tissue, the water soaking into the paper and siphoning all over the floor.

When I arrived home, the other dogs would tiptoe through the mess and cower in the garden. Oscar would hurl himself at me, sobbing with relief that I had reappeared, then bring me lengths of paper to play with. Or he used to grab one end of a bigger bit, and roll over and over until he was bandaged like a mummy.

Clearing up the mess was all part of the game. As fast as I picked up the chewed bits and put them in a bucket, he took them out, killed them again, shaking them vigorously, and spread them all over the floor.

He had an inexhaustible supply of energy. In spite of a voracious appetite, he kept his trim, whippety figure. He could easily outrun all the other dogs, and kept up easily with cantering horses. He was not a yappy dog. Admittedly, he barked at the dustmen and joined in the general howling when I had to leave dogs behind. Neighbours assured me that they complained only until I was out of earshot, and then remained totally silent until my car turned into the end of the lane on my return.

They all sometimes sang with trumpets or violins on the radio, and Jeannie always joined in when Louise played the mouth-organ some misguided person had given her. I returned home one afternoon to find she had invited two friends to tea. They were having a concert for glockenspiel, recorder, mouth-organ and Scottie.

Feeling rather cheerful one morning, I burst into song as I drove along.

'Let us with a gla-had so-home mind,' I began.

Oscar, on the seat beside me, pawed at my leg and whined. I ignored him.

'Pr-r-raise the Lord for He is kind,' I continued. Oscar lifted his nose and yipp-yipped experimentally.

'For Hi-his mercies aye endure, ever-her faithful, ever sure.'

'Eeeeeee, yipyip, yarooooooh,' yodelled the poodle.

I joined in, pitching my voice to harmonise.

'Yi-hi, yooohooo,' I warbled. 'Eeeeeargh, ooooooh.'

He rolled his eyes and changed key. I obligingly slid up half an octave and harmonised. 'Oh, woooohooo,' we sang.

I paused to draw breath, and discovered, to my intense embarrassment, that we had arrived at the town centre. I had stopped automatically at a red traffic light. The driver of the car pulled up alongside was leaning across to peer into my car window, an expression of utter disbelief on his face. People passing on the pavement were nudging each other and pointing. My face assumed the same hue as the traffic light as I sat waiting for it to change and allow us to escape.

A few days later, I called at Park Farm to check a group of sick calves. They were much better, and the farmer followed me to the car to collect a bottle of antibiotic, so that he could carry on with the treatment himself. He looked at the dogs.

'Your Poodle don't grow much,' he observed.

'He's not supposed to,' I explained. 'He's what they call a toy. He's very tough, though, and keeps up with the others.'

A sly grin spread over the farmer's face.

'Got a good voice, too, I hear,' he said.

*   *   *

Not long afterwards I paid a visit to the animal sanctuary. Zoë had another oddity for my inspection.

'If you look at him this way,' she held a kitten sideways before me, 'he looks normal. And if you look at him this way,' she turned him round to face the other direction, 'he looks normal.'

'Well,' I said, 'I didn't really see him properly, but—'

'But if you look at him like this,' she switched him round like a conjuror so that he faced directly towards me, 'you can see the trouble.'

Solemnly, the kitten and I stared at each other. His eyes were round, bright, golden yellow, and odd. They were not a pair. The left was half as big again as the right. Separately, each eye was perfect, and he could apparently see normally, but his lop-sided stare was unnerving.

'The rest of the litter have gone, but nobody wants this one,' said Zoë sadly, 'and if he can't sell himself as a kitten, nobody will take him as a grown cat. I've got too many cats, and the Society's inspector is coming next month, so there's only one answer.'

She sighed heavily and handed him to me.

'I've got too many cats, too,' I claimed, 'but it seems a pity to kill a healthy kitten.'

His coat shone like polished ebony, and his purr throbbed through his whole body. I rubbed the top of his head, and he turned and looked at me, unblinking.

'All right, I'll take him,' I said helplessly, and he nipped my finger, affectionate, satisfied.

Liz and Louise were enraptured.

'Have you ever seen eyes like that before?' they demanded.

'Never,' I admitted.

'It gives you a funny feeling to stare at them,' declared Liz, 'sort of giddy.'

'He's probably a magic cat, bending you to his evil will,' giggled Louise. She walked stiffly across the room, pretending to be hypnotised. 'Yes, O master,' she intoned, 'I obey and will get you some milk.'

Disconcertingly, the kitten jumped off my lap and followed her to the kitchen, where he watched her fill the milk dish. Crouching over it, he purred and lapped at the same time. Liz shivered.

'Weird,' she said. 'Makes me feel ill. What shall we call him?'

'Black, shiny, and makes you feel ill,' I pondered. 'IPECACUANHA.'

'Ippy-what?' the girls protested.

'Ipecacuanha,' I repeated. 'I remember it from pharmacology. Black, shiny, makes you feel sick.'

The kitten returned, jumped back onto my lap, and seized my fingers in his front paws, then kicked them with carefully sheathed claws in his hind legs. He liked his name.

He grew rapidly and, apart from his strange eyes, was a very handsome cat. His black coat almost glittering in the sunshine. He remained always in the house or the garden, never leaping over the wall or the gate like the other cats. In some ways he seemed very clever, and I often had the uncanny feeling he understood speech. In other ways he was remarkably stupid, and would be lost at the end of the garden, unable to find his way back to the house. He loved people, and was effusively affectionate, but he ignored all the other animals. They behaved as if he were not there. I wondered if the world looked strange or lopsided through his unequal eyes.

The road outside our house was sometimes busy with traffic, and we were normally very careful to keep the gate closed to protect the various animals. One morning when Ippy was about six months old, the postman left the gate open, and we realised a short while later that Ippy was missing. The other cats, of course, came and went as they pleased, but I was worried Ippy would get lost.

My fears were justified. He had apparently vanished from the face of the earth. I put a large notice on the garden gate, and another on the notice board in the surgery waiting room. I telephoned the local paper and put an advertisement in the Lost and Found column. I think Liz and Louise were secretly rather relieved, but they knew I missed him.

'If anyone finds him,' they comforted me, 'there'll be no trouble identifying him. After all, he was unique.'

'Was?' I demanded tearfully.

'Is, is,' they corrected themselves hastily.

About a week after his disappearance, little Miss Grimes staggered into the consulting room during the morning surgery. Panting, she rested a heavy cat basket on the floor and subsided gratefully into the chair by the examination table. Of indeterminate age, she lived alone in a small terrace house in the middle of the town.

'You put my Fluff to sleep last month,' she began, 'because you couldn't get him better.' There was a short, accusing silence, while I reflected that there was no cure for old age. 'You told me to let you know when I felt ready for another cat,' she continued, 'and you would help me find one.'

'It looks as if you've found one for yourself,' I smiled.

'No,' she disagreed, 'he found me. Walked into my house, large as life, sat in my Fluff's chair and looked at me. Made me come all over queer!' She turned and began to unstrap the lid of the basket.

'I brought him down for you to see, and make sure he's healthy.'

She opened the basket, and lifted Ippy onto the table. He pushed his head into my hands, purring delightedly.

'Hello, little chap,' I laughed. 'Where have you been?' I turned to Miss Grimes. 'He's—' I began.

She snatched him back jealously, and clutched him to her skinny bosom.

'He's a handsome cat,' I finished lamely. 'What do you call him?'

'Blackie, of course,' she said pityingly.

Ippy regarded me, inscrutable, waiting. I said nothing. He ducked his head under her chin and pushed his nose into her neck.

'He loves me,' she claimed, almost weeping.

'Yes,' I agreed, 'he does, and he's clean and healthy, and I know he'll be happy with you.' Miss Grimes put him back into the basket and buckled the straps.

'You know,' she confessed, 'I had a strange feeling when I came in here. I thought you would tell me there was something wrong and take him away from me.'

'No,' I said, 'I'd never do that.'

Liz and Louise were philosophical when I told them. 'We've got lots of other cats,' they said, 'and we mustn't be greedy, and it will suit Ippy very well to be a witch's cat.'

6

From a very early age, both my daughters helped in the surgery and accompanied me on visits to patients. This had instilled in them a very strong desire to be anything but vets when they grew up. They both loved animals, and we had the usual array of dogs, cats and different small rodents, but they decided a vet had a terrible life, ruled by the Tyrant Telephone, and with distressingly little free time.

I naturally wanted both to have every opportunity, and hoped they would decide on definite careers. In her early teens, Liz said she wanted to work with horses. This is a phase many girls go through, but she seemed determined, so I thought about finding her a good pony. We were far from rich, and this decision would mean giving up all idea of a proper holiday, and making do without too many new clothes, but we seemed agreed on priorities.

For many years, since our time on the Isle of Wight, the girls had shared Old Jack, a New Forest pony bought from a riding school in his youth, and ridden every day by his lady owner until he was twenty. She then decided he was too old to work any more, and retired him to a little paddock behind her garden, with a stable he could use if he wished. He was well fed, and she visited him every day, but it was a lonely, boring life. When he was nearly thirty, his owner decided to go and live in Minorca, and asked me if we would look after the old lad in his declining years. I had a big chestnut mare and her four-year-old daughter, and he was delighted to come and live with two such charming ladies.

I had bought ponies for the girls from time to time, but they never showed much interest, and the ponies were sold on to more appreciative owners. They inspected Jack without enthusiasm. He was a strangely angular fellow, with an enormous jug head, big bony joints and little boxy hooves like a donkey. His nondescript bay coat had no shine, and stuck out in different directions. It was possible to spend an hour grooming him, and leave him looking exactly the same as before. He was a friendly chap, and joined in the children's games with an easy good nature.

He was a little too tall for them to get on his back without a saddle, so they invented their own methods. Louise would pull his head down and stand astride his neck. When he lifted his head, she slid down his neck, over the bump of his withers, landing more or less in the right place. She would then gleefully turn round to face his tail, slide off over his rump, and do it all again.

Liz had an easier method. She found a short ladder, and Jack would stand perfectly still, braced against it, while she climbed up and slid across his back. As he walked away and the ladder fell, he always gave a little skip and she promptly fell off again.

To make matters safer, I found a saddle that fitted him, and we constructed a bridle from the box of spare parts I kept in the tack room. When he was cast in the role of Indian pony, they still rode him bareback, but when he played cowboy horse, he was saddled, and lolloped amiably around the garden and paddock, shrieking children on his back and under his careful feet. At weekends and on evenings when I was at home, I rode out on the mare or the filly, and Jack seemed quite happy to be left with his other equine lady friend.

One weekend, an equestrian visitor decided to accompany me, and both mares were saddled up and led out into the yard. Jack crashed around his stable, trumpeting desperately and trying to leap out over the lower door. Fearful for his safety, I threw both sets of reins to my companion and asked her to take the mares out into the road, while I let the hysterical old pony out into the paddock. He raced across the grass, jumped the hedge into the garden, galloped across the cabbages and runner beans, leaped the fence into the yard, skidded through the open gate and triumphantly joined us in the road.

Liz had watched the performance open-mouthed, and

offered to fetch his tack and join us on the ride. I was very doubtful.

'It will have to be a short ride, then,' I suggested. 'Hacking along the lanes and across the fields is a bit different from playing cowboys and Indians in the garden. And he's not shod.'

Jack listened, swivelling his ears like semaphore flags. Obviously delighted to be out and working again, he pranced along like a two-year-old, his tough unshod hooves whispering on the road in sharp contrast to the clatter of the mares' feet. When we started a sedate trot, he nipped the older mare until she retaliated with her heels, squealing angrily. Excited by the commotion, her daughter bucked and began a fidgety canter.

'Take it easy,' I warned, trying to control my scatty old steed. What a hope! Within seconds, all three had set off in a headlong gallop across the field. Swerving to a stop at the hedge, Jack shook his ugly head and danced joyfully.

From that moment, Liz and Louise developed an interest in riding. They took Jack to gymkhanas, put up jumps in the garden, and practised bending races in the paddock. They were careful not to ask the old pony to do too much, but he was tireless. Louise, at the time still smaller and lighter than her older sister, entered him in a small local hunter-trial, and we discovered Jack's amazing cross-country abilities. Obstacles which could not be jumped were scrambled over. Nothing stopped him. All his rider had to do was close her eyes, hang on and pray. He acquired a local reputation. Owners of less courageous mounts tried to get behind him, hoping he would give them a lead over the jumps. His collection of rosettes on the girls' bedroom wall ran all round the room.

Now, after nearly ten years, he was approaching forty, an incredible age. Liz and Louise rarely rode him, because they had grown while he, of course, had not. One of their friends, a slightly built tiny girl, took him to a gymkhana when he must have been at least thirty-seven, and he won a trotting race, hacked five miles home, then skipped and bucked all round his field, chivvying the mares and telling them how clever he was. If Liz was serious about working with horses, she would obviously need something capable of hard work.

I telephoned Miss Thynne, a lady who bred and sold superior children's ponies. Liz pointed out she was not a superior child, and would be happy with an ordinary pony, but I was determined she should have the best. We made an appointment to visit Miss Thynne's stud one Saturday afternoon when I was free. One of my colleagues usually did her work, so I was just another customer.

Her ponies were incredibly beautiful. And extraordinarily expensive. As the afternoon wore on, and the presented ponies became more and more expensive and out of reach, I became more and more despondent. Liz seemed quite cheerful. At last, Miss Thynne said she had shown us everything for sale, and she was sure we would like a cup of tea while we made up our minds. We all trooped into her impressive old house, and Liz and I sat on hard chairs in a cold stonewalled room, while our hostess went to the kitchen to see about tea. Liz idly picked up a copy of *Horse and Hound*.

'Oh, good!' she said. 'It's this week's.'

'You shouldn't read things in other people's houses,' I whispered, 'not without asking.'

'Just a minute,' Liz exclaimed, 'look at this! Four-year-old part-bred Arab gelding. Well-handled and recently backed. In Horsham. Mummy, that's only fifty miles. We could go there tomorrow. All these posh little ponies are too small. I'm going to grow a bit more yet, so I might as well have something to last.'

We drank our tea, and I mendaciously told Miss Thynne we had not made up our minds and wanted to think about it. She was quite happy about this.

Next day, we rang the owner of the Arab, and drove out to see him. The owner accompanied us to the back of her house, and we looked at a neat little grey mare in a stable there.

'This is the mother of the one I'm selling,' she explained. 'She's half Arab and half Connemara. Her son is by an Arab, but he is too flighty for me. To be honest, I'm scared of him.'

We went through a gate into small paddock, and Liz clutched my hand and squeaked, 'That's the one! Perfect!'

At the far end of the paddock, a stocky Arab pony grazed, unconcerned. He was a rich dark grey with a lighter silver mane and tail. As he turned, his flanks shone pink in the sunshine. Mrs Holton, his owner, explained.

'He was foaled chestnut,' she said, 'but began to turn grey when he was a year old. He's registered with the Part-bred Arab stud book as a chestnut, so you would have to change that.'

'What name did you give him?' I asked.

'I called him "Cara Mansour", a mixture of friendly Irish for the Connemara part of his ancestry, and highclass Arab.'

'What a mouthful,' scorned Liz. 'I shall have to call him "Manny".'

Manny had heard voices, and stood gazing at us, ears pricked so that they almost touched. Making up his mind to investigate, he floated towards us, his tail carried so high that the long silver hair fell forward and cascaded over his back. Stopping a few feet away, he snorted explosively. Liz stepped forward, hand outstretched, knuckle up in case he snapped in excitement.

'Beautiful Manny,' she breathed. 'Beautiful, perfect horse.'

Manny sniffed Liz's hand, then investigated her arm and nuzzled softly at her face. Suddenly, he snorted again, wheeled, and galloped off, kicking his heels and squealing.

'Can I try him?' begged Liz.

Mrs Holton looked doubtfully at her slight fourteen-year-old form. 'Are you sure?' she asked. 'My groom backed him a few months ago, but I've never ridden him. I prefer my gentle mare. He's done very little work, and has not been off the lead rein.'

'Mummy is going to buy him for me to ride,' explained Liz patiently, 'so can I try him, now, please?'

Doubtfully, the old groom brought out a saddle and bridle, and shook a bucket to attract the little horse's attention. He came at once, and licked up the few grains of oats. He made no objection to being tacked up, and I legged

76

my daughter up into the saddle. The groom held grimly on to the leading rein, but relaxed and lengthened it when he saw that Liz was perfectly happy and calm.

'He feels marvellous,' she crowed, 'very bouncy but not at all unseating. I think he would do what I told him if he understood—whoops!'

A sudden freshening breeze blew a long branch from the hedge, startling Manny and making him dance excitedly. Liz waited for him to calm down, then asked him to stand still, walk on, and stand again. He obeyed, arching his neck submissively. She slid off, smilingly thanked the groom, and caressed the horse's neck, untangling the silver mane with her fingers and crooning to him lovingly.

Mrs Holton turned to me. I've had several inquiries,' she claimed, 'and a definite offer from a riding school, but I'd like your daughter to have him.'

There was no doubt in Liz's mind that Manny was the horse for her. Mrs Holton delivered him the following evening, and we went for a short ride together so that he could get acquainted with Jack and my gelding, Jubi, before we turned them out together in the holiday camp field.

When we first bought Manny, Louise would accompany Liz on old Jack, but he was really too old to go far. Also, she had suddenly grown very tall, and besides being too heavy, found that her feet nearly touched the ground on each side of him. As a great honour, she was allowed to ride Manny sometimes, but she very badly wanted a proper horse of her own. I promised to keep my eyes and ears open, wondering with slight desperation where the money was to come from.

Then my accountant, bless his heart, found I had been paying too much income tax, and was owed enough refund to pay for a proper holiday for all of us. Alas for my plans!

*   *   *

Filled with curiosity and with a tinge of apprehension, I drove through Reuben Lee's scrapyard and parked the car in front of the dingy bungalow. He was known locally as the King of the Gypsies, and was greatly feared and re-spected by the didikais and the few true gypsies who remained. He kept half a dozen trotting ponies, and some-times, passing his field, I had seen him, perched precari-ously in a racing sulky behind a flying pony, circling the field at speed. A pony normally trots on diagonally oppo-site legs, advancing the left front and right hind together, then the opposite pair. To race in harness, the pony is taught to swing both right legs, then both left legs together, giving a marginal increase in speed. This is achieved in training by hobbling the legs together on each side with long leather hobbles, and the effect on a high-spirited pony in early training is quite spectacular.

Gypsies do not often seek medical or veterinary advice, preferring their own remedies, and I wondered what disas-ter had befallen. Sick or injured dogs are knocked on the head, so I guessed my patient was one of the ponies. I had brought the horsey box of tricks with me—farrier's tools, dental rasps, tranquillisers, emergency instruments, every-thing I could think of. My knock on the front door of the grimy bungalow was answered by a prim, bespectacled lady who told me that Mr Lee was expecting me, she was on the telephone, and good afternoon. She closed the door and I turned to find that a short swarthy man, dressed entirely in black, had appeared noiselessly behind me. A black felt hat covered his lank, black hair and obscured most of his face.

'Round 'ere,' he said, and stepped catlike between a broken-down lorry and a pile of disintegrating cars. We came out onto the field I had seen from the road. In the far corner was a beautiful Reading Van, smoking wisping from its chimney. Advancing towards us was another black-garbed figure, leading a prancing, stilt-legged pony. They stopped in front of me, and man and pony inspected me carefully.

'What—' I began.

'My best trotter,' he said without preamble. ''Angs 'er 'ead to one side, goes all crooked, 'asn't won a race fer weeks.'

As I patted her neck and spoke to her, she nuzzled softly

at my face. There was a faint, foetid odour on her breath which gave me the germ of an idea.

'I'll fetch some things from my car,' I said.

Wordlessly, the man holding the horse jerked his head, and the other gypsy followed and watched while I opened the box and took out a dental rasp, a bottle of disinfectant, a syringe and some ampoules of tranquilliser. Reaching into the car, I took a torch from under the dash. I flicked the switch hopefully but nothing happened. I had forgotten to renew the battery. With an unladylike curse, I tossed it aside. I offered the man a bucket and asked him to fill it with clean water. He materialised beside me when I returned to my patient, and men and pony watched with interest while I poured from the bottle into the bucket, and swished the rasp in the strong-smelling milky liquid.

With infinite tact and patience, I opened the little mare's mouth but could see nothing without the torch. I picked up the rasp, and slid it experimentally over the teeth on one side. She backed away nervously. I pulled the rasp forward again, and began to slide it along the upper row of teeth. She jumped forward, the rasp hit something in her mouth and was knocked violently from my hand. With a scream of rage and pain, she reared up, striking out with her forelegs and throwing me to the ground. Lying there dazed, I saw a small bloody object by my outstretched hand, and an objectionable stink filled the air. Clambering to my feet, I picked up the smelly object and held it out to Mr Lee.

'Bad tooth,' he cried. 'You knew straight away and just knocked it out.'

He pushed his hat back, and a beam of delight spread over his dark face. I thought it tactful not to explain that I had meant only to inspect the pony's mouth, and would normally use an anaesthetic for removing a tooth. In fact the pony had knocked the tooth so violently against the rasp that she had removed it herself. ''Ow much,' he demanded.

I mentioned a sum, and he produced a thick wad of notes from a back pocket and peeled off the right amount.

'You're looking for a good horse.' It was a statement, not a question.

'Yes, for my second daughter. She's very tall, so it needs to be a fair size.'

'Bring the missie here Wednesday, six o'clock.'

Turning on his heel, he stalked back towards the van, throwing the reins of the pony to the other man behind him, and I continued, shaken, on my rounds.

On Wednesday, at six, Louise and I drove to the scrapyard, and clambered through new heaps of metal debris to the field. Reuben stood there, holding the most spectacular pony I have ever seen, before or since. His basic colour was bright silvery white, and he was covered all over with half-crown-sized black spots, each spot ringed with a circle of mixed black and silver hairs, as if the colour had run. He was not very tall, about fourteen and a half hands, (a hand is four inches), but broad and muscled, giving the impression of great power. His long mane and sweeping tail were a mixture of black and silver, and his hooves were striped like old-fashioned bulls' eyes.

Louise gasped with delight and took a step towards him.

'Don't look too keen,' I muttered. 'They'll put the price up.'

The pony was wearing a Western saddle and ornate silvermounted bridle, and Reuben tugged gently at the reins to keep his head up and neck proudly arched. He looked magnificent. Louise walked all round him, felt his legs for lumps and bumps, and peered into his mouth to check his teeth.

'Seven?' she suggested.

'Seven year old, little missie,' replied Reuben, smiling.

'Can I try him?' she asked.

Without comment, Reuben handed over the reins.

'I'm not riding in that awful thing, thank you,' she said, disparagingly. 'We've got a proper saddle in the car.'

I fetched my own precious saddle from the car and, to my surprise, it fitted perfectly. Louise hopped up, tightened the reins, and squeezed him on.

'Walk on,' she commanded.

He walked away, then trotted, cantered, and finally did a flying gallop all round the field.

Louise pulled him up, and slid off.

'You try him, Mummy, he's lovely.'

Accustomed to my long-legged thoroughbred, he felt as if he had four wooden legs, but he was very obedient and easy to ride. After circling the field, I dismounted and inspected him more closely. That great crested neck had aroused suspicion. My fears were justified.

'He's a stallion,' I accused.

'Oh, yes, Lady, he's full horse,' affirmed Reuben. 'Quiet as an ol' lamb.'

I was horrified. 'I can't buy a stallion for a young girl,' I protested. 'He'll kill somebody, probably my daughter.'

'No, Lady,' disagreed the gypsy. 'Quiet as an ol' lamb, he is.'

'Can he jump?' asked Louise.

A gleam appeared in Reuben's eye. He heaved two old oildrums out of the hedge, balanced a mighty pole across them, and stood back.

'Take him over that,' he suggested.

The jump looked enormous, at least four feet high, and solid. Louise walked the spotted pony up to it and let him have a good look, then trotted to the far side of the field, wheeled, and cantered back with a determined air. The pony stopped momentarily, gathered his feet, and cat-jumped off his hocks. He cleared the pole by inches and cantered on, shaking his great head.

Reuben slapped his thigh and yelled with glee.

'Yes,' he shouted. 'He CAN jump.'

'I don't want a stallion,' I insisted, 'however quiet he is.'

The light in Louise's eyes went out. Slowly, she shook her feet clear of the stirrups, slid off the saddle, and stood with the pony's head cradled in her arms.

'Take him on trial for a week,' said Reuben. 'The missie can handle him. Next Wednesday, bring me the pony or two hundred and fifty pounds.'

I gulped. It was a high price, and if we accepted him after trial, we would have to pay the asking price, no haggling.

'That's too much.' Louise unbuckled the girth and pulled my saddle off the pony's back. 'You can't pay that much for a pony for me. That's more than Liz's Arab cost.'

'We can pay it if we don't go away for a holiday again this

year.' I stifled a very small sigh. A nice hotel where someone else did the cooking and washed up was my idea of heaven.

Louise brightened. 'We don't really need to go away for a holiday,' she declared. 'We've got the sea, and the downs.' She saw my crestfallen expression. 'And when you have your holiday from work, you and Jubi can come with us.' She stroked the horse's massive neck. 'We'll have to think of a name for him.'

'Ocelot,' I said unthinkingly, realising immediately that I had thus committed myself to buying him. I shook hands resignedly with Reuben. 'Two hundred and fifty pounds, next Wednesday,' I agreed.

We had come prepared to buy, with a.borrowed trailer hitched behind my big old car. Ocelot loaded with no trouble. Reuben looked as surprised as I felt.

Gypsy horses are not allowed to run free, and Ocelot had been stump-chained, tethered by the roadside, all his life. Jack had been taken to a distant field to keep my old mare company, and Jubi and Manny were in a little field I rented from the local council. It had several drawbacks. It was on the main road, and had an invitingly wide grass verge beside it, encouraging holiday motorists to park and use the edge of the field as an emergency lavatory. Immediately opposite was a holiday camp, whose visitors seemed impelled to feed the horses all sorts of unsuitable titbits, including meat pies, sausage rolls, and polythene-wrapped packets of sandwiches.One side of the field bordered on a new housing estate, some of whose residents tilled allotments a short way along the main road. Our field provided a short cut, which did not worry me until they started cutting the wire fence to get their wheelbarrows through. I was getting very tired of being telephoned by the police in the small hours, to tell me the horses were wandering up and down the main road, having found the latest hole in the fence.

It seemed wiser to put Ocelot, who had been reduced to Ozzie, by himself in a tiny half-acre field belonging to one of our neighbours, which we were allowed to use from time to time. As a precaution, we kept him tethered, and Louise spent every evening after school getting acquainted. The first time she rode him on the road, I went with her on Liz's bicycle, but he was bombproof in traffic and his manners were impeccable, so I stopped worrying. At the weekend, we all rode together, and Ozzie was polite to the geldings, so we decided to put all three together in the holiday camp field.

The spotted horse's delight when he realised he was free was a joy to see. He thundered across the field, tossing his head, kicking at nothing, squealing with excitement.

'This is all very well,' fussed Louise, 'but how do we catch him again?'

I walked into the middle of the field, carrying a halter. 'Ozzie!' I shouted. He came at top speed. Gypsies are totally unsentimental about their animals, which are taught from an early age to have a deep respect for humans. I stood my ground, looking braver than I felt, and the great spotted beast skidded to a stop and stood motionless while I slipped the rope over his head.

However, we discovered that if the human ran away from him, he followed in gleeful pursuit, enormous yellow teeth and flashing heels much in evidence. As far as I knew, he never actually hurt anyone, but we had no more trouble with trespassers.

The two sisters had always spent a lot of time together, complete opposites but good friends, and that summer they were constantly on horseback. Off duty, I often rode with them, and when I was working, they invited privileged friends to stay for the weekend and ride my horse. We sunbathed on the beach, and swam in the sea, with or without the horses. We walked miles with the dogs, and I borrowed the trailer and towed Manny and Ozzie to shows and gymkhanas beyond hacking distance.

Jumping was not Manny's forte, but he did his best, and Liz rode him gracefully and correctly. Ozzie was either very very good, or absolutely awful. Some days, he returned festooned in rosettes, at other times, he galloped round the ring, apparently knocking the jumps down just for the hell of it.

There was one major problem at the end of the summer. Ozzie behaved so well, we often forgot he was a stallion, until one day, Louise unthinkingly took him for a ride on the beach with two of her friends. One was riding a gelding, and the other a mare. Ozzie seized the gelding by the neck and bit him savagely, and it was only Louise's fearless determination which stopped him killing it.

I gave her two options. We could sell him back, at a loss, or take a chance and castrate him, a very risky operation for an adult horse. Having a touching faith in my surgical ability, Louise decided we must geld him. The operation was successful, and after a few weeks Ozzie was safe to ride with any other horses. His jumping improved, and he became well known in cross-country competitions, but the gypsies never forgave me.

* * *

Liz persisted in her ambition to work with horses and become a qualified riding instructor. If I was disappointed that she was not attracted to an academic career, I think I hid it pretty well.

Manny accompanied her to the stables where she began her training the following year, and they underwent some intensive schooling together. Liz took him hunting, entered dressage competitions, and took part in hunter trials, and the little horse always gave all he had. After taking her examinations and getting some letters after her name, Liz worked in several different establishments. Manny went with her to some of them, but as a paid instructor she had little time or opportunity to ride him. She was expected to work from early dawn to late evening, and needed all her energy and dedication to cope with giving instruction, mucking out, grooming, cleaning tack, and schooling difficult horses. I was astonished at her tenacity and proud of the way she stuck at the job, which is far less glamorous than many starry-eyed teenagers believe.

Louise adopted Manny for a time, and won many rosettes at local shows, but eventually, he had to be sold. He went to a young couple who kept him at livery at a top class riding school, sharing him and loving him as much as Liz had. Indeed, visiting friends in the neighbourhood some years later, Liz called at the riding school, and was amazed and delighted to find him still there, still belonging to the same people, and still, to their amusement, taking off with them at great speed when they rode over the downs. She insisted he recognised her and was glad to see her, but I think it was mostly due to the packet of Polos she always carries in her pocket.

7

Above the clatter and roar of the washing machine I thought I heard a bell ring, and switched off the machine to listen. There it was again, not the telephone, but the front door. Drying my hands on the kitchen towel, I padded barefoot through the sitting-room into the tiny entrance hall and opened the door. A well-dressed lady stood on the doorstep, holding a pale child by the hand. She held out her other hand, smiling.

'How do you do?' she said. 'I'm Norah Cameron, from the white house next door. I understand my daughter Mary is having tea with you today.' I blinked.

'Is she?'

'This is number 234? And you are Mrs Barber, Louise's mother?' I admitted this was true.

'Mary and Louise are in the same class at school, and Louise has invited her to tea. I called to make sure . . .' her voice trailed off.

Called to check us out, I suppose, I thought to myself. 'I'm so sorry,' I said aloud, 'do come in. Tuesday is my afternoon off. I was about to make a cup of tea.' This was not strictly true. I had been thinking that a cup of tea would have been a marvellous idea if there had been time to stop. She came in, glancing round the room. I was thankful I had done the housework before starting the washing.

'Please, sit down,' I begged. She perched warily on the edge of the settee. It wobbled slightly and three long black noses appeared inquiringly from beneath it, sniffed, and disappeared.

'How nice to have time off to yourself during the week,' she gushed. I smiled noncommittally, thinking that one free afternoon a week hardly compensated for working every Saturday and alternate Sundays.

'I'll put the kettle on,' I said. 'The girls should be home soon. I'm afraid they make their own social arrangements and often forget to tell me until the last minute.' As I spoke, the back door flew open and Liz hurtled into the kitchen.

'Louise has invited that puny girl from next door to tea,' she warned, 'and her mother will probably . . .' She saw my face and stopped. I pointed towards the sitting-room. '. . . will probably be calling to see if you mind,' she finished diplomatically. She dropped her satchel on the floor and marched into the next room. 'Hello,' she said, 'I'm Louise's sister. We're going to see the horses before tea.'

Mary nodded eagerly.

'Louise said I could ride Ozzie,' she claimed, 'so I changed into trousers.' She was wearing very elegant velvet ski pants. Liz said nothing. As I carried in the tea tray, Louise burst into the kitchen, began to say something, then noticed the visitors.

'Sorry, Mum,' she cried. 'I forgot to ask you, but you usually let us have friends to tea on your day off. Can Ceilidh come in? He's a bit muddy.' The question was rhetorical: the lurcher was already in the sitting-room. He sniffed at Mrs Cameron, who shrank back. He moved politely to Mary, who was entranced, and stroked him. He rolled on his back, kicking his legs and groaning with ecstasy as he scrubbed his itchy back on the hearthrug.

'Isn't she sweet?' Mary trilled.

'He,' said Louise. 'Ceilidh is a he.'

'I can't tell from his name. How was I supposed to know?' pouted Mary.

Louise called Jeannie from under the settee and rolled the unprotesting bitch onto her back.

'See these little buttons?' she demanded, 'they're her teats, where she fed the Pups when they were babies. All females have teats, and males have the other bits, like Ceilidh.' She indicated the dog's obvious masculinity. 'See?'

'I see,' Mary nodded. 'Like the biology lessons at school, but I never could understand what it was all about.' Louise had lost interest.

'Come up to my room,' she commanded, 'and I'll show you the rosettes Ozzie won last Saturday. I'll lead you round the field on him if you like, but you'll have to borrow a pair of my jeans. Those trousers are much too posh.'

I turned to Mrs Cameron. She sat open-mouthed, her teacup frozen halfway to her mouth. Her complexion was mottled purple and red. My daughters' frankness often had this effect. She rose shakily to her feet and I escorted her to the door.

'Mary won't be late home,' I promised, 'and I'll see they do their homework after tea.'

Liz was ferrying saddles and bridles through the kitchen and stacking them in the back of the car.

'Silly woman,' she said, and grinned wickedly. 'Good job she wasn't with us that day at Langford Chine. You remember, that day we saw the hippies?'

'I'll never forget it,' I said quite truthfully, and began to empty the washing machine, gazing unseeingly out of the window. Only four years ago, I thought. We had a heatwave in May . . .

*   *   *

'I can't see anything wrong with it,' complained Liz. Louise peered over her sister's shoulder.

'It's a perfectly good picture of a horse,' she declared. 'Jolly good, in fact. Can I have it to show my friends?'

'No! No!' I cried. 'That's the whole point. Look at it, and you'll see why.' Liz examined her drawing critically, head on one side, then her brow cleared.

'I see,' she agreed, 'like the rabbits.'

'Exactly,' I said.

'It started as a picture of a mare and foal,' she explained, 'then I realised I had made the mare's back too short, so I added a bit and turned it into a gelding.' Louise nodded approval. 'But when I had finished putting in the mane, I had given him a big, crested neck, so I had to put the other bits in and turn him into a stallion.'

'Perfectly reasonable,' I agreed. 'We know it's a good picture. Your teacher knows it's a good picture. But some of

88

your friends and their parents would think it was rude. Put the picture on your bedroom wall, but don't take it back to school.'

'OK,' Liz agreed. 'Fiona Peasgood has the same trouble with pigs. They live on a farm and her brother is always drawing tractors. Fiona draws pictures of pigs, but she always does sows and litters and puts in the udder and teats. People laugh. It was her auntie who caused all the fuss over the rabbits, wasn't it?'

Liz had been given a Dutch rabbit for her birthday, a delightful little black and white doe, full of character. To her joy, she found that one of her school friends had a buck of the same breed, so they decided the rabbits should get together and have some babies. Accordingly, one Saturday, I left Liz at the friend's garden gate, promising to collect her, and her rabbit, when I had finished my shopping. Half an hour later, I returned to find her standing at the gate, trembling with distress. The friend's mother towered over her, red with fury, and turned on me as I approached.

'How dare you allow children to do such things?' she demanded. 'If these filthy arrangements have to be made, it should be done by grown-ups when the children are not there.'

'What filthy arrangements?' I was flabbergasted. 'They only wanted to mate Jennifer's rabbit with Liz's little doe, so that . . .' The silly woman squealed and put her hands over her ears.

'Stop it!' she cried. 'Take your nasty-minded child away. I've put Jennifer to bed, and I shall . . .' I interrupted her.

'I'm sorry if we have offended you,' I said, 'but it's wrong to punish Jennifer. My children regard sex as a fact of life, like eating and drinking.'

'And going to the lavatory,' added Liz wickedly. The woman slammed the garden gate and ran into the house, redfaced and gobbling with fury. Why was it, I thought, that country folk are so often more prudish than city dwellers?

'Are we going sailing with Sam tomorrow?' asked Louise, changing the subject.

89

'He's bringing his family over to the Island for the weekend,' I said shortly. 'We'll go to Langford Chine tomorrow if you like. Take a picnic.' I wanted to put as much distance as possible between myself and the quay. Sam had been visiting me now for almost a year, and the relationship was causing me some concern. From time to time, he suggested leaving his wife and sons and living with us, but I always imagined he was secretly relieved when I refused. The girls and I had become accustomed to our single-parent life, and had adapted mentally, emotionally and financially, but I had no wish to inflict such trauma on another woman whose only sin was that her husband found her boring. In any case, as I pointed out, the idea was totally impractical. We could not live in London, and he could not possibly commute. Why not remain as we were, I beseeched him, loving friends, always glad to see each other, but each having full and separate lives? Relationships, however, do not remain static, and he was becoming possessive and jealous, towards the girls as well as myself. It was disturbing.

The next morning was hot and windless, a perfect day for a swim and a picnic. I put all problems out of my mind and resolved to enjoy the day. To their deep disgust, the dogs were left at home. There was no shade in the car park at Langford, and the beach would become very hot.

'Zeeta will probably have a fit tonight,' said Liz resignedly.

'No, she won't,' I promised. 'I'll give her half a tablet tonight instead of her usual quarter. She'll be fine.'

We packed a large amount of food and drink into the cool box, and stowed it in the car, and I drove the few miles to Langford Chine.

'Looks as if the world and his wife have decided to come here,' grumbled Liz. 'Rows and rows of cars.'

'They'll probably all be sitting within a hundred yards of the bottom of the steps,' I consoled her. 'We'll walk along the beach a little way and find a secluded spot for our picnic, then I'll come back to fetch the box while you two sunbathe.'

It was agreed that this was a good idea. We descended

the steps to the beach, left jeans, tee shirts and shoes in a tidy heap on the pebbles, and picked our way through and between pinkly roasting bodies to the water's edge. Liz turned right.

'Let's go this way,' she suggested. 'The beach is usually empty just round the corner.' We splashed along through the little waves, picking up pretty shells and pebbles, totally absorbed in our finds. Liz suddenly stopped.

'There's crowds and crowds of people,' she complained. I looked up. There *were* crowds and crowds of people, sitting, squatting, walking in the sea, all stark naked.

'Good Heavens!' I said inadequately.

'It's the Festival,' cried Louise. 'You know, the Pop thing we could hear last night from all those miles away. Some of the hippies have come to the beach.' She was right. It was strangely silent. Nobody ran or played or shouted. The young people sat around driftwood fires, or made solemn little sandcastles; even the few children were quiet and subdued. They looked very, very old. Just in front of us, a lad emerged from the sea. The cold water had excited him and his young manhood was obvious. The girls stared at him.

'Do all men look like that?' demanded Liz.

'Well, yes. More or less,' I admitted.

'Eeeerargh! Yuk!' she exclaimed, while her sister made horribly realistic retching noises and pretended to be sick in the sea.

'Don't be ridiculous,' I said crossly. 'You know about stallions and farm animals. Men are just the same.'

'Oh, no!' contradicted Liz. 'Male animals are beautiful, all proud and muscled. That man is just sticking-out ribs and sharp shoulder blades.' She watched him walk away. 'And a nasty little white bum,' she added. Louise gazed round.

'They're all so white and skinny,' she shuddered. We turned round by mutual consent and began walking back.

'They all come from the city,' I explained. 'They don't live a healthy life. We are very lucky to have all this.' I waved my arms, including the sun, sea and sky in one comprehensive gesture. Liz was scornful.

'It's all right for holidays, I suppose, but it gets boring, especially in winter.'

'Boring?' I was utterly flabbergasted.

'Boring,' she insisted. 'You've got your job, and Sam comes and takes you out, and it's OK for kids like Louise, but what can I do? We don't do much at school, and there's nothing else. Even the pictures close in winter. Come on Louise, race you to the next breakwater.' They splashed off like frolicking puppies, Louise heading for deeper water, Liz staying prudently close to the shore. She didn't really like the water much. For me, the sparkle had left the day. I pondered seriously.

Competition was intense for the few grammar school places on the Island and Liz, with no academic ambitions, had seemed content to go to the comprehensive school in the next village; but although she enjoyed the lessons, she obviously found the work far too easy. The chief employers on the Island were farming, sailing, light engineering and tourism, and opportunities for girls were strictly limited. Did I really want them to be shop assistants or chambermaids? Even if they eventually opted for a non-academic career, they must surely have more choice than that. We must return to the mainland.

I stopped and looked around. The girls had found friends and were shouting, swimming, squealing with glee. I waved to them and, pointing to the steps, made eating motions. They understood. I was going to fetch the picnic box. Deep in thought, I was startled when a figure detached itself from the crowd, seized me in a fierce hug and swung me off my feet. I stiffened with fear and resentment, then relaxed. It was only Sam.

'What on earth are you doing here?' I demanded. 'You're supposed to be with your family.'

'The boys are fishing with their mates from the next boat, and Hannah has gone shopping in Newport. Shopping! On a day like this!' he exclaimed. 'Let's go back to your place,' he suggested with an evil leer. I was not in the mood for games.

'How did you . . .' I began.

'Get here? We're staying for a week, so I brought the car over.'

'. . . know we were here?' I finished.

'That was easy,' he smirked. 'I found your dogs left at home and knew you must be here or at Blackgang. Blackgang would be jolly crowded so it had to be here. Not exactly lonely even here, is it? Let's go back to your place. The girls will be all right for an hour or two.' I pushed him away, angry and miserable.

'Go back to your blasted family,' I sobbed. 'Leave me alone!'

'But I haven't seen you for a week,' he protested. 'I want you. Listen! I can't enjoy my holiday unless we . . .'

'That's all I am, isn't it?' I said disgustedly. 'A creature, a thing you need to play with for a time, then you go back happily to your family. Do you ever think how I feel? You do not!' We were having our first major quarrel very publicly. He seized my arm and pulled me away to a less crowded spot. We sat on the pebbly beach.

'Listen!' he begged. 'I do love you. I love the girls like a father. Their own father must be mad to let them grow up and never try to see them.'

'He can't love anybody,' I said sadly, 'not even himself.' By now, I was completely depressed. I knew that if . . . no, when . . . we left the Island, my relationship with Sam would end. I was just part of the scene, the sea, sailing, being jolly. Living elsewhere, I would have little attraction for him. I held out my hand.

'Goodbye, Sam,' I said quietly. 'You had better fetch Hannah from the shops and go back and see what your boys are doing.'

He stood up and stamped off furiously without looking back. I watched him go. He fitted Liz's definition of a male very well. I felt bereft and alone. Drowned in misery, I sat for a minute, perhaps two, then scrambled up briskly. The girls would be hungry and wondering what had happened to me.

I would look through the back pages of the *Veterinary Record* this evening, I promised myself, and see what jobs were available on the mainland. We would have to sell the calves, and those nice ladies who had bought Minky's kids had seemed very keen to have her, too. Did I have their telephone number? Full of plans, I climbed the steps up to the car park . . .

*   *   *

The machine had pumped itself dry and was whining protestingly.

'Wake up, Mum!' said Liz, reaching across to turn it off. 'I'll go and change while you do the feeds.' She stamped noisily up the stairs.

'Come on, Louise and Mary,' she called. 'We're nearly ready to go, and there's lovely things for tea when we get back.'

I measured barley and pony nuts into buckets, reflecting ruefully to myself that the present, although much less exciting than my past, was probably less stressful.

Only a few weeks later, however, I began to wonder. We had spent a wet Sunday morning doing some overdue housework. The girls had tidied their room and attacked the kitchen and bathroom with Vim and elbowgrease. I had restored some semblance of order to the sitting-room.

'It's no good,' declared Liz despairingly, 'we'll have to get some different furniture. This room is a cross between a kennel and a junk shop.'

'It's clean and tidy,' I protested.

Liz gazed at the floor. 'And a new carpet,' she said. She stared out of the window. 'And the curtains are awful.' She turned to the settee in the corner. 'And that object,' she accused, 'is the worst of all.'

'But I made it.' I almost wept. It was a single bed, pushed against the wall between the door and the fire. I had plugged the wall behind it, and hung a padded backrest. It was covered with blankets and multicoloured cushions. The effect was hideous and uncomfortable, but Jeannie and the Pups loved it. Their stumpy little legs were unable to hoist their disproportionate bodies onto the seats, but my homemade settee was high enough for them to disappear underneath it. The hot water pipes from the stove ran

94

under the floorboards, the blanket hung in front of them, and they spent a large part of their time indoors in their own private cosy cave.

I stood in the doorway, and tried to see the room as a visitor. The girls' friends liked visiting us. They enjoyed the animals and the *laissez-faire* attitude, but most of them had houseproud mothers who dusted and polished, and never, ever let the dog into the sitting-room, let alone a horde of cats, a cage-hating parrot, and a half-tame squirrel, to name but a few.

The door where I stood led to the kitchen, the utility room where we kept saddles, dogbeds and sacks of animal food, and then the backdoor and yard. A door on the other side of the room led to a tiny hall, with the stairs on one side and the front door, leading to the garden, on the other. The sitting-room was thus the through route from anywhere in the house to almost anywhere else. A definite worn track led from door to door.

The hearthrug was scorched and holed where live coals had fallen out when I made up the fire. The curtains, Percy Phone Parrot's favourite hate, hung in orange tatters. The armchairs—Heavens, why had I never noticed the armchairs? Percy Phone had ravaged the tops of the backs, apparently convinced that the foam padding held treasures he could never find. The backs had been used by successive cats to test their claws, shredding the upholstery, and the fronts were similarly rent by dogs and puppies clawing their way up. The cushions, thanks to Oscar, had a curiously lumpy look. I had snipped, patched, and repaired, but the result was a cross between a kennel and a junk shop. I could understand the girls' diffidence about bringing new friends home.

'We can't afford new things,' I said bleakly.

'Sit down, Mum, and listen,' ordered Liz.

I sat, and listened.

'Gail's auntie has just died,' she began, 'and left them her house in Chichester. It's a nice house, Fully Furnished' (she often spoke in capitals when she wished to make a point), 'and it's convenient for school and Gail's dad's work. So they're moving.'

Bully for them, I thought. We don't have a rich auntie, dead or alive.

'So,' continued Liz, 'they are selling a lot of stuff from their bungalow, and Gail says there's a practically new Three-piece Suite we could have for Almost Nothing.'

I stood up. 'When do we go and look at this furniture?'

True to Gail's word, we bought the settee and chairs for very little, and I found a carpet in the Great Sale at the local department store. The girls made new chintz curtains to replace my orange rags, and the room began to look like anyone else's. Plastic covers on the backs of the chairs protected them from Percy Phone, and he decided he disliked the texture of the new curtains and left them alone. The seats had blankets on them, whipped off when visitors came. It looked very smart.

Jeannie and the Pups hated the new settee. It was much too low. They tried very hard to live underneath it—my goodness, how they tried. They would push head and shoulders underneath, and pedal frantically with stubby hind legs, grunting with the effort. When they succeeded, they had to lie flattened and spreadeagled, and any movements they made produced strange effects in the people sitting above them.

One evening, when both girls were out, I could stand it no longer. Searching through the shed, I found the discarded legs of the old settee. In the utility room, I unearthed a saw, a screwdriver, a hammer, and a handful of nails and screws. I had a busy and constructive evening.

Liz was the first one home. She had been to a meeting of the local Riding Club. As president, I should really have gone too, but after a hard day's work could not face the prospect of two films about Badminton, and the inevitable quizzing in the interval from members trying to get free advice about their animals.

Liz sat down on the settee, and leaped up again as if stung.

'What have you done to it? It feels terrible.'

She lifted the blanket and peered underneath. Three black, whiskered faces blinked contentedly in the sudden light. A square block on the foot of each leg lifted it up four inches. The blocks were fitted almost straight, and were nearly the same colour as the legs, and if you descended carefully, it hardly wobbled at all. Liz sighed, and let the blanket fall.

'I expect they would have dislocated something if you hadn't raised it. I expect we'll get used to it.'

When Louise came in, she was less sanguine. I was accused of wrecking the house, ruining everything, and turning the place into a pigsty. From a few asides, I gathered she had quarrelled with her latest boyfriend, so I said very little, and by morning, she found my improvements quite amusing.

Gradually, over the next weeks, the room reverted to normal. We forgot to replace the plastic covers when visitors departed, and the cats returned to their favourite perches on their backs. Percy Phone gleefully tore the exposed upholstery, and having got his beak back in training, had another go at the curtains, producing a very pretty fringed effect. Oscar attacked some of the new cushions, though with less enthusiasm than before. A distinct worn track appeared on the carpet from door to door.

A few weeks later, I was washing up the breakfast dishes. The girls were supposed to be getting ready for school, but were in fact discussing the schedule for Chichester Show which had arrived that morning. I glanced through the door into the room. The chairs were covered with snoozing cats, legs and tails hanging nonchalantly. The breeze from the open window lifted the tattered curtain and disturbed a pile of peanut shells and sunflower husks on the television set, where Percy Phone was moodily eating a late breakfast. Contented snores emanated from beneath the wobbly-looking settee, which was distinctly taller than its attendant armchairs.

'Come on, you two,' I called. 'You'll miss the school bus, and I've got a long operating list this morning, so I can't run you in.'

'That's all right, Mum,' replied Louise. 'Mrs Darwin said she had to make allowances for us, because we come from a broken home.'

Liz was incensed. 'We don't come from a broken home.

There's nothing wrong with this home.' She looked around and giggled suddenly. 'Mind you,' she added, 'some of the things in it are pretty well busted up.'

'That's not what she meant, Twittish Person,' cried Louise. 'She meant Daddy doesn't live with us.'

'I know what she meant, and I'm not a Twittish Person,' said Liz, 'and anyway we saw Daddy about six months ago, and I wrote to him last week. What more do we want?'

'You want to hurry up, or you'll never get to school,' I said. They hurried off down the garden path, bickering amiably over the show schedule. I put away the plates.

'Come on, dogs,' I called. 'Let's go and earn some money to keep our busted-up but unbroken home together.'

They paused by the door, and looked at each other uncertainly. What on earth was I jabbering about?

'In the car,' I commanded. 'Might have time to go walkies on the beach at lunchtime.'

Relieved, they poured out of the open door and gathered behind the car. That was better. 'Walkies' and 'Beach' they understood. All was right with the world.

8

I wound a short length of broomhandle into the slimy rope and passed it to the man behind me.

'Don't pull on it yet,' I warned, 'just keep a bit of tension on it.'

Pete was a good cowman and could manage most calvings very well. My heart always sank to my boots when he called for help. If he couldn't do it, it must be a really bad problem. He had been very apologetic about getting me out of bed at 3 a.m., but it was a fine night and I enjoyed the drive to the farm in the moonlight. Ceilidh and Oscar had come with me, but Jeannie and the Pups had stayed firmly in bed.

Pete preceded me to the calving box, carrying a bucket of warm water. I poured in some disinfectant, shudderingly removed my cosy jumper and donned the clammy rubber calving gown.

I soaped my hands and arm liberally. Peter had already washed the back end of the patient, and he held the tail helpfully to one side.

'Can't feel any legs or a head,' he said, 'just a tail.'

I slid my arm into the nice warm cow, and felt a tail and a little calf bottom.

'It's a breech,' I said, 'coming backwards with its hind legs tucked right up by its ears.'

Grunting with the effort, I pushed further into the cow and felt from the calf's bottom along one leg, until I reached the hock joint halfway along it. I hooked my fingers into the joint and eased the leg back until I could slide further along it and grasp the foot. Cupping my hand carefully round the sharp little hoof, I worked it back and into view, and looped a rope round it.

Pete held the rope, while I resoaped my arm and fished

for the other leg. There was more room now, and it did not take so long.

'Keep your leg slightly in advance of this one,' I said, 'and it will tilt the calf's pelvis and make it easier.'

Much straining by the cow, and helpful heaving on the ropes, and a nice live heifer calf was born. Pete was delighted.

'One of my best milkers,' he crowed. 'First heifer calf she's had in six years. We'll keep this one.'

I felt inside the cow again, and my suspicions, aroused by the small size of the calf, were confirmed.

'There's another one,' I said.

The cow's womb had not yet contracted down, and there was plenty of room to rearrange and extract the second twin, also a heifer. Pete's grin nearly split his face in half.

'Good thing you called me soon enough,' I declared. 'If you had left her straining until morning, she would have been dry, and it would have been really difficult.'

I pushed a handful of pessaries into the womb to prevent any infection, and could feel the powerful muscles already contracting down very satisfactorily.

'I think she'll cleanse all right,' I said, 'but if she holds on to the afterbirth, give me a ring and I'll come and take it away.'

Pete fetched a bucket of clean water, and I took off the rubber apron and washed the blood, dung and sticky drying birth fluids from my arms and the side of my face. It was quite cold in the early dawn, and I was grateful for the warmth of my nice thick jumper.

On the way home, tired but contented, I glanced at the clock on the dash. Half-past five. The patients for my morning operating would be arriving at the surgery at eight o'clock for their premedicating and tranquillising injections, and before that there were the horses to feed, and the girls to breakfast and get off to school. Hardly worth going back to bed for an hour.

'How about walks for dogs?' I suggested.

Ceilidh and Oscar signified approval, so we stopped at the field behind the shops, and they galloped off joyfully

100

into the morning mist. I followed more sedately, feeling the after-effects of two hours' hard physical labour, and we circled the field. As we neared the car park on our return, a figure loomed out of the mist and I recognised Mr Ruskin, the newsagent, towing his fat labrador Julie, on a lead.

'Good morning,' I greeted him, 'looks like it might be another fine day.'

'Damned dogs everywhere,' he returned disagreeably. 'Thought I might have the place to myself at this hour. Get away, blast you.' He aimed a kick at Oscar, who was sniffing excitedly around the labrador. From the dogs' behaviour, I gathered she was in season, and they were both very reluctant to leave her and follow me back to the car. Mr Ruskin disappeared grumpily into the mist, tugging crossly at Julie's lead. I called at the horses' field, gave them a token breakfast (they were full of grass and much too fat) and went home to call the girls out of bed and cook our morning meal.

Oscar apparently forgot all about Julie, but Ceilidh had fallen in love. At every opportunity over the next week or so, he hopped over the gate, or pushed through the hedge, and disappeared to the shops. There he sat in the middle of the paved precinct, gazing up at the window above the newsagent's shop, where his love yawned back at him.

On Friday of that week, I finished the evening surgery dead on time, returned home and fed the animals, then cooked my own supper. Both daughters were at a birthday party, due to be returned home at ten o'clock. Until then, I had the place to myself, in blessed peace.

Ceilidh asked to be let out into the garden, and I unthinkingly opened the back door. He ran off, and I put a big fat trout under the grill. The girls did not like fish, except nasty little fingers in shiny packets in the deep freeze, so I usually treated myself when they were out. I toasted some almonds, made a tossed green salad, took the gently spluttering fish from under the grill and carried a loaded tray into the sitting-room. Subsiding into my chair with a happy sigh, I balanced the tray on my knees and picked up the knife and fork.

The sudden shrill of the telephone startled me and

produced the usual dentist's waiting-room effect in the pit of my stomach. I never knew what disaster was about to be unfolded. I put the tray carefully on the floor, and padded out to the shrilling monster in my bare feet.

Before I could say a word, Mr Ruskin's sour tones grated in my ear.

'Your grey mongrel is sitting outside here howling. If you haven't collected him in two minutes, I'm going down to kick his blasted ribs in.'

He slammed the receiver down, and I returned to the sitting-room to collect my shoes.

Five cats sat around my supper tray, cleaning their whiskers. The almonds had been licked clean and spat out, the salad was scattered all over the hearthrug, and of the trout not a morsel remained. Head, bones, skin, succulent pink flesh, all had gone. It was entirely my own fault for putting the tray on the floor, but I had been looking forward to that trout all day, and I nearly wept.

In a very bad temper, I backed the car and went to fetch Ceilidh. I heard him serenading his beloved as I approached. He stopped when he saw me and stood wagging his tail shamefacedly. I was in no mood to sympathise, and ordered him crossly into the car. He stood and looked up at the window. I smacked him sharply on the rump, which did not worry him, but hurt my hand. He followed me meekly and got into the car. I drove home without further comment, made myself an omelette, and went to bed early.

I watched him carefully the next day, and all went well until lunch time. The telephone rang while I was feeding the girls' pet rabbits, and I ran back into the house, leaving the kitchen door open. By the time my caller had rung off, Ceilidh had gone. My lunch took priority, and on my arrival at the field fifteen minutes later, there was no sign of him. A call at Mr Ruskin's shop produced only a torrent of abuse, so I returned dispiritedly, to hear the telephone shrieking imperiously.

'Yes?' I snapped. It was Carol.

'We've got Ceilidh here in the surgery. I think you had better come straight down. He's had an accident.'

102

I called the other dogs in from the garden, bundled them into the car, and we covered the mile to the surgery in record time. Ceilidh was sitting on a blanket in the preparation room, his left front leg hanging uselessly and appearing twice its usual length. He was panting a little but did not seem unduly distressed.

'Looks like a broken humerus,' I said. 'Have you X-rayed him?'

'No,' replied Wendy. 'I thought you had better see him first.'

Very gently, I explored the dangling leg. He wagged his tail and huffed at me. Feeling the length of the leg, moving it carefully back and forth, did not hurt him and I could not feel the teeth-on-edge grinding of a broken bone. My heart sank right out of the soles of my feet. A wave of utter despair engulfed me.

'Radial paralysis,' I said. Wendy nodded.

'That's what I thought,' she agreed. 'No pain. No movement at all.'

'What happened?' I demanded.

'Mrs Fishandchipshop brought him in,' she replied. 'She's in the waiting room. She's very upset.'

Mrs Melville from the fish and chip shop sat weeping in the waiting room. She had three elderly Siamese cats which needed frequent attention, so I knew her well.

'Oh, Mrs Barber,' she wailed, 'I'm so terribly sorry, but he came out so quickly, and I really wasn't going very fast, but I didn't have a chance. He crashed into the front bumper of my car just as I drove out of the car park. Have I killed him? Is he terribly badly hurt?'

I tried to comfort her. 'I thought it must be a car accident,' I said. 'He has damaged the nerve which runs along the top of his shoulder. There's no sensation in the leg, and it's totally paralysed, but there's a chance that it will repair itself, and then he will be all right again.'

I did not tell her how slender my hopes were, and she went home consoled.

From enquiries later, I gathered that Ceilidh had called briefly at his lady-love's house, but even his ardour had finally been killed by her total lack of interest and the animosity of her owner, so he had wandered off across the field to seek more congenial company. The only other dog in sight was Mr Pugh the greengrocer's long-haired Alsatian, Honey. Her temperament matched her name, but Ceilidh did not know this. With a yelp of pure terror, he turned and fled, memories of Bandit and Robber still fresh in his mind. Thinking only of home and safety, he crossed the car park at top speed, running strongly. Looking behind him, he did not see Mrs Melville's car until he hit it full tilt. Horrified when she recognised him, she had gathered him up and taken him straight to my surgery.

I had to forget my own troubles while I did the afternoon calls and took the evening surgery, but my depression returned when Louise questioned me that evening. Ceilidh was lolloping about quite unconcerned on three legs, the useless left fore leg trailing on the ground.

'Will it ever get better?' demanded Louise. 'What can you do about it? Can't you mend it? Isn't there a nice operation he can have?'

'In the same order,' I said, 'I don't know. Very little. No. And no.'

I explained what had happened, tracing the course of the injured nerve across the front of his shoulder.

'It runs very close under the skin there,' I pointed out, 'hardly any protection at all. A really hard bang on the right spot, and the nerve is bruised, or crushed, or even completely cut.'

'How can you tell how bad it is? How soon will it get better?' Louise was distressed. I tried to be optimistic.

'It's worth keeping him for about three or four weeks,' I answered. 'If there's going to be any repair, it will show by then. There will be movement and a bit of feeling coming back.'

'Supposing it doesn't get better?' Louise was anxious to know.

'Some dogs and cats get about quite well with a back leg missing,' I admitted, 'but it's more difficult to balance without one of the fore legs. And Ceilidh would be at a particular disadvantage because he had rickets and his bones and joints are all crooked anyway.'

'So if he doesn't get better—' her voice tailed off miserably.

I was determinedly cheerful. 'We shall have to find a way to stop the paralysed leg trailing on the ground. He can't feel it scraping, but the hair and skin will rub off, even the flesh if we're not careful. Then it will hurt when the feeling comes back, and he won't be able to use it properly.'

Over the next few days, we invented bandages, straps, slings, every sort of contrivance to keep the useless leg off the ground. Once he had rearranged his weight and changed his balance, his tripedal support gave the lurcher no problems at all. Within a week, he was jumping over the gate, and his speed, although marginally less, still enabled him to catch a rabbit on the horses' field. Eventually, I invented a sort of waistcoat, with a hole for his good front leg and a neat little pocket for the bad one. I made several coats, because he resumed his normal life, running after the horses on the beach and over the downs, keeping up with the other dogs easily. He even picked a fight with a big hairy sheepdog which made unwelcome advances to Jeannie.

Twice a day he had his physiotherapy, which did no good but made me feel I was helping, and stopped the girls nagging me for doing nothing. I stretched the injured leg to its fullest extent, and nipped the sensitive web between the toes with my fingernail, looking eagerly for any involuntary twitching of the muscles, or any sign of resentment or pain. There was nothing. Sometimes, we imagined a slight tremor in the muscles over his shoulder, but when I pinched the foot again, he never flinched. Liz once shouted that he had a different look on his face when I was deliberately trying to hurt him, but we realised it was because he could hear Oscar barking at a neighbour's cat, and wanted to go and join in the fun.

Three weeks went by, four weeks, five. After three months with no feeling or movement returning, we had to admit he was not going to recover. By this time, he was running about on three legs as if it were quite natural. He could even balance on two legs to lift one hind leg and pee against the trees. He could jump the garden gate, and seemed perfectly happy. The idea of putting him to sleep —killing him—was unthinkable. Against my better judgement, I decided to amputate the paralysed leg and keep him with three legs.

One morning, he was taken to the surgery by himself, injected with premedicating tranquilliser, and put on the operating list. Once on the table, he was just another patient, and the operation went without a hitch. He flatly refused to stay in a kennel once he was round from the anaesthetic, and made such a fuss that I decided to take him home the same evening. He was groggy from the shock and loss of blood, and the removal of the dead weight of the useless leg had upset his balance. For the first two or three days, I wondered if we had done the wrong thing.

Oscar appointed himself chief nurse and comforter. For the first time, he failed to jump up onto my bed, and slept curled up with the lurcher on the sheepskin beside my bed. He walked close by his friend, helped to lick the wound when I removed the dressing, and ate from the same dish, thus encouraging the bigger dog to take his share. They were completely inseparable.

I think that without Oscar's obvious love and concern, Ceilidh might have given up. As it was, by the time the stitches were removed and the hair had grown over the operation site, he had recovered his former spirits, and took up a normal life again.

*   *   *

What happened next was so bizarre that it could not be dismissed as sheer coincidence. It had been a busy morning surgery and I was looking forward to a much needed cup of coffee as I dealt with the last patient. Mrs Melville's new Siamese kitten did not want his flu injection, and he said so, very loudly. He had no desire to go back into his basket, and when I insisted, raked his claws across the back of my hand, catching them painfully on the knuckle. His owner bore him off, still bawling, and I tottered into the preparation room, where Wendy was putting out the coffee mugs.

'Sorry, Mrs Barber,' she said, 'you've got one more patient before you can have your coffee. Zoë from the Sanctuary.'

'Better put out an extra mug,' I replied. 'I'll see her in here.'

I gingerly wiped the blood off my knuckles. 'Good job I'm not operating today. Scrubbing up would be jolly painful. Hello, Zoë. Have a cup of coffee. Where's the patient?'

'I didn't know how she would react with that little Siamese, so I left her in the van. Two sugars please, Wendy.' She sipped the coffee appreciatively.

'How's Ceilidh? Getting about all right?'

'He's very well,' I answered. 'I get the odd comment from other people. Dear old ladies tell me he should be put out of his misery.'

'Never saw a less miserable dog in my life,' she laughed. 'I'll go and get this greyhound. Thanks for the coffee.'

She went out to the car park, and returned with a small, beautifully marked greyhound bitch. Her left hind leg stuck out sideways and upwards, and did not touch the ground as she walked.

'She was a gypsy lamping dog,' explained Zoë. 'The gamekeeper caught them at it one night, and took a pot-shot at her. Broke her leg.'

'What's a lamping dog?' Wendy wanted to know.

'Poaching, at night,' I explained. 'You shine a powerful torch, and the dog runs down the beam and catches the rabbits and so forth, dazzled by the light.'

'The gamekeeper doesn't seem to mind about the rabbits,' said Zoë, 'but objects to the and-so-forth, especially his pheasants.'

Wendy scooped up the dog, and deposited her on the table. I inspected the deformed leg carefully.

'It's been done a long time,' I said. 'Set in this position, can't move the joint at all. It doesn't seem to give any pain.

'I can't possibly find her a new home in this condition,' complained Zoë. 'Nobody wants a handicapped animal. Greyhounds are difficult enough to place at the best of times. Poor Tania! You'll have to go.'

'Mike is really the orthopaedic expert. Why not leave her here for him to see this afternoon?' I suggested.

So it was arranged. Mike came in a little early, gave Tania an anaesthetic, and examined the leg very thoroughly. Like me, he decided nothing could be done.

The next morning, I had a long operating list. I met Wendy walking back up the road with Tania on a lead.

'She's very clean,' she said. 'Greyhounds are not usually house-trained, but her kennel was dry this morning.'

'It's a great pity the gypsies didn't do something about that leg when it was first broken,' I said. 'She's very beautiful.'

Tania pushed her head into my hand, looking up with soft brown eyes.

'Zoë rang. She wants you to put her to sleep,' declared Wendy. 'Nobody will ever adopt her, not like this. Poor little Tania.' I smoothed the greyhound's soft velvet head.

'Put her back into the kennel and give her something to eat,' I ordered. 'I'll take her for a walk with my crew at lunch time and see how they all get on.' Wendy grinned happily.

'That's what Zoë said you would say,' she exulted.

I had a definite feeling that I had been manipulated.

At lunch time, I decided to walk along the beach to blow the ether fumes out of my head. Ceilidh and Oscar were intrigued by this new female companion, and pushed each other jealously to sit next to her. Tania appeared faintly embarrassed by the attention. Jeannie and the Pups, who clung ever closer together as they grew older, did not think much of her. Three large black noses sniffed from the parcel shelf, then they went back to sleep until we arrived at the beach. I kept Tania on a lead at first, but she was so quiet and friendly, I let her off. She stayed close by my side, then, when the two male dogs began playing and barking in the waves, she joined them. By the time I went back to work, it seemed as if she had lived with us for years.

The deformed leg gave her no pain, but was very inconvenient. It never touched the ground. When she walked, it remained sticking out at her side. When she ran, it waved in frantic circles. She found it awkward to sit in a chair, having to arrange the rest of herself round the bad leg. I considered amputation, but since the leg caused no pain, decided that surgery was not justified.

(Two years later, the decision was taken out of my hands. Chasing a rabbit at full speed one day, she tripped over the leg, vaulted high in the air, and snapped it cleanly just above the original break. I was no longer in general practice, having taken up a slightly less arduous job with the Ministry of Agriculture, but a colleague still in practice made a pretty job of amputating the leg, and Tania was so much more comfortable, I regretted we had not done it before.

One three-legged dog used to cause comment. Having two three-legged dogs is a sure way to be noticed. I have learned to ignore the unkind things some people say.)

Tania proved to be a happy addition to our household. Her coat was brindle velvet, and her expression, like her character, soft and gentle. Her main fault at first was that she obviously considered that cats were put on this earth for greyhounds to chase. My cats rapidly educated her. Not only did they refuse to run away, they actually seemed pleased to see her. She would stand, quivering with frustration, while a purring cat rubbed its head under her chin. If she barked or tried to intimidate the cats, she received a smart tap on the nose with unsheathed claws to remind her of her manners.

She was not very bright. She knew her name, and understood 'Walkies' and 'Dinner'. Like all the dogs, she became wildly excited if I changed my shoes, put on a coat, or brushed my hair, all of which meant Going out. If I spoke quietly and calmly, she understood 'Come Here', but if she disobeyed and I raised my voice and repeated the command, she cowered down or ran away. This could be dangerous if we were riding or walking along a narrow lane and a car approached. Fortunately, she usually followed Ceilidh and copied everything he did.

During that winter, we were keeping the horses in a big fifteen-acre field belonging to a local businessman. He had a landing strip in the field for his aeroplane, and during the summer the grass was cut for hay, but kept clear of stock. In September the little plane was put away, and we were allowed to graze the horses in the field. The grass was plentiful even in the coldest weather, and they needed hay only if deep snow covered the ground. I gave them a feed of corn twice a day, and topped up the water trough and made sure their rugs were comfortable. The field was bounded on three sides by a river, and access to it was by a bridge with a gate at each end.

Unless the weather was very bad, the dogs liked to come with me when I fed the horses in the afternoon, enjoying a ramble over the rough grass. One very cold and windy afternoon, we visited as usual. While I dealt with the horses, the dogs wandered off on their own business. Jeannie and the Pups earnestly investigated an interesting hole in the river bank, throwing clouds of loosened soil into the water. Ceilidh and Tania, followed by Oscar, chased a rabbit across the field, and vanished in the hedge on the far side. I put the empty feed buckets back in the car and shouted. Jeannie and the Pups came at once. If I had time, we walked along the opposite bank to a small recreation ground where they were sure to meet some of their friends. Followed by my musketeers, I began to walk slowly along the towpath, calling the other dogs.

They appeared on the opposite bank, and were obviously worried to find the river between us. Oscar worked out the problem straight away, turned and ran along beside the river, over the bridge, along the towpath, and joined us. After a short hesitation, Ceilidh followed. Tania went to the water's edge, whining desperately. She walked into the water, found it was deep and cold, and backed out again. I began to walk back towards the bridge, encouraging her to follow. She started to trot agitatedly along the bank, then suddenly belly-flopped into the water and tried to swim across. Her crooked leg made it impossible for her to swim straight, and with a despairing wail, she floundered out onto the mud.

I galloped smartly back to the bridge, and appeared on the same side as the poor bewildered greyhound, waving my arms and yelling at her. Wild with relief, she ran up, her bad leg flailing the air, and followed Ceilidh back along the towpath to where the others patiently waited for her to sort herself out. I encouraged her to run and chase about, and her short dense coat rapidly dried.

I told the girls about her escapade that evening. Liz was not impressed.

'I reckon that when brains were given out, our Tania stood in the back row,' she declared. Louise was even more disparaging.

'She probably forgot to queue up at all,' she said.

9

In the spring we moved the horses back to the old orchard, and the dogs delighted in my daily visits to feed them and to straighten or change the waterproof rugs. At first, Ceilidh did not enjoy himself. The Bellmans' house was at one end of the plum orchard, standing in a large wooded garden entirely surrounded by a high stone wall. Bandit and Robber had a kennel in the garden, but spent most of the time roaming free inside the wall. An ancient notice on the drive gate warned visitors to beware, a warning backed up by the dogs' ferocious barking when anyone passed the gate. The sound always sent Ceilidh scurrying back to the safety of the car.

One day, the electricity meter reader called at the Bellman house. He saw the notice on the gate, but disregarded it because it looked old and faded. Walking confidently up the drive, he rat-tatted on the door. There was no reply, so he explored the little path leading round the side of the house. To his horror, the two guard-dogs appeared from their kennel, hackles up and growling threateningly. If he had stood his ground, or walked away slowly and calmly, he would have been safe, but he turned and fled.

Within a few strides, the dogs were upon him, and although he was not badly bitten, his clothes were ripped and savaged, and he was terrified. A passer-by heard his screams, and rushed bravely to his rescue. A few days later, a gale blew down a tree, which fell against the garden wall. The dogs discovered it, and used it as a bridge to climb to the top of the wall and jump down into the road.

Outside their home territory they were harmless, but such was their local reputation that people passing by fled. An ambulance was called to an old lady who collapsed in fright, and the police were summoned to catch and destroy

112

the 'dangerous dogs'. I felt deeply sorry for the misguided and misunderstood animals, but could sympathise with the local feelings.

The Bellmans bought two Dobermann pups, who were too small to be thought of as guard-dogs, and in any case were friends with the whole world. Ceilidh forgot his fears and began to enjoy the visits to the orchard. A large ginger cat called Snap added to the fun. He lived in the end house of the row backing onto the horses' paddock. He was usually sitting in the sun when we arrived, and disappeared briskly through a small hole in the fence when he saw the dogs. As a formality, they barked at him, but the hole was too small for any of them to see through, except perhaps Oscar.

One wet April evening, after an unusually busy surgery, we arrived at the orchard much later than usual. I removed the dogs' collars, because there were thickets of bramble, fallen trees, rabbit warrens, derelict greenhouses, all sorts of places where they might have been trapped. Jeannie and her daughters rushed off to find a rabbit and Tania and Ceilidh followed them. Oscar's collar tangled in the long hair at the back of his neck.

'You really are a scruff,' I told him, 'you'll have to have a bit of a haircut this weekend.'

Finally released, he looked round for the others, could not see them, so wandered off in the opposite direction to see if Snap was about.

It was a miserable evening, and I made a quick job of changing the horses' waterproof rugs. I carried the heavy buckets of food across to the shelter of the hedge, and hung up the nets of hay. They all seemed perfectly happy, ignoring the raindrops dripping off their ears and sides. They were so fat, they could withstand any weather.

Shivering, I decided to forgo our usual stroll round the edge of the orchard and head straight for home and a nice fire. Loud calls and a prolonged blast on the car horn produced the three musketeers, panting and wet. They shook themselves vigorously, and hopped into the car and up onto the parcel shelf, where they sat busily licking the mud off their feet. Another shout brought Ceilidh cantering lopsidedly into view, followed by Tania. I called Oscar, and suddenly knew, with heart-stopping, utter conviction, that I would never see him again.

An hour later, I had searched the orchard, and had not found him. An hour later still, still searching, I saw car headlights approaching across the grass, and recognised Mike's car. He jumped out.

'Are you OK?' he called. 'Liz and Louise phoned me. They said you came here to feed the horses hours ago and they are terribly worried. What's happened?'

I told him, rain and tears streaming down my face. He considered.

'It's very late now, and Oscar will have found somewhere out of the rain to lie up. Much better to go home, and come back in the morning when it's light.'

I agreed with him, and drove home to apologise to my poor distressed daughters, feed indignant hungry cats and dogs, and crawl into bed. We all went back to the orchard at first light, and spent three hours searching. We turned over piles of fallen branches, burrowed under collapsed dead trees, ransacked derelict greenhouses, and shudderingly stirred through a noisome ditch at the far end of the paddock, full of stinking effluent from the neighbouring chicken farm. We found nothing.

At half-past eight we had to go, the girls to school, and I to my morning surgery. During the day, I telephoned the Police, the RSPCA and nearby animal shelters. I advertised in local newspapers, and on the radio. That night, I had a curious dream, which I have never forgotten, and which I am sure was Oscar's memory of the last twenty-four hours, sent to me telepathically.

I was hurrying along through wet grass, in the rain. The fact that the grass towered above my head seemed perfectly natural, because I was small. I was very worried, because I had lost somebody, but knew roughly which way I had to go. Then the dream changed. It was daylight and I was on a wide, smooth road. Enormous noisy things swished by, then suddenly, one of them stopped. The door opened, and I thankfully jumped up into what I thought of as a small room. Straight away, I realised I had made a dreadful mistake. It was the wrong place, and the wrong room, and the wrong people. I turned to escape, but it was too late. The door was closed, and the car moving.

Much later, I was sitting under a chair or a low table, close to a fire. The door was closed, but every now and then it opened, and each time I peered out in a wild hope that somebody had arrived. I was always disappointed.

During the next few weeks, I spent every possible moment looking for Oscar. Friends, colleagues, and clients all helped. We searched fields, hedges, ditches, roads, gardens, parks. I advertised again on local radio, and put leading advertisements in newspapers. There were reports of lost Poodles and strays. None of them was Oscar. I put notices on gates and walls near where he disappeared, offering rewards for information. Gradually, we pieced the story together. He was seen at nine o'clock on the day after he disappeared, outside the orchard, probably having followed Snap through the hole in the fence. At different times that day, he was noticed walking along the main road which would eventually have taken him home; then, at one point, he vanished.

The people who picked him up, skinny, bedraggled, collarless and frightened, probably thought they were rescuing a homeless stray. In fact, by failing to tell anybody, they stole him, and in so doing, they took Ceilidh's greatest friend and robbed me of my dearest companion. We shall never forgive or forget.

*   *   *

'It's only a dog,' they said. 'Why make such a fuss about losing a Poodle? It's not as if you had lost a proper human friend.'

How little they understood. People, however close, retain their own characters and personalities. Animals give themselves freely and generously. A properly schooled horse willingly gives control of his body to the mind and wishes of his rider. Such a rider suddenly finds he is eight feet tall and his body has half a ton of thundering muscle. A trained sheepdog, totally under the shepherd's control, becomes an extension of his master's body, rounding up the sheep with no effort. A dog kept as a companion, accustomed from his wild past to obeying a pack leader, submerges his personality in that of his owner. When the owner is happy, the dog rejoices. When the person is sad or angry, the dog becomes irritable and snappy. They give us total love and devotion, whether we deserve it or not. To lose such a companion is like losing part of one's self.

If the animal is old or sick, the parting can be anticipated, and is no shock. A violent end by accident is a shock, but the wound is clean. To lose a friend, as I lost Oscar, not knowing whether he was alive or dead, or whether he would return or not, is the most painful of all. I admit it, I made a fuss, and wept, and mourned. I knew that in many ways I was lucky. I had an interesting job, a comfortable home, two lovely daughters, and many, many people had far more to worry about than I had. The fact that others are less fortunate has never been much consolation, and I continued to grieve.

The girls understood, and were plotting something. My birthday fell about five weeks after Oscar's disappearance, and they whispered together, and suddenly stopped talking when I entered the room. The Saturday before my birthday in the middle of May dawned bright and sunny, with a promise of heat to come. It was my weekend off, and we all got up early and went for a ride in the cool of the morning, then took the dogs for a short walk on the beach before the holiday-makers were up and about.

After a late second breakfast, I decided my bedroom needed spring-cleaning and rearranging. We took down the curtains, rolled up the rugs, and with much effort and grunting, pushed the heavy bed to the other side of the room. In the patch of dust and fluff thus indecently exposed, I found Oscar's squeaky rubber rabbit and a much-chewed toilet roll covered in tiny tooth marks. I collapsed in fresh floods of tears. Liz and Louise looked at each other and went out. I could hardly blame them. It must have tried their patience severely to have to live with so much woe and misery.

Abandoning the bedroom, I went down to the garden

and began to cut the grass . . . it could hardly be called a lawn. Jeannie and the Pups retired, panting, to their shady lair behind the compost heap. Tania went back to bed in the cool house. Ceilidh stretched out on the grass, so that when I finished, there was a dog-shaped patch uncut.

Having had two breakfasts I didn't need lunch, and went on working in desultory fashion, digging out weeds, putting in little plants to replace some of those eaten by Liz's rabbit. Teatime approached. The girls had been gone for nearly four hours. I put the kettle on, set out the teacups, and lifted the cake tin off the top shelf of the larder. The garden gate rattled, and looking out of the window, I saw Liz and Louise staggering wearily up the path, carrying a basket between them.

I ran out to meet them, and they put the basket down, opened the lid, and lifted out a very, very small Poodle puppy. He was less than four weeks old, far too young to be on his own, but his mother had refused to have anything to do with him, and the breeder had reared him by hand. For this reason, she had let the girls have him for half-price.

I gave them only a token amount of pocket money, because I paid all the feeding, shoe-ing and other expenses for the ponies, but they both had Saturday jobs. Liz had saved hard for a new saddle, and Louise had her heart set on a fluffy white jacket and a pair of cowboy boots. They had drawn out their savings and spent every penny on a new puppy for me. Not only that, they had walked to the breeder's kennel and back, a round trip of nearly nine miles, in the blazing midday heat, because they thought I needed cheering up.

I mourned Oscar no less, but realised how extremely fortunate I was, and applied myself to bringing up the new puppy. We called him Louis. For the first couple of weeks he needed feeding every three hours. During the daytime, this was no problem. The nurses at the surgery helped, and in the evenings my daughters did their share. At night, he was solely my responsibility.

I had a long working week. As well as the normal working days, I was on duty on alternate weekends, day and night. Two or three nights each week, depending on the rota, I took the evening surgery, which might not finish until nine o'clock, then transferred telephone calls to my house. Only very rarely did the vet on duty have an undisturbed night. On my evenings off, and the following mornings, I took my horse out on the beach. I had one half day off each week, to do the shopping, organise the household, and catch up on the thousand other things that women are supposed to spend their time doing. Feeding Louis every three hours on top of all this wore me out so effectively that I had no energy left to mope.

He slept at first in a box by my bed, but complained so bitterly the first night that I lifted the box onto the bed. It fell over, and he crawled out, ensconced himself on the pillow behind my head, and fell asleep quietly. When he was hungry, he woke me by chewing my ear. I sleepily put on the light, added hot water from a thermos to his milk mixture, and fed him. After his feed, I put him gently on the floor on spread newspaper and he obligingly produced a minute puddle. Lifting him back on the bed, we both went back to sleep.

After a time, the midnight feeds became less frequent, and he learned to get on and off the bed by himself, visiting the earthbox in the corner as necessary, clambering up onto the bed via a stairway I had made with a chair and a pile of cushions. By the time he was three-and-a-half months old, his last feed was late in the evening, and he slept all night without disturbing me.

No Poodle could ever have replaced Oscar in my heart, but Louis developed his own character, and made his own place.

10

'I don't know a lot about parrots,' I confessed. Mrs Zabrowski lifted the cage onto the consulting room table and opened the door in the side.

'I asked especially to see you this morning because I know you have a parrot yourself,' she replied.

'All Percy Phone has taught me,' I said bitterly, 'is that parrots are noisy, destructive and not very lovable.'

'Solly is quite different.' Mrs Zabrowski had put her hand into the cage and was scratching the grey parrot's head. The bird's eyes were closed and it pushed its head ecstatically against her fingers. 'She is very good company. My husband is away a lot, and I talk to her all the time.'

'How do you know it's a female?' I asked.

'I just know,' she replied. 'She's so intelligent and beautiful. My husband says she is a male and calls him Solomon, but I call her Solly.'

I felt rather confused.

'What symptoms is he—sorry, she—showing?'

'She seems perfectly all right most of the time, but then she faints, usually in the evening.'

'Faints?' I was puzzled.

'Falls off her perch onto the floor of the cage, then gets up and shakes herself and seems normal again. I can't describe it.' Mrs Zabrowski took a packet of cigarettes out of her bag, followed my glance to the 'No Smoking' notice on the wall, and apologetically put them away again.

'Sorry. I'm trying to stop, but it's difficult when I'm so worried. Look—would you take her home with you and see what she does, then you'll know how to make her better?'

'Well,' I said doubtfully, 'perhaps it would be a good idea for me to see one of these attacks for myself, then I could consult one of my colleagues at the Veterinary College who knows a lot about this sort of bird.'

'Good. That's settled.' Mrs Zabrowski looked happier. 'I'll ring you in a few days to see how she is.'

'And I'll contact you if there are any developments before then,' I promised.

I took Solly home at lunch time. Percy Phone was in his cage so I prudently shut the door, then put Solly's cage on the table next to him. They eyed each other.

'I'll leave you two to get acquainted,' I said, 'and let you out this evening.'

I made a sandwich, cut a slice of fruit cake, then returned to the patient dogs waiting in the car outside. It was the height of the holiday season, and the beach was covered with people who would not be pleased to have a pack of dogs sniffing at their picnics or pee'ing on their sandcastles, so we went to see the horses in their weekday field. I had some afternoon visits to do on that side of the town, and there was a public footpath beside the horse field, leading over a stile and across the meadows. I sat on the stile and ate my lunch while the dogs whoofled about in a ditch and hunted rabbits in the hedge. Ceilidh nearly caught a baby one, and huffed and puffed to me about it, very pleased with himself.

I was not on duty that evening, and went home when I had finished my visits. Louise was just finishing her homework.

'I've just made a pot of tea,' she said. 'Liz has gone to tea with Caroline. She says her dad will bring her home and she won't be late. Why have we got another beastly parrot? Isn't one bad enough?'

'Solly is the sort of parrot I really wanted,' I replied. 'She talks, too.'

'Hasn't said anything so far,' muttered Louise.

I let both birds out and they climbed to the tops of their respective cages and glared at each other. Percy Phone turned his back. Solly crossed cautiously on to his cage.

'Peek-a-boo!' she said coyly.

We found during the next few days that her repertoire was amazing. I don't know if she really understood the meaning of the words she said, but she always said the right thing at the right time. When I got home and fell into a chair, she made gusty sighing noises: 'Uh-huh! That's better! Let's put the kettle on.' When I unthinkingly did as she suggested, the sound of the kettle being filled caused an excellent imitation of rattling teacups, followed by the unmistakable gurgle of tea being poured out. She called all the dogs 'Fred' and frequently caused pandemonium with her rendering of two cats fighting.

She liked to sit on my lap and have her neck scratched, and insisted on sampling any food she saw us eating. Taking it carefully in her beak, she always said, 'Nice, very nice,' even if she subsequently spat it out. She occasionally spoke in a deep, gruff man's voice, which was disconcerting at first. If we were in different rooms, she would call out, 'You all right?' 'I'm all right,' I answered. 'Good,' she would say.

She strutted into the kitchen one day, and I heard her say admonishingly, 'No, Solly. Naughty girl!' There was an almighty crash, and I rushed out to find a pile of plates dislodged from the draining board onto the floor. Solly walked away, saying loudly in her gruff man's voice, 'Blasted parrot, look what it's done.' I almost forgave the two broken plates.

That first evening, she was less forthcoming. Obviously missing her owner, she climbed down from the cage, beak-and-clawed her way down the table leg, and approached my chair. Passing Ceilidh asleep on the rug, she stopped and inspected him.

'Hello, Fred,' she said, and whistled.

Ceilidh opened one eye, growled deep in his throat and shut his eye again. Solly leaned forward, turned her toes in and continued towards me. Louis lay in his usual place across my feet. He rarely sat on my lap, but ejected any cats he found there, and prevented their return. They had developed the habit of creeping onto my lap from behind, jumping onto the back of the chair and edging over my shoulders. Louis had just persuaded Fanny to go away, and had settled on my feet, content to have me to himself. Solly looked at him.

121

'Hello, Fred,' she said. 'Walkies!'

He ignored her, but Tania scrambled to her feet and rushed to the door.

'Tania!' I said, exasperated, 'you are a silly bitch.' She gazed at me, pop-eyed. 'A silly bitch,' I repeated. 'Go and sit down.'

Puzzled, she sat down again with a great sigh. Solly, meanwhile, had climbed the leg of my chair and sat herself on my lap, pushing her head under my hands. I sat, dreamily scratching her neck, until I suddenly noticed Louise's expression of gleeful anticipation, tinged with anxiety. Before I could move, Percy Phone heaved himself off the arm of the chair and onto my lap. Bowing politely, he approached Solly, making the friendly chirruping noise he used when he felt sociable. She bowed back, equally polite.

'Peek-a-boo!' she said, and pushed her head back under my hand.

Percy Phone stood close to her, chirping softly, and she nibbled the nape of his neck. He was obviously enraptured.

Greatly daring, I moved my hand and tickled his head. Immediately he screamed with fury and slashed at my fingers, just missing them. Solly obviously thought he had attacked her, and faced him furiously. Terrified, hardly daring to breathe, I sat quite still, expecting them both to turn on me, but to my unspeakable relief, first Solly, then Percy Phone belly-flopped to the floor, and strutted back to the cages. From then on, they ignored each other, and I always felt sorry for ruining a beautiful friendship.

At nine o'clock Louise went to bed, and shortly afterwards, unable to stifle my jaw-cracking yawns any longer, I followed suit. When I covered the parrots' cages, Solly said, 'Night-night, dear,' in her light female voice, and, 'Goodnight, Solomon,' in her deep gruff voice.

I read in bed for a short while, then switched the light off, but knew I would not sleep until Liz came home. Shortly after ten, a car drew up, and light footsteps came up the garden path and round the side of the house. The kitchen door opened and closed. A friendly greeting from the Pups was quickly 'shush-ed', and then a loud crash as a chair over-turned. There was another, louder exclamation, and

Liz stamped up the stairs, switched on my bedroom light and confronted me angrily.

'Why didn't you tell me?' she demanded, shaking. 'You could have *warned* ME.'

'Wha-wha-what?' I stammered, sitting up and organising my sleepy wits.

Liz sat on the end of my bed, trembling, and I realised she had been badly frightened.

'I was walking across the sitting-room in the dark,' she said accusingly almost in tears, 'and somebody coughed. I stopped and said, "Who's there?" and a man's voice said, "Hallo?" in an inquiring tone. I dived at the light and your chair fell over and I saw it was another blasted parrot. Why do you want another one? Isn't Percy Phone bad enough?'

By now I was trying hard not to laugh, but she saw my expression and we both had hysterics.

'I suppose it was funny really,' she gasped. 'Sorry to wake you up. I'll go down and pick your chair up and make us a hot drink.'

Solly stayed with us a week, two weeks, three, and showed no signs of fainting. Liz observed one morning, 'That new parrot has got a dreadful cough. She nearly choked.'

'Parrots don't cough,' I replied. 'She's probably imitating her owner. I know Mrs Zabrowski smokes very heavily.'

Solly's owner wanted her to stay until she had demonstrated her symptoms and I was quite happy for her to live with us. Not only was she great entertainment, but Percy Phone's sulks meant he was almost quiet and we had a rest from his constant screeching complaints.

We were having some repairs done to the outside of the house, and one of the workmen came in one afternoon to get the tray of tea mugs. He was smoking a cigarette, and when he stopped to admire the parrots, puffed a lungful of smoke at them. Solly swayed, fell off her perch, and lay motionless on the floor of her cage. After a few seconds, she got up, shook herself and appeared normal again.

I telephoned Mrs Zabrowski and told her I thought Solly might be allergic to tobacco smoke. She was very upset to think she had been causing her beloved pet distress, and declared it was just the spur she needed to make her give up the habit completely.

The house was very quiet without Solly, until Percy Phone recovered his spirits, and I was almost glad to hear him shouting again. About a month later, Mrs Zabrowski rang me.

'I was wondering,' she said diffidently, 'if you could look after Solly again for me, for about two weeks.'

I was delighted. 'I must pay you,' she added, 'or I can't ask you.'

'All right,' I agreed. 'I'll charge you five pounds a week for looking after her, and pay you five pounds a week for entertainment. That makes us quits.' She laughed.

'Are you coming this way soon?' she asked.

'As a matter of fact, I'm calling on one of your neighbours tomorrow afternoon,' I said.

'Good. Call here afterwards, and we'll have tea, and I can explain.'

Solly seemed pleased to see me, and after our mutual greetings Mrs Zabrowski pushed her into her cage, and carried her into the adjoining room. 'She talks more if she can hear you but not see you,' she explained, 'and I want you to hear her new words.'

We sat silent, drinking our tea. Suddenly, there was the sound of high-pitched barking. I stood up, recognising Louis' bark, but Mrs Zabrowski lifted her hand, and I sat down again. Incredulous, I heard a good imitation of my own voice.

'Shut up, Louis!' it said tetchily. I was filled with remorse. Did I really sound so cross all the time, I wondered? There was my voice again.

'Ceilidh!' it called. 'Come here, my beamish boy.' I blushed. The absurd things we say to our pets sound ridiculous in public.

I opened my mouth to speak, but my hostess shushed: 'There's more. This is why she can't be here while my sister-in-law is visiting.' Solly sang a song, and rattled through a few nursery rhymes. Mrs Zabrowski offered more cake, and we ate and drank in companionable silence.

'Oh, Tania.' I was getting used to hearing myself speak

from the other room. 'Tania,' said my voice, exasperated, 'you are a silly bitch!' There was a sigh. 'A silly bitch,' the voice repeated.

'That's what's worrying me,' Mrs Zabrowski declared. 'My sister-in-law comes next week to stay for a short holiday. She mustn't hear Solly say her new words.' I was puzzled.

'We were careful what we said in front of her. I hardly ever swore, and I told the girls to be careful of their language.'

Solly's owner wrung her hands despairingly. 'You don't understand,' she cried. 'My sister-in-law is what you call strait-laced. She has no sense of humour, and her name is Tania.'

So Solly came to stay with us until the coast was clear. It was the first of many visits, and she almost became one of the family. After a while it was understood that we would look after her whenever the Zabrowskis were on holiday, and she provided an endless source of entertainment.

One evening, when she was again staying with us, the girls were sitting doing their homework while I tackled a pile of mending.

Liz got up from the table and headed towards the kitchen. 'Homework makes me thirsty,' she claimed. 'I'm going to put the kettle on.'

'Good idea!' approved Louise, 'I've nearly finished. Can we put the TV on? We're missing "Top of the Pops"!'

'Oh! Catastrophe!' cried her sister, diving towards the set. Crimpy suddenly got up from her place on the hearthrug, and ran in front of her, an infuriating habit she still has. Trying not to tread on the silly cat, Liz stepped awkwardly high, banging her knee sharply on the side of the bookcase.

'Oh, sh . . .' she began.

'Stop!' I shrieked. 'Not in front of Solly. You know how she picks up everything you say. If you must swear, do it under your breath or go outside where she can't hear you. I had a card from Mrs Zabrowski today. They are leaving Canada next Tuesday and hope to pick Solly up on Wednesday, a week today.'

'Blasted parrot,' said Liz. She saw my protesting expression. 'It's all right,' she reassured me, 'she knows that already. Blasted parrot. It will be a relief to be able to speak without thinking first.'

'In your customary fashion,' I muttered to myself. 'Oh, by the way,' I added, 'try to keep your clothes as clean as possible. The washing machine is on strike. I've arranged for it to be looked at, but he can't come until Tuesday, my half-day. I'll have to wash your blouses and underwear by hand this weekend.'

Percy Phone loved, 'Top of the Pops'. Sitting on top of his cage, he yodelled, crowed, flapped his wings and shouted, 'Geroff! Oyez! Oyez! Yeehar!' He subsided during a rare quiet song, and Solly obviously thought it was her turn. She looked straight at me.

'Mary had a little lamb,' she informed me.

'Oh yes?' I said. 'So what?'

'It's fleece was black as soot,' the parrot continued.

'Oh, no,' I despaired, 'not one of Louise's silly rhymes.'

'And into Mary's bread and jam 'is sooty foot 'e put,' finished Solly, ending with the maniacal screech Louise always gave when she thought she had said something funny.

'Mrs Zabrowski will not be amused,' I scolded.

'That's nothing,' said Liz. 'She taught her the one about Baa Baa black sheep, why did . . .' I put my hands over my ears.

'Don't tell me,' I begged. 'I can plead ignorance when Mrs Z complains.'

The following Tuesday, I arrived home slightly later than I had planned, and found a bemused young man in the kitchen.

'Washing machine,' he said. 'I knocked on the door, and somebody told me to come in, but there's nobody here except the parrots.'

'Hello, darling,' called Solly. 'Put the kettle on. Peep, peep, peep, peep, peep, peeeeep! Seven o'clock. Here is the news.'

'The other one doesn't say much,' said the young man, 'but the grey one never stops, does it?'

126

I hauled the washing machine out from under the draining board, and pointed out its deficiencies. He looked doubtful.

'Hasn't been serviced for some time, has it? Needs a new hose here, and a gasket here.' He fetched the necessary parts from his van. The dogs sitting in my car watched with interest. He returned and began to dismember the machine. Solly and Percy Phone stalked out into the kitchen and watched him.

'I've just got to slip up the road to see someone,' I said. 'I shall only be a few minutes.'

'That's OK,' he answered. 'This will take at least half an hour.'

I had not had time during the morning to visit a neighbour's elderly cat. It had a variety of minor complaints, but with care could remain comfortable for a little while. I liked to call and check progress every month.

When I returned, the parrots had put themselves back in their cages, and Solly was unusually silent. I went upstairs and changed the sheets on the bed and hoovered the carpets. When I came down, the mechanic was just leaving.

'All fixed,' he said. 'It should be good for another ten years now.'

The girls were very pleased when they came home from school.

'Oh, good. I can wash Ozzie's numnah and girth in the machine now,' said Louise.

'Definitely not,' I answered. 'Everything will be covered in little black and white hairs for weeks, however well you rinse out the machine afterwards. Listen, I didn't have time to ride this afternoon, but we could go now and just school them in the field if you like. The tide is right up, so we can't go on the beach.'

The dogs thought this was an excellent idea, too. It had been a very boring day, they made me understand. Stuck in the car all the time that interesting-looking chap was playing in their kitchen; then, when I finally allowed them in the house, they had been positively hounded from pillar to post by that noisy sucking machine. Their lovely smelly blankets had been whipped from underneath them, replaced by boring old clean ones, and I had hardly had time to spare them a kind word.

Ceilidh and Tania danced a three-legged polka all round the yard while the Pups earnestly investigated the contents of the horses' feed buckets. They decided they liked sugar beet pulp with flaked maize mixed in it.

'Will it hurt them?' asked Liz anxiously.

'No,' I reassured her, 'but the sugar beet will go through them unchanged, like a bulk laxative. We had better leave the kitchen door open tonight.'

At the field, Louise spent an arduous half hour trying to persuade Ozzie to jump over the poles balanced on oil drums in the corner of the paddock. She seemed very happy that the horse absolutely refused to do anything so pointless.

'If he misbehaves at practice,' she explained to me, 'he'll be angelic at the gymkhana on Saturday.'

Liz concentrated on doing a turn on the forehand and a shoulder-in. Jubi, I discovered, had lost a shoe, so he had the evening off and I walked the dogs round the adjacent fields and along the river towpath. We went home early because the girls had homework to do. They seemed to need the usual accompaniment of loud pop music to aid concentration, so I retired to the kitchen to cook the tea, closed the door and switched on a Beethoven concert. The Emperor Concerto made a suitable background to the music of frying mushrooms and sausages.

When I carried the tray into the sitting-room, Liz and Louise seemed full of suppressed mirth.

'Did the washing machine say anything about Solly?' asked Liz.

'He thought she was rather chatty,' I replied.

'That's not all he thought,' declared Louise with unholy glee. 'No need to worry about my nursery rhymes. You should hear what else she can say.' Solly ate a peanut.

'Hello, darling,' she greeted me. 'Pop goes the weasel.'

We ate our tea in unaccustomed silence, waiting for her to speak again. She demanded a piece of sausage, but otherwise said nothing.

The girls switched on the television. I picked up a book,

and forgot the parrot. The cops and robbers on the screen had a noisy shoot-out, much approved by Percy Phone, who yelled encouragement. In the sudden silence when the shooting ended, Solly lifted her wings, looked up and said, 'Christ! It's a bleeding parrot!' I dropped my book.

'Oh, no,' I groaned. 'And she goes home tomorrow. There's no time for her to forget it.'

The bird turned to me scornfully. 'Sod off, you noisy bastard,' she said.

11

For the third time that afternoon, I checked the telephone. It seemed to be working perfectly well.

'I don't understand,' I fussed, 'why is everything so quiet?'

'Mum, why don't you just relax and enjoy this lovely Sunday afternoon?' begged Liz.

It was my weekend on duty, and although I had been moderately busy on Saturday, the evening surgery had ended at seven o'clock, and there had been no sudden emergencies since then. Lynne had telephoned at ten that morning to say there were no appointments for the emergency Sunday surgery, and she could cope alone with the dressings necessary for two of the hospital in-patients.

Liz had invited her friend Caroline to stay for the weekend. I had left the girls to look after the telephone for an hour while I walked the dogs, then all three had been for a ride—Caroline was slightly over-horsed on my horse, Jubi, but had managed him quite well, according to Liz. They had all come back undamaged, anyway. While they were out, I had done the ironing, made some cakes, and hoovered the carpets. After lunch, we all trooped out into the garden. Liz and Caroline were sitting surrounded by bits of bridle and stripped saddles, bars of glycerine soap and pots of leather dressing. They told me I should have been ashamed of my saddle, it obviously hadn't been cleaned for yonks. Not knowing how long a yonk was, I was unable to argue.

Louise, lying on a blanket in the full sunshine, decided her tummy had had enough cooking, and turned over to toast her back.

'It's nice and restful for you when the phone is quiet,' she mumbled. 'When you are off duty, you rush about, riding and walking and making the most of your free time, but when you're on duty you have to stay in, and can take it easy.'

'If you think this is easy—' I stopped struggling with the lawnmower, and mopped my brow—'come and have a go yourself.'

'No fear,' she replied. 'Not until you get a proper motor mower. That push-me, pull-me thing is murder, especially on this so-called lawn.' I inspected the lawn, wounded with hoof marks, bare in patches where the guinea pig runs had been, and dug into holes by Arfer, Liz's rabbit.

'All these lumps and bumps would be lethal to a motor mower,' I explained. 'I'll have to stick with this one.'

'I'll help, Mum,' offered Liz. 'I'll water the vegetables for you. Where's the hose?'

'Jeannie and the Pups were playing with it this morning,' I replied. 'It's in a tangle under the hedge.'

Liz straightened out the hose, threaded one end through the kitchen window, and fixed it to the tap, then carried the free end past her somnolent sister to the far end of the garden.

'Can you turn the water on, Louise?' she called.

'I've just got comfortable,' groaned her lazy sibling. 'Mum will do it.'

'I want to go and put the kettle on,' I said. 'You really are a lazy cat, Louise. Gosh, I could do with a nice sit-down and a cup of tea.'

I went into the kitchen and turned the tap on. There was a loud scream of rage and shock from Louise, and I rushed out to find her leaping frantically out of range of several fountains surging skywards from the hose. The dogs' teeth had obviously punctured it in several places.

'Not much water coming out this end.' Liz appeared from behind the runner beans. 'What's the matter with Louise?' She saw her furious, dripping sister. 'Serves you right, you should have got up and made yourself useful,' she said unfeelingly.

The uncut patch of grass was very wet, so I thankfully put the mower away, and went in to make the tea.

'You had better take that bikini off—what there is of it,' I suggested, 'and put on some dry clothes.'

Louise started up the stairs, and at that moment the telephone rang.

'I'll take it,' she called. She had a brief conversation, then ran into the kitchen.

'It was Mr Burden,' she cried. 'His daughter's new pony has got tetanus.'

'It can't have,' I protested, 'he only bought it last month, and all its boosters were up to date. What symptoms is it showing?'

'I didn't ask,' said Louise, crestfallen. 'He just said it had tetanus and he wanted you to go and see it.'

'Can Caroline and I come with you?' begged Liz. 'We could carry things, and I've never seen a horse with tetanus.'

I drained my cup. 'It hasn't got tetanus,' I said crossly. 'Can you look after the phone, Louise? We shouldn't be long.'

This suited her very well, as there was a film she wanted to see on television.

Caroline and Liz squeezed into the back of the car, leaving Ceilidh his usual place next to me. It was not far to Eastgate, Mr Burden's farm.

'Wasn't Mr Burden the man who gave you Jubi?' asked Liz.

'That's right,' I said.

'Gave you such a beautiful horse?' gasped Caroline.

'He wasn't worth much at the time,' I pointed out. 'Mr Burden turned him out in a field next to his stallion, and they had a fight through the barbed wire fence.'

'Nearly cut his leg off,' interrupted Liz, 'you should have seen the blood. Mummy took ages trying to sew him up, but he had lost a lot of skin.' She shivered theatrically.

'Don't exaggerate,' I laughed. 'It was quite a mess, though. Mr Burden didn't want to have to nurse him for months, and sent for the knacker. I offered him the same price, and he gave me the horse.'

'How did you get him better?' asked Caroline.

'I took him to the beach every day, and paddled him in

the sea. It took two years to heal, and he still has a nasty scar.'

'Yes, I saw it when I groomed him this morning. I wondered how it got there. Gosh, I wish someone would give me a horse.'

'Where would you keep it?' Liz asked.

'My cousin has got a spare stable and plenty of grazing. Dad says if I save up and buy a pony, he will help with its keep.'

'How much have you saved so far?' I asked.

She sighed. 'Thirty pounds.'

Liz giggled. 'That would buy one foot.'

While we were talking, we had arrived at Eastgate Farm. Mr Burden stood outside the stable, waiting for us.

'Damned pony threw my daughter, so she won't ride it. Been standing in the stable doing nothing, except eat. Now this happens.'

I was horrified. 'Mr Burden,' I protested, 'when I examined this pony for you last month, I told you I thought it had had laminitis, and gave you advice about feeding and exercise. Bring my case, Liz, I'll have a look at it.'

It took only a brief look, and my worst fears were verified. The pony stood in the middle of the box, a look of utter desperation and agony on its face. The poor beast knew that if it lay down, it would probably never get up again, but standing on its acutely inflamed feet was so painful, it stood rigid, sweating, hardly daring to breathe. Wordlessly, Liz handed me a syringe and the bottle of pain-killer, then ran her hand reassuringly down the pony's neck and pressed her fist into the jugular groove, to bring the vein into prominence. My daughters were well trained. The injection took effect almost at once. The pony did not move, but his expression became less anguished.

'Is this going to happen very often?' Mr Burden demanded.

'It mustn't!' I cried. 'Quite apart from the pain it gives, sooner or later you will cause permanent damage to his feet.'

'Don't bother with any more injections,' ordered the farmer. 'I'll go and ring the knacker. My daughter doesn't like him now, anyway. She wants a prettier pony, not just an ordinary brown one.'

'Oh no,' groaned Caroline. 'You can't have him shot when he could get better.'

'Now listen,' he said. 'You know what I paid for that pony. The knacker might give me sixty pounds, he's very fat. You can have him for sixty pounds, pony, saddle, bridle and all.'

Liz grabbed my hand beseechingly. 'The tack is worth more than that,' she whispered. 'The saddle is too big for this pony, but it's just what I want for Manny.'

'How much money have you got?' squeaked Caroline. 'We could buy him between us. You have the tack, I'll have the poor pony.'

Liz sagged despairingly. 'Only twenty pounds. I spent a lot a few weeks ago.'

Yes, I thought, spent it on a puppy for me.

'I'll lend you ten,' I offered. 'You can pay me back in money or work.'

'I'll clean your tack, mow the lawn and wash the car every week,' cried Liz ecstatically.

'Careful,' I warned, 'we have witnesses.'

'Well, have we got a sale or not?' demanded Mr Burden impatiently. 'I want him away from here today.'

'He can't be moved until he can walk,' I argued. 'Midday tomorrow.'

He stamped off. 'Midday, not a minute later. And don't go sending me any bills for today's treatment, either.'

I left two very excited girls looking after the pony. I told them to make him walk on the smooth road, even though the first steps would be excruciating. Caroline asked me to ring her father, and assured me he would be delighted, and would pick them up from the farm later that afternoon.

It all turned out very well. I had to explain to Caroline and her father exactly what laminitis was, and how they could cope.

'It's a sort of allergy,' I told them. 'Too much food, too little exercise, or the wrong sort of food, and it has this dreadful effect on his feet. The sensitive parts try to swell up, but they're sandwiched between the horny parts of the hoof, so they can't swell. The pain is frightful. Try biting your thumb nail quite hard.' Caroline obeyed, looking puzzled. 'Now hook your thumbs together, and try to pull them apart.' Caroline did so, and squealed with pain. 'Yes,' I said, 'you have got a tiny bit of your thumb nail inflamed. Imagine the whole hoof feeling like that, with all the pony's weight on it.'

The girl shuddered. 'How can we prevent it?'

'Easy. Just make sure he is exercised every day, and is not overfed. Nice fresh spring grass is especially dangerous. Work him hard, and half-starve him.'

I smiled, knowing they would understand. Caroline loved her pony. Liz was delighted with her saddle. I had my car washed, tack cleaned, and washing-up done every day for several weeks, but somehow, Liz never got around to mowing the lawn.

*   *   *

An occasional wild animal added variety to the patient list, and spice and excitement to our lives. We never charged for treating them, although they often caused headaches. Our clients included a young falconer, who knew a lot more about birds, particularly birds of prey, than we did, and was always ready to care for them. He often flew his birds at shows and exhibitions, and to accustom them to the noise and bustle of crowds, could be seen striding along the High Street, a hooded falcon on his gauntleted fist.

I called briefly at home one chilly evening, to make sure Liz and Louise were all right, and to leave the dogs in the warm house while I took the late surgery. I had lit the fire at lunch time, and the house was warm and welcoming. After a good drink, the dogs dispersed to their favourite snoozing places—the musketeers under the settee, Tania to her basket in the dog-room, and Ceilidh and the infant Louis to my armchair.

'Will you feed them for me if I'm not back by about eight o'clock?' I asked. 'The meat is all cooked and cut up, you'll just have to mix in the biscuit.' Liz looked up from her maths homework, and nodded. It must have been difficult

135

to hear me. The loud pop music which was apparently essential to concentration on homework thumped from the record player, punctuated by screams and yodels from Percy Phone. I prepared to leave, hoping the homework and musical background would be finished by my return. A sudden loud rat-tat on the door startled me. My neighbour stood there, wild-eyed.

'Quick! Quick!' she cried. 'There's an eagle in my garden!'

I followed her along the road and into her garden. She stopped on the path and shone her torch on to the flowerbed. Bending down, I saw a small kestrel sitting under a rosebush. Gently, I nudged the back of its legs with my fist, and it stepped back and perched, clutching my knuckles.

'It looks much smaller than I thought,' said my neighbour, disappointed. 'What will you do with it?'

'I'll take it to the surgery,' I replied, 'and ring Jim Thorburn, the falconer. He'll probably keep it until he is sure it can fly and feed properly, then let it go.'

The surgery that evening was quiet, probably due partly to the atrocious weather. Jim agreed to come and fetch the kestrel, and suggested I should just keep it warm, and not try to feed it. I perched it on the desk, where it sat, unmoving, unblinking. Nobody even noticed it until old Mrs Pearce came in.

''Ere,' she said, 'I brought a 'edge-og' in last week, wiv a bad leg.'

'That's right,' I answered. 'How is it?'

'You give me some powder,' she went on, 'and I sprinkled it on, and the leg healed lovely. So I put some on my old moggy's bad ear, and that healed lovely, too. Then I put the rest on my old man's hand when he cut it in the garden, and now that's getting better, as well.'

I was beginning to feel I had been over-generous with my free medicine for the hedgehog. Mrs Pearce took out her purse and, with a grand air, offered me twenty pence.

'So I thought I ought to pay for the powder, all things considered.'

136

It actually cost a lot more than that, but I took the coin and dropped it into the appeal box on the desk. Mrs Pearce watched, and suddenly saw the kestrel.

'Oooh!' she cried. 'a stuffed owl! Innit lifelike? Looks almost alive.'

She bent and peered closely at the kestrel. The bird yawned widely and blinked its eyes. Mrs Pearce fell back with a shriek, then left, muttering to herself that she didn't think it funny, frightening a body like that.

Jim turned up a little later, and bore the bird off to his home, where it would be expertly cared for. At other times, wild animals found temporary refuge in our house. A hedgehog was brought in one day, hopelessly entangled in plastic garden netting, which had cut into its legs. Liz and Louise spent a painful, prickly half-hour disentangling the vicious green strands. I decided the infected wounds on its legs needed a few days' care, so after relieving the spiky creature of its creepy-crawly parasites, we put it on the hearthrug. The girls were charmed to see it slowly and trustfully uncurl, and lap at a proffered saucer of milk.

I transferred our guest to a big cardboard box in the dog-room, where it ate chicken giblets, eggs, and tinned cat food. It had an enormous appetite, producing waste in proportion, and soon generating a strong aroma, in spite of frequent cleaning. We were all relieved when I pronounced the wounds healed, and we were able to set it free.

Some wild animals caused a lot more trouble. Mrs Lloyd, a local smallholder's wife, rang one morning in great distress. She had found a badger in the corner of their old cowshed, and had tried to pick it up, protected, as she thought, by a stout pair of gardening gloves. The gloves were no match for the badger's powerful jaws, and after a trip to the cottage hospital to have the deep wounds dressed, she rang me in despair.

'There's a wire loop on its neck,' she said, 'so tight it has buried itself in the flesh. It smells awful, and the badger seems sick.'

I had to visit a farm close by, and arranged to see Mrs Lloyd and her badger afterwards. She led the way to the old building, heavily bandaged hands carefully folded.

'I can't do anything about it now,' she explained, 'not with all these dressings on my hands.'

The badger, quite a small one, crouched miserably in a dark corner, almost hidden in dirty straw.

'Do be careful,' warned Mrs Lloyd, 'don't touch it!'

I had no intention of risking my hands.

'Can we have a look through your husband's workshop?' I asked. 'Might give us some ideas.'

Ten minutes later, I returned with a pair of pointed wire-cutters, a sheet of weldmesh, and a bucket of warm water with a handful of salt dissolved in it. It was quite easy to trap the badger under the weldmesh, and standing on the ends to hold it down, I manoeuvred the points of the cutters through the mesh and snipped the wire round the creature's neck. Nothing happened. The wire was so deeply embedded, it remained in place. Removing the weldmesh, I chivvied the badger into turning round, and repeated the snipping operation on the other side, making it possible to work the two rusty semicircles of loop free. Keeping the badger imprisoned under the wire, I washed the neck wound as well as I could with the salt water.

'Do you want some disinfectant?' asked Mrs Lloyd.

'No,' I replied, 'it would make her smell different, and the others in her group might not accept her when she goes back.'

I picked up the weldmesh and stepped back.

'It seems much livelier already,' declared the small holder. 'What do we do now?'

'The sooner she goes back to the sett, the better,' I said. 'Why not shut her in here for the night, with some food and water, and see how she is in the morning?'

Food was a slight problem. Apart from earthworms, I had little idea of a badger's diet, but knew they were not fussy eaters. Eventually, we provided a handful of worms from the compost heap, half a tin of dog food, and some peanuts. With a bowl of water, these offerings were left on the floor close to the badger, and we closed and bolted the heavy door.

Next morning, Mrs Lloyd telephoned.

'The food was gone,' she said. 'So has the badger. It dug

138

its way out under the wall. I don't know if it ate the food first, or whether I just gave the rats a free supper. It must have felt better, though, to have managed all that digging.'

For her kindness to the badger, she was left with painful bites and a big hole in her cowshed floor, but she did not expect gratitude.

Some of our own temporary guests, however, were more entertaining—like the small orphan which came into our lives one summer morning. I had gone for a ride along the beach and was now making for home. As my horse Jubi stepped from the sand onto the bottom of the paved boat ramp, he stopped and looked at me over his shoulder. I patted his neck.

He half turned and gazed at the distant sea, like a small boy begging for one last paddle, but I turned him firmly in the direction of home. We both enjoyed these peaceful Sunday morning rides when I was off duty. Occasionally, one or other of my daughters would accompany us, but having spent Saturday evening at a disco, a party, or similar teenage entertainment, they generally preferred to lie late in bed.

Sometimes, we headed towards Pagham and I would leave the beach and take Jubi home, turning him loose in the garden while I had my breakfast, and returning him to his field later in the day. On this perfect June day, I had ridden the other way, towards Littlehampton. We had waded belly deep in the sea and contemplated the horizon, the only sound the soft sucking and gurgle of the waves as they rocked hypnotically back and forth. Refreshed, we jumped some small breakwaters on the way home, and cantered splashily in the little waves at the water's edge, the spray salty on my lips and glittering on his mane like diamonds.

It was still not quite eight o'clock, but the sun was well up, and felt hot on my back as I walked him gently on the wide grass verge beside the holiday camp. The path had been mown the day before, and Jubi dropped his head and hoovered up the rows of cut grass. I slid off the saddle and walked slowly beside him.

'Hey! Can you help me?' I vaguely heard a voice. 'Hey! You with the horse.'

I looked around, and saw a girl inside the holiday camp, holding something in her cupped hands.

'Are you calling me?' I shouted.

'Yes,' she replied. 'Can you take this?'

I led Jubi over to the fence.

'I found it on the ground, under a tree,' she explained. 'It seems too young to look after itself but I'm working here and I can't cope with it.'

Carefully, she pushed a small baby squirrel through the chainlink mesh into my hand. It appeared undamaged, but was indeed very young.

I bundled him into my chiffon scarf, judging it would be fine enough to restrain any parasites he might have, and put him carefully in my pocket. Arrived at the field, I gave Jubi a good breakfast, then put him back with the others. I took two big haynets out of the back of the car and hung them on the trees by the gate. The grazing in that field was very sparse, and we had to feed them while they were there, but the field was near home, close to the beach, and a convenient place to keep them at weekends and during school holidays.

Caroline's pony, Whiskers, had temporarily joined our family group, and she rode him every day with Liz and Louise on Manny and Ozzie. He was worked hard, was fit and in good shape, and had had no recurrence of his laminitis. He was astonishingly fast and would jump anything his rider pointed him at. When all the girls rode together, they sometimes had a madness and galloped fast on the sands—not racing, they assured me, just seeing who could go the fastest—and Whiskers was rarely last.

I refilled the water trough and left them pulling at the haynets while I drove the short distance home. Liz was padding around the kitchen in a dressing gown, and the mingled aromas of toast and frying bacon drifted out of the window.

'Louise is still asleep,' she said. 'I took her a cup of tea, but I don't think she woke up enough to drink it. The pot's

140

still hot.' She took my special mug out of the cupboard and filled it up.

'Toasted bacon sarnies?' she suggested. 'You have these, and I'll make myself some more.'

I took a heaped plate and steaming mug out into the garden, and sat on the grass to enjoy my breakfst, surrounded by hopeful dogs. Suddenly, I remembered the squirrel, took my food back to the kitchen, and ran to the car to fetch my coat. The little bundle was safe in the pocket, and I unwrapped him carefully. There were no visible lodgers, but to be on the safe side, I took him into the dog-room and puffed flea powder over him.

'Could you open a small tin of Carnation, Liz?' I called. 'And put a teaspoonful or so into an egg-cup with a drop of hot water from the kettle?'

I fed him from a plastic hypodermic syringe, and he grasped it with tiny hands and sucked avidly until the barrel was empty and his rotund little stomach full. I put him for his own safety into an empty mouse cage, and returned to my congealed sandwiches and lukewarm tea.

We called him Cyril, and during the next few weeks he grew and thrived. After a few days, he objected violently to the cage, shaking the metal mesh door and chattering angrily, so I turned him loose. He rarely touched the floor as he raced round the room, leaping from chair to mantelpiece, from bookcase to passing human, and back to the furniture. The dogs ignored him, and he prudently kept away from the cats. He weaned himself onto sunflower seeds and peanuts filched from Percy Phone's cage while the rightful occupant was elsewhere, pieces of fruit, bread, biscuit and chocolate supplied by obliging humans, and different seeds and bits of fat from the bird-table in the garden.

He continued to regard me as a source of warmth and comfort, and when he felt sleepy, would dive down the front of my jumper, or wriggle down my back. I got quite used to ironing, working in the garden, or doing the housework with a little bump just above my waist. He had an insatiable curiosity, and when he was awake and active, it was difficult to read, write, knit, or carry out almost any

141

household activity. He learned from bitter experience that the iron was hot, but that did not stop him climbing up the flex and pulling it down on his head. Liz handed in some French homework with several long scrawls across it, and her explanation that the squirrel did it was greeted with total disbelief. I got out my instant camera, and took a photograph of her sitting at the table, writing, with Cyril perched on her wrist, his hands clasped round the top of the pen, an expression of concentrated fury on his strange chinless face. I sent the picture to the teacher concerned, and she not only apologised to Liz, but came to tea to meet Cyril for herself. He ran up her arm, inspected her face closely, and bit her nose.

Cyril took to spending most of his days outside. The house next-door had long been empty, the acre of garden around it a wilderness full of birds, squirrels and other small beasts. At first, he still came in at night to sleep in an old woolly sock on the hearth, but eventually, he stayed out at night, too. The girls insisted they often saw him when they walked past the house next door on their way to school. They said he was smaller than the other squirrels, and did not run away, but stayed chattering at them. I never saw him again.

12

It seemed as if my animals were taking it in turn to worry me. No sooner had Ceilidh recovered his old spirits than I realised that Jeannie was far from well. She had been slowing down recently, and we often had to wait for her to catch up when we walked on the beach. At eleven years old, this was to be expected, so at first we were not unduly worried.

I drove the car to the top of the Downs one bright Sunday morning, opened the door and invited the dogs to come for a walk. They all fell out in a heap, as usual, but Jeannie stayed half-sitting, half-lying, where she had landed on the grass. Concerned, I stroked her and comforted her. She was panting and obviously distressed. Her gums, even her tongue, were pale and bloodless. She had apparently suffered an internal haemorrhage.

I dragged a blanket out of the car and tucked it carefully under and around her, and left her to rest while we took the others for a shortened walk.

By the time we returned, she was wandering about, apparently unconcerned, trailing the blanket behind her. She greeted us joyfully and was pleased to be gently picked up and deposited in the car. She even tried to scramble up to her usual place on the parcel shelf, so I pushed her up, and she sat contentedly, the Pups flanking her on either side.

She ate her dinner as usual that evening, and over the next few days seemed to make a good recovery, but I was worried. Carefully prodding her tummy, I was sure I could feel a lump inside her, so I took her to the surgery and asked Mike, one of my colleagues, for his opinion.

Jeannie liked sitting on the table with everyone fussing around her. She enjoyed having her tummy felt, made no objection when Mike stuck needles in her and took blood samples for analysis, and she kept perfectly still to be X-rayed.

Mike's verdict was discouraging.

'Tumours on the liver, possibly spleen, too,' he said. 'I could do a laporotomy, open her up and have a look, but there's not much point.'

His diagnosis confirmed my own fears, and he agreed with me it was best to let her go on quietly, as long as life was comfortable and she was happy.

'When you decide to let her go,' he added, 'I'd like to see if, by any faint chance, the main growth is on the spleen and operable.'

Alas, the tumours grew rapidly. Within a very few weeks, her belly was obviously swollen and caused her some discomfort. She had two more attacks of internal bleeding and we had to leave her behind when we took dogs for walks. The Pups stayed pressed close to her side except when I took them on the beach. When Jeannie pottered out into the garden, they walked with her, almost leaning on her and seeming to hold her up.

One evening, she ate only half her dinner, backed away and crept back under the settee. She had had enough. I discussed it with the girls, and we agreed unanimously that the time had come to let her go.

To my surprise, she came out from under the settee, and sat close to the fire, probably feeling cold. We all sat on the floor with her, and said Goodbye.

'Do you remember when she was a little puppy, and she made a pudding on the kitchen floor?' sobbed Louise. We all remembered.

'What about the time she had a false pregnancy and stole Lottie's kitten.' Liz smoothed the Scottie's black head. 'Silly old thing, weren't you, Jeannie?'

'Not silly,' I protested, 'just very maternal. Remember that pig?'

Both girls groaned and giggled through their tears.

'How could we ever forget Dolly?' they said . . .

*   *   *

'Ah! She's a good mother,' Perce Lillywhite approved. 'Fifteen 'er 'ad this morning, like shellin' peas.'

'She's huge,' I said, awestruck.

'The missus calls 'er Queen Mary. She do walk about with 'er nose in the air, and looks like she oughter be wearing one o' they funny 'ats.'

Her Majesty lay on her side in elephantine bliss, a long row of pink piglets snuffling and pulling at the udder which ran the whole length of her belly, milk dribbling from their greedy mouths.

Liz and Louise gazed longingly at the squealing piglets. It was the first day of the summer holiday and they had decided to come with me on my rounds. We had had a fairly eventful morning, and now the last call before lunch was to Perce's smallholding. He kept hens and a few pigs and reared calves for a local dealer. The calves had been suffering from pneumonia and, having dealt with the sick babies, I had tried to persuade the old man that the calf-house needed more ventilation, not less. Grumbling, he had removed great wads of dusty straw from the air vents, and had been forced to agree that the atmosphere in the shed was immediately more breathable.

He had suggested we might like to see the new litter of pigs.

'You said fifteen. She's only got fourteen,' declared Louise.

'Yes. I took away the dolly pig. Old lady's only got fourteen titties, see? Couldn't feed fifteen, so I took the little 'un out.'

'Where is it, then?' Liz demanded.

Perce jerked his head backwards. 'Be'ind you, in the drain.'

The girls bent to inspect the tiny pallid body, lying half in the cold, dirty water. It opened its eyes and gasped.

'It's alive,' squealed Liz accusingly. 'It's alive and you threw it away.'

Louise peeled off her cardigan, picked up the piglet and wrapped it up tenderly. She cradled it in her arms like a baby, the rubbery snout poking out from the blue woolly.

'Can we have it?' she pleaded.

145

'It'll die, little maid,' answered Perce, 'but take if it tha' wants it.'

When we reached home, the girls disappeared in the direction of the bathroom, bearing the still-gasping piglet.

Sue had arrived, a teenage friend who spent all her school holidays with us. She looked after the girls while I was working, cooked the supper and was a priceless treasure.

'You have your lunch, Kate,' she said. 'I'll see to them when they've finished washing the little pig.'

I ate a hasty sandwich, and hastened off to deal with the afternoon surgery and the late calls.

When I returned that evening, the piglet, pink and shiny skin glowing through a coating of fine silvery hair, was sleeping peacefully in a box by the Aga. Sitting with her chin on the edge of the box, Jeannie regarded the snoring infant with a fond, maternal eye. Sue and the girls were sitting at the kitchen table, eating their tea.

'Jeannie's adopted it,' they informed me. 'We washed it clean, rinsed it and dried it, and it's had about four bottles of Carnation.

'Don't keep calling her "it",' protested Liz. 'Her name's Dolly.'

Dolly lived with us, in the house, for nearly six months. At first, she was fed every two hours during the day, from a baby's feeding bottle, then she graduated to a pie-dish on the floor. Supervised by Sue, the girls added porridge oats to the milk, then we offered proper piglet weaner pellets and grower's meal. She also ate meat and biscuit at dog-feeding time and devoured all the household scraps.

Her table manners were atrocious. We fed her eventually in a large washing-up bowl, and she would paddle her front feet in the meal and splash it all over the floor in her haste to gulp it down. Then she would investigate cat and dog dinners, pushing the rightful diners aside. As she grew bigger and stronger, we had to banish her to the old dairy at mealtimes. She learned this very quickly, and as soon as I started mixing meat and dog-biscuit, would trot out to the dairy and honk impatiently until someone appeared with her bowl.

146

While she was very small, Jeannie kept her clean and tidy. Housetraining later was no problem: pigs are very clean animals. At first, copious newspaper in the porch provided an acceptable lavatory, but at a very early age, Dolly discovered the Great Outdoors, and would stand and grunt by the door to be let out. When she outgrew the cardboard box, she took over one of the dog-baskets. Jeannie would lie beside her, one hairy black arm possessively across the pig's face, and they would snore in contented harmony.

Dolly obviously thought of herself as one of the dogs, and would join in any game with my daughters or their fascinated friends. She learned to sit on command and walk to heel. She chased sticks, and played tug-of-war with the dogs. She played rough, and often sent children and dogs flying, but was always gentle with Jeannie, her adoptive mother. Not many people go for an evening stroll with six dogs, several cats, two goats and a large pig.

She sometimes wished to join us in the sitting-room in the evenings. A big pig on a stoneflagged floor in an enormous farmhouse kitchen is no problem, except that when she slept by the Aga, there was no room for cats and I had trouble reaching the saucepans. That same pig occupying all the hearthrug is something else, and when she developed ambitions to join us on the sofa, I put my foot down with a firm hand. Pigs, I decreed, do NOT live in sitting-rooms.

Alas, she grew and grew. By the beginning of winter, she was as big as a small pony. An acquaintance kept pigs on a free-range system, and agreed to take her on.

For the winter, she lived in a large covered yard with a dozen other gilts.

'Gilts—gold plated pigs?' suggested Liz.

'No, dear,' I said, 'it's the proper farm name for a maiden pig.'

'The farmers call me "maiden" or "maid". Does it mean I'm a pig?'

'Idiot,' giggled Louise. 'It means you're not married yet.'

'Pigs don't get married. How can they be maidens?'

147

'It means they haven't had any babies yet. Same thing.'

Well, I thought, almost the same thing anyway.

The following spring all the pigs were turned out into the fields, with huts for shelter. In the fullness of time, Dolly produced her first litter of eight piglets—quite a respectable first effort. We visited to congratulate her, and she graciously accepted two packets of Polos, a bar of chocolate and a pocketful of dog-biscuit, then returned importantly to her babies.

'Next time,' Liz vowed tearfully, 'we'll have a small kind of pig.'

'Next time,' I promised myself, 'they are NOT bringing it home.'

*　　*　　*

. . . I had agreed with Mike that when we decided that life had become more of a burden than a pleasure for Jeannie, he was to do an exploratory laporotomy. This would cause her no more concern than putting her to sleep, and if he thought the case was hopeless, Mike would see to it that she did not come round from the anaesthetic. I telephoned him in the morning, and arranged to leave her at the surgery before I did my morning rounds.

Next day, the girls got up without protest, ate their breakfast without chatter, and departed for school without their usual banter. Before leaving, they knelt briefly on the hearthrug, and reached under the settee to give Jeannie a last, loving pat.

Arrived at the surgery, I lifted the old Scottie off the parcel shelf where she sat wedged between her two daughters, and carried her into the preparation room. She was not worried. She had been there before and no one had hurt her. Depositing her on the table, I reached into the cupboard for the bottle of tranquilliser and took a new syringe from the tray. Mike breezed in.

'Whew!' he whistled. 'Looks as if there's a Rugby football in there.' Gingerly, he tapped the side of her tummy with the tips of his fingers. Jeannie looked up at him through her eyebrows, frowning.

148

'OK, old lady, we'll make you more comfortable, one way or another.' He scratched her neck and turned to me. 'Got a couple of routine spays to do first, then we can concentrate on her,' he said.

'I'll call back at lunchtime,' I promised.

Knowing Jeannie would not like to be shut in a hospital cage, I spread a blanket on the floor by the radiator and lifted her down. She sprawled uncomfortably on her swelling belly until I folded the side of the blanket to support her shoulders.

She put her chin on her outstretched paws and dozed off. I stroked her lightly.

'Goodbye, rotten dog,' I whispered. She thumped her tail once, and I departed, dry-eyed, to do my round of visits.

The news at lunch time was no surprise.

'Totally inoperable,' announced Mike. 'I don't know how she had survived for so long.' He went into technical details, but I was not listening. Carefully, I wrapped the hairy body, a neat blue line of stitches across the bloated shaven belly, carried her out to the car, and put her on the back seat. The other dogs sniffed at the bundle, then ignored it.

I buried her deeply against the hedge, next to Zeeta and Nina. The pups did not appear to pine, and carried on with life as before.

They became, if possible, even closer, and sat for long hours in their usual favourite place behind the compost heap, a few feet from their little mother's grave.

For some time, Penny had been diabetic, not severely enough to need injections of insulin, but I had to be careful with her diet, and she had special pills in her food. After her mother's death, her symptoms increased, and within a few weeks, she quietly died in her sleep, as unassuming in death as she had been in life. Boadicea did not seem to fret. She moved out from under the settee and took to sleeping on Liz's bed, toiling up the stairs at nine o'clock each night, and keeping us all awake with her snores. She ate well, came for shortened walks, and enjoyed splashing in the edge of the sea. She seemed especially fond of Liz, and lay at her feet, upside down, waiting to have her tummy tickled.

One evening, halfway up the stairs, she suddenly stopped and cried out. I carried her down again, and ran to get my bag from the car. When I returned, she was dead. It was just three months since Jeannie had died. My dear musketeers had left us, as they had lived, together.

13

I put away the last of the plates and saucepans, tottered into the sitting-room and collapsed into my chair. My afternoon off had so much crammed into it that it usually became the most hectic time of the week. Jubi had taken me for a brisk canter along the beach at lunchtime, and I had walked the dogs along the river towpath to the little recreation ground by the main road. They had met several of their friends and galloped themselves to happy exhaustion.

Returning to the house, I had hoovered, tidied, polished and scrubbed and then made a heap of cakes and pies. While they were baking, I returned briefly to the horses' field to give them their evening feed and haynets. This evening, the telephone blessedly silent, I would go to bed really early. Sighing contentedly, I stroked Louis' ears and rubbed Ceilidh's back with my toes. Two cats, perched on my shoulders, dug in their claws as I moved.

'I've made a chicken curry for tomorrow,' I began, 'and put it in the bottom of the fridge. All you have to do . . .'

'Sshh,' interrupted Liz. 'Listen!'

I listened. The television was switched off and the record-player disconnected while the girls did their homework, a serious matter these days. The fire popped and crackled quietly, the cats purred and a faint snoring came from beneath my chair. I shrugged my shoulders.

'All you have to do,' I continued, 'is . . .' Liz waved her arms.

'Sssh,' she repeated, 'I heard a lion.'

'A lion? In Marshton?' I laughed. 'You've been watching too many wildlife programmes.' There was a short silence, then I distinctly heard a coughing roar.

'I heard a lion!' I squeaked incredulously. Without looking up from her book, Louise said, 'No big deal. There's a

151

circus on the West End car park. Mary and I went and had a look at it after school. That's why I was late home. I did tell you but I don't expect you heard.' She looked up reproachfully. 'You were conducting Mahler with a wooden spoon and didn't even notice I was late.'

'Do you want to go to the circus?' I asked. 'How long are they staying in Marshton?'

'No, thank you,' said both girls together, and Louise added, 'They're here for another week, until November 10th. There's going to be a big firework display on Friday. I hope they make sure all the animals are shut up safely.'

'They're probably all used to noise and flashing lights,' considered Liz comfortingly, 'and anyway, they wouldn't take any chances with valuable performing animals.'

'There's a menagerie,' said Louise. 'Shall we go and look at it after school tomorrow?'

'OK,' replied her sister, 'but I only want to see the horses. I hate to see the lions in those little cages. I've finished my homework. Can I put the telly on?'

They went off to school next morning agreeing to meet off the bus and visit the menagerie before coming home. I spent most of the morning in the operating theatre and took the dogs for a walk along the wet, windy beach to blow the anaesthetic fumes out of my head, then went briefly to the house to light the fire and make sure everything was ready for the girls' return. I was due to take the evening surgery and would probably be late home. I had two farm visits to make in the early afternoon, then returned to the surgery. A highly excited Carol pounced on me as I entered.

'Oh, Mrs Barber,' she cried, 'can you do a visit for Mike? He's gone to a calving at Jefferies. He rang back and said it might be a Caesarean. Wendy's gone there with the Caesar pack'—we kept packs of instruments for different operations ready sterilised—'and you'll just have the time before evening surgery.'

I had been hoping for a cup of tea and a chance to tidy the inside of my car. 'OK,' I said. 'Where is this visit?'

'At the circus,' replied Carol excitedly. 'A lion with a septic leg. Mike rang his friend at London Zoo and found out which antibiotic to use, and the dosage. It's all written down here.' She handed me a notepad. 'Wendy got a new bottle out in case you didn't have enough. All you have to do is go and inject it.'

I was doubtful. As a student, I had seen lions and other big cats treated at a big safari park. They were enticed into a small cage, one side of which then moved to squeeze them against the opposite side. Different parts of their anatomy could then be examined or manipulated with little danger. I doubted whether a travelling circus would have a squeeze cage. Feeling rather like Daniel, I drove to the West End car park.

The dogs put their noses to the open top of the car window and inhaled deeply, snorting explosively, then breathing in again slowly. They had never known such a fascinating range of smells. Even my feeble senses could distinguish elephant, horse, big cat, trampled grass, cooking smells from the waggons, and an all-pervading stench of diesel.

'You'll have no trouble with him, Miss,' the lion man assured me. 'It's the old man. Ran a nail into his leg. I've bathed it with antiseptic but it needs an injection.'

'Do you have a squeeze cage?' I asked hopefully. He laughed.

'All the bloody cages are squeeze cages,' he answered. 'Hardly room to turn round. They've got good accommodation at the training quarters but the travelling pens have to be small. Funny thing, they don't seem to mind much.' We had walked past the horse lines at the far end of the rows of tents, and he led me to a cage containing a morose-looking black maned lion, slowly and carefully licking a swollen paw. He flexed the foot, shooting out wicked talons, and snarled with pain. Ignoring the claws and the horribly visible teeth, the lion man put his arm through the bars and scratched the great, hairy head.

'Easy, boy, easy,' he crooned. 'We'll have you feeling better soon.' The cat rubbed his face on the man's arm and purred thunderously.

'Go in the little door at the other end' commanded the lion man, 'walk in calmly, inject him and back out straight away. Don't fall over and try not to let him know you're

153

worried. The door is a bit low. You'll have to duck in. Easy, old man. Easy now.'

I wondered if my insurance policy covered death by lion. Making quite sure the little door was open, I advanced the few paces across the cage, removed the needle from the hypodermic syringe and held it firmly between thumb and forefinger, then stroked the surprisingly soft and smooth skin of the lion's haunch with the back of my hand. He took no notice, so I tapped him smartly twice with my knuckles, turned my hand over and flicked the needle through the tawny skin into the bunched muscle beneath it . . .

Liz and Louise crept along the horse lines.

'We shouldn't be here,' whispered Liz. 'That sign said Private.'

'I didn't see a sign,' said Louise.

'Only because I told you it was there so you shut your eyes,' responded her sister.

'We're not doing any harm, as long as we don't upset the horses. Oh! Look at those four Arabs! Aren't they beautiful? I wish . . .' her voice tailed off. 'Arabs wouldn't suit me,' she decided. 'I'm better off with Ozzie. Oh, look, Liz, there's a big spotted horse, and that wide cob must be a rosin back.' She was very proud of her knowledge of circuses. They became aware of a disturbance at the far end of the horse lines. Somebody ran round the corner.

'Quick! Quick!' called a voice. 'The vet's hurt. She came to inject the lion, and . . .' The girls stared at each other in horror and raced towards the corner, shouting, 'Mummy! Mummy! Where are you?'

There were boots by my head, legs rising up, anxious white faces peering down. I sat up groggily, my head spinning. Liz and Louise hurled themselves upon me.

'Mummy! What did the lion do to you? Are you bleeding?' They were frantic with anxiety. I shook my head and stars exploded all around. The lion man laughed.

'The lion was good as gold,' he declared. 'Didn't even

know he'd been injected. Your mum backed out of the cage so fast, she forgot to duck, hit the back of her head on the door and knocked herself out.'

I held my aching head in my hands. Dangerous work, I thought to myself, treating wild animals.

*   *   *

If the experience with the lion literally knocked me cold, it was nothing to what I went through on another occasion, when I had to conquer one of my worst phobias in the cause of duty.

We now had three people in our branch of the practice, and the weekend rota had been altered, giving us one weekend on duty, one off, then one where we worked Saturday morning, remained on call until the evening, then had Sunday off. This was my half-and-half weekend, and I had so far been let off very lightly. Now, it was seven o'clock on a wet and windy November evening, and I was being asked to climb up a ladder to rescue an injured swan.

'Oh, no!' I protested, 'I can't do that! Heights terrify me. I get giddy if I stand on a chair!'

'I've tried the RSPCA,' Mr Robinson insisted, 'and just got the answer machine. There's no one at the bird sanctuary and the police say it's not their pigeon. I told them it's nobody's pigeon, it's a swan.' He guffawed merrily at his own joke but I was not amused. Mr Robinson was the caretaker at the college of further education on the other side of the town. He had seen a flying swan hit the electric wires beside the college, and fall onto the flat roof. Alarmed, he had shinned up a ladder to investigate and found the bird, apparently with a broken wing, crouched against a chimney stack.

'Didn't touch it,' he said, 'a swan can break a man's leg, you know. Very dangerous, they are!'

I agreed that an angry swan defending its nest or its young could do some damage, but assured him that an injured bird, in the dark, was unlikely to hurt him. Mr Robinson was adamant.

155

'I'm not risking myself,' he said. 'You'll have to come and collect it.'

I agreed and, sighing deeply, returned to the kitchen, where I had been about to feed the dogs and cats.

'Do dogs want dinners, or come in the car?' I asked.

Ceilidh, Tania and Louis surged to the back door, panting excitedly. I put their filled bowls into the larder, spread seven cat dishes on the floor for impatient moggies, and sallied forth into the dripping darkness.

As usual, Tania sat on the back seat, sharing it on this occasion with my largest cat basket. Ceilidh sat bolt upright on the seat beside me, trying hard to see through the streaming windscreen. Louis perched on the back of my seat while I backed down the drive, then edged forward to drape himself round my neck like a fur tippet.

We arrived at the college to find Mr Robinson waiting impatiently, rain dripping off his cap and the end of his nose.

'You go up the ladder,' he pointed, 'only three floors, then across the flat roof to the chimney straight in front of you. The swan's sitting by the stack.'

I knew that if I stopped to think I would never do it, so summoning up my meagre reserves of courage, I started up the ladder, looking straight ahead at the wall. The ladder whipped back and forth under my weight, and I don't know if the wind made it tremble or if I did. The rain lashed my numb hands, and hurt my eyes if I tried to look up.

The top of the ladder barely reached the parapet, and I fell forwards ungracefully and crawled thankfully away from the edge on all fours. The swan crouched where the caretaker had said it would be, and made no protest when I picked it up, tucked it under my arm and crept back to where I judged the ladder to be. There, I realised I had a problem. The only way to get back down the ladder was the reverse of the way I had come up—approaching the edge of the roof backwards on all fours, then feeling over the edge with my foot, trying to find the top rung. The very thought froze my blood. With a heavy wet swan tucked under my arm, it was impossible. I stood, a yard back from the edge irresolute, and slowly panicking.

'Have you got it, love?'

Never was human voice sweeter. The RSPCA inspector's rubicund face appeared, then a hessian sack was heaved across to land at my feet.

'Put the bird in there, then hand it to me,' he ordered. The swan was not very enthusiastic about being pushed backwards into the sack, but it had no choice. The inspector threw over a piece of rope, and I tied the neck of the sack securely. Inching to the very edge of the roof, I handed him the sack and he hooked it onto his belt, then sank from view.

'I'll take it to the sanctuary and ring you tomorrow if I'm worried,' his voice floated up. I turned my back on the parapet, sank on to all fours, and crawled cautiously backwards. Swallowing hard, I hung one foot over the edge and searched for the top rung. My foot hung in space for a few heartstopping seconds, then lodged on the stop. From the ground far below, I heard the inspector's arrival. It seemed he had a reception committee—perhaps the press had got hold of the story. Popping flash bulbs sparked like little fireworks, and muffled exclamations could be heard. I dismissed them from my mind and concentrated on the descent. When I reached the bottom, I was drenched in sweat, my hands were bleeding, and everyone had gone home.

The dogs were waiting patiently in the car. Ceilidh yawned creakingly as I climbed in. 'Very boring evening,' his expression said. Louis wrapped himself welcomingly round my neck and licked the rain off my cheek.

I drove home and gave them their dinners, and was relieved to find my stew had not boiled dry. After a hot bath, I put on pyjamas and a thick dressing-gown, and settled by the fire to eat my supper. Reaction suddenly set in and my hands shook so that I couldn't hold the knife and fork. The girls had gone to visit my parents, and I had arranged to drive over for lunch next day and collect them, so I was alone in the house. I poured myself a generous whisky, which made me feel worse, and crept shivering and supperless to bed.

Next day, quite recovered, I described my adventure to

the family. They were not impressed. The local paper came
out on Thursday. On the front page was a big photograph
of a bedraggled swan, firmly held by a beaming inspector.
Banner headlines proclaimed, 'Heroic Rescue By RSPCA.'
   Nobody even mentioned me.

14

'Someone's got to do it,' they said, looking at me.

'Oh, no,' I protested. 'Not me. I haven't done any meat inspection since I left College.'

'Nor have we,' they pointed out, 'and you left College after us.'

I was taking a much-needed coffee break, halfway through a long morning's operating, and had found my employers, Harry and Sean, sitting in the prep room, waiting to discuss a new job we had been allocated by the Ministry. It seemed that Yandle's slaughterhouse at Barkington were exporting beef to Europe.

'Why have you suddenly got to do the meat inspection?' demanded Wendy. 'Who usually does it?'

'District Council meat inspectors,' I answered. 'Highly trained and very efficient.'

'But now we belong to the Common Market,' interrupted Harry, 'so we have to comply with EEC regulations, which state that meat for consumption in Europe must have been inspected by a vet.'

'And vets with the necessary expertise are very thin on the ground,' continued Sean, 'which is why Kate is going to Birmingham on Sunday week for retraining. Come on, Kate!' he went on. 'It's only going to be three half-days a week. The Ministry VO will do the other days.' I knew further protest would be useless. They had not bothered to point out that they were the employers and I the employed. They didn't have to. I put down my mug.

'Come on,' I said to Wendy, 'we've still got that big mammary tumour to do, and two dental operations.'

I had ten days to get my domestic arrangements organised. Liz was temporarily in Surrey, running a big livery yard. She saved up her time off and came home for a long weekend about once a month. I phoned her and told her I would be away for the next weekend. She was worried about the animals.

'Will Louise be able to look after everybody?' she asked.

'It's OK,' I assured her. 'She's working at that garden centre at Lavender Green.' (Louise seemed to change her job with her underwear, and had little idea what she really wanted to do.) 'She wants Debbie and Tracy to stay, and they will help feed and so on. They think it's all a big adventure, and I shall be home before the novelty wears off.'

I promised to move Jubi, my horse, to the small field near home where Louise was keeping Ozzie, to make it easier for her to feed and visit him. During the week, I made sure there was enough food for people and animals prepared and stored in the freezer, but on the Sunday of my departure the horse was still in a field five miles away. I got up very early, and drove to the distant field, leaving loudly complaining dogs behind. There I parked and locked the car, tacked up the horse, and rode him to the little field. We were able to take a short cut along the beach, but the tide was coming in rapidly, and we had to jump the last two breakwaters. I turned him into his new field, where he was delighted to rejoin Ozzie, and staggered the half mile home with the heavy saddle and bridle.

I now had to fetch the car, so I borrowed Liz's bicycle and pedalled manfully back to the distant field. Arrived there, I fished in the pocket of my anorak for the car key, and found a hole. No key. For certain, I had dropped it on the beach, now covered in surging waves. Remounting the trusty bicycle, I headed for the nearest telephone box to ring Harry and enquire the whereabouts of the spare key. I found I had no money, and had to pedal home.

Harry was not pleased to be called from his bed at half-past seven on his Sunday off, and even less pleased when we realised there was no spare key for my car. After much discussion, the manager of the local garage was recalled from the golf course and persuaded to cut a new key. He arranged to meet me later at the field where I had left the car, to make sure the new key worked. All this took

160

time, and I finally left for Birmingham at four o'clock in the afternoon, six hours later than planned.

The partners had booked me into a bed and breakfast guest house on the outskirts of the city, and I left armed with the address, and a sketch map showing me how to get to the abattoir where my retraining was to take place. I was not exactly filled with confidence. As far as I am concerned, a map is a piece of paper which helps me get lost.

I found Birmingham—even I would have had trouble missing it—but I managed to sail past the turning leading to the guest house. Racing along the motorway with the lights of the strange city extending for miles on both sides, I was amazed at the amount of traffic. I decided to turn at the next interchange, but it seemed an awfully long way away. Suddenly, I saw cars apparently floating in the air above me, and when I looked down, there were others passing far below. To my intense dismay, I realised I had reached Spaghetti Junction.

When I finally arrived at the guest house, the proprietors were about to retire for the night. It was, they pointed out, half-past eleven. I was due at the abattoir at seven the next morning. Breakfast, they told me, began at seven-thirty. I got up at six o'clock, and was grateful for the makeshift meal left in the breakfast room for me. Rather to my surprise, I found the slaughterhouse without too much trouble, arriving at the meat inspectors' office on the stroke of seven. They had been working for an hour.

My first and enduring impression of that slaughterhouse was the noise. Spoken communication was possible only by yelling into each other's ears. The walls, roof and all possible equipment was metal, which echoed and reverberated. Even the belts round the slaughtermen's waists were metal chain, with metal scabbards to hold their knives hanging almost to their knees. The doors of the stunning pen clanged deafeningly shut, then opened with a crash. The hide stripper, attached by long chains to the skin of the dead beasts, rose gradually to ceiling height, then dropped hide and chains to a metal chute twenty feet below. The carcases were split by enormous reciprocating electric saws, while metal trolleys laden with clanging metal trays thundered across the tiled floor, and men yelled at each other to be heard.

There were four meat inspectors. Two at a time entered the slaughter hall, one to inspect and stamp the carcases, pushing most on their way on the overhead rail to the cooling room, diverting any needing closer examination into a side room. The other man inspected the heads and offals, cutting into hearts, lungs, livers and cheek muscles, looking for evidence of parasites or infection. The pace was frenetic, with barely enough room to stand. Every half-hour, the two on duty returned to their office, seized newspapers and tea mugs, and sent the other two into the fray. This continued until about four o'clock, when the hall was pressure-hosed and scrubbed to immaculate cleanliness, and everybody went home. I returned to the guest house, utterly drained.

I had not done any useful work. My initial entry into the slaughter hall had been greeted with jeers and catcalls from the score of men working there. The meat inspectors assured me this was their normal reaction to visitors and was not to be taken personally. When the men realised I was to be there all day—all week, even—they could not have been kinder. Provided I did not interrupt the flow of work, I was allowed to go to any part of the hall. I spent most of the time behind or beside the meat inspectors. They had to make a thorough examination of the meat, cutting into glands, slicing across livers and hearts, and satisfy themselves it was healthy, but, in doing so, they were not allowed to damage the appearance or saleability. There were recognised ways of doing this, which I had to learn. From time to time, one of the inspectors would adjourn to the side room to make a more detailed inspection of the detained carcases, cutting away bruised areas, trimming where necessary, sometimes condemning whole sides of beef. I relearned valuable lessons.

There were no facilities for women. I had to share the men's changing room, and when the interminable mugs of tea had the obvious effect, had to divest myself of boots, hard hat and protective overalls, and go through to the office part of the building, in search of the typists' washroom.

Having started work at six, the men stopped for a meal at eleven o'clock. I looked into their mess room, took one breath of the tobacco smoke-laden, frying oil-redolent air, heavy with the smell of sweat and old socks, and decided I wasn't hungry. John, one of the meat inspectors, said he was going to look at the lairage, and invited me to join him.

'We inspect everything as they come off the lorries,' he told me, 'and anything not fit is killed straight away, even if it means opening up the hall again when we have just cleaned it. Everything else is left to rest here for a few hours. It makes the meat set better,' he added practically.

About a hundred cattle and twice as many sheep were standing or lying in pens in a large barn. They had bedding and water, and appeared relaxed and unperturbed by the noise from the adjacent hall. The lairage was well organised.

'Calves are always killed as soon as they arrive,' said John.

'Their crying upsets some of the old cows in the lairage, and the men hate dealing with them, so they do it quickly to get the job over.' He saw my sceptical expression. 'You wouldn't believe what a soft-hearted crew they are,' he went on. 'There was a very small lamb in a bunch of sheep, and none of them would kill it. It lived here for years. The men called it Daisy and took turns leading it to the park down the road to graze.'

'What happened to it in the end?' I asked.

'We had a new man in the lairage,' he answered, 'and he put Daisy with a bunch of sheep and she went through the race and was slaughtered. The whole place went into mourning, and none of the men would touch mutton for weeks!'

They suggested I should arrive later the next day, which meant I could have a proper breakfast. I stopped on the way, and bought biscuits and fruit to eat at lunch time. My ears were becoming accustomed to the noise, and I found I could hear people speaking to me. I had no equipment, so one of the slaughtermen reluctantly lent me an old knife.

They were immensely proud of their knives, which were kept honed to razor sharpness on enormous steels hanging from their belts. I was allowed to cut glands on the sides of beef, and was inordinately pleased with myself when I found flukes in one of the livers. Carried away with enthusiasm, I let the knife slip, and it sliced across the top of my hand. Horrified, I looked at the blood dripping off the ends of my fingers.

I woke up at the first aid post, having been carried there unconscious by the biggest slaughterman.

'What's the matter?' demanded the nurse scornfully. 'Can't you stand the sight of blood?'

*   *   *

I returned home with my memories of meat inspection refreshed and my mind and body exhausted. The appointment at Yandle's was taken up immediately, starting at six on the first Monday. It was a small establishment, killing fifty cattle on a busy day, and occasionally taking a few sheep. Old plain dairy cows were slaughtered for export on three days a week, and on the other days, prime beef was produced for Yandle's own shops and for sale to local wholesalers.

I found that my 'half-days' began at six a.m. and rarely ended before three or four in the afternoon. The partners suggested I could do the evening surgery after this, but the worm finally turned. I pointed out that by the time I had got home, showered and changed, I had had an eleven-hour day, and could not be expected to produce my best tableside manner for an evening surgery. They changed the rota.

News of my new appointment spread rapidly round the practice, provoking a fairly predictable response—chiefly shock, horror and outrage. I was first noticed by some of our clients who came to the back door of the slaughterhouse in the afternoons to buy tripe for their dogs. The stomach of the cow, like that of other ruminants, is a complicated affair, with four compartments. The first is essentially a big bag which, when full, occupies about half the belly space.

Freshly eaten food arrives here and ferments, giving off gas which the cow gently burps up. When she is full, she sits down or stands in a quiet place, and chews the cud or ruminates. Small amounts at a time of the fermenting mass are regurgitated, chewed and reswallowed, going this time to compartments two, three and four. The lining of the first two compartments is tripe.

Before being offered for sale for human food, it is cooked and bleached, but for dog food it is purchased raw, or green. The stomachs are merely emptied, hosed down and hung up to drain. I tried it with my animals for a short time. The dogs all loved it. Three of the cats liked it, but four refused to touch it and left the kitchen in disgust while the others were eating. I tried cooking some to make it more palatable, but this was a bad mistake. The house stank for hours. As a food, green tripe is cheap and very nutritious, but, for my dogs at any rate, it had a major drawback. It caused flatulence.

After their meal, the dogs would sprawl in the sitting-room with satisfied grunts, and within a very short time the air would be filled with disgusting green smells. For kennelled dogs, this presents no problems, and owners of boarding and breeding kennels bought tripe by the dustbinful.

Emerging from the back door of the slaughter hall one afternoon, I literally bumped into Mrs Gladstone, who bred Alsatians. At first, she did not recognise me. I removed my hard hat and commented on the warmth of the day.

'Good Heavens!' she cried. 'Has there been an accident?'

'I hope not,' I replied.

'But isn't that why you are here? Surely you don't . . . ?' For the first time, she noticed my bloodstained white boiler suit, PVC apron and welly boots. She stared in dismay at the slaughterman's belt with its pendant knives and steel.

'Surely you don't work here?' she gasped. I explained about vets having to inspect meat for export.

'You actually work in there?' she pointed to the entrance to the slaughter hall. 'It must be absolutely ghastly for you!'

'Well,' I replied, 'it is a bit noisy, but you get used to it.

The men are a cheerful lot, and careful with their language when I'm around. In fact,' I continued, 'confidentially, when the partners are in a bad mood, the nurses are grumbling and the clients being difficult, I'm quite glad to come here!' She stared uncomprehendingly.

'But they kill animals, and bleed them, and—and . . .' she stopped, shuddering theatrically. If she had been a vegetarian, I could have respected her feelings, but I loathe hypocrisy and tact was never one of my strong points.

'What about the lamb chops you probably had for lunch?' I demanded. 'Or the roast beef you cooked last weekend? They were parts of animals, which were killed so that you could eat them. If you can't acknowledge that, then you shouldn't eat meat.' We had been joined by her husband, who listened with interest.

'I admit to being a carnivore,' he said, 'but surely a slaughterhouse is a distressing place to work?'

'We mostly kill cattle here,' I said, 'and perhaps a few sheep. They really don't seem to worry at all. They are used to being driven about and shut in small spaces. The men here are not cruel, and handle them as gently as possible. I'm not so sure about pigs. They are too intelligent. But we have no facilities for pigs here.'

A loud voice hailed me.

'Oi! Inspector! We've got a traffic jam 'ere! Can you come and do some work?' I returned to my sides of beef, shiny brown and purple livers, floppy pink lungs and writhing intestines. I attacked a row of suspended heads, cutting hidden glands, slicing cheek muscles to look for parasitic cysts. I reflected to myself that most people would consider Yandle's a horrendous place, but to me, the meat and offals bore no relation to the animals I had inspected a short time before. Once they fell out of the stunning pen and were hung up over the bleeding trough, they became carcases. Just meat. I find the insides of animals far more interesting than their outsides, and had to confess I did not find the slaughterhouse at all distressing.

At the end of each day's work, the men cleaned the hall and I returned to my office to complete the paperwork necessary for export. By this time, the cows for the next day would be arriving, having travelled a hundred miles from markets in the South West. I watched them unload, and inspected them as they entered the pens in the lairage.

There are still some farmers whose concern for their animals is greater than their love of profit. When their old dairy cows reach the end of their useful lives, they are taken directly to the nearest abbatoir and killed within a very short time of leaving the familiar farm. However, cows taken to a market might make a better price, because there is competition from several buyers. Those matrons I inspected had been loaded on a lorry very early in the morning, transported to market and herded into pens. They had been poked and prodded, passed through a noisy sale ring, chased into different pens, and loaded onto another lorry. After a four-hour journey, they finally arrived at their destination. Small wonder they were tired. They queued at the drinking bowls, then most of them lay down to rest. Some picked over the straw bedding. They would be left in peace until the following morning, then filed one at a time through the race to the stunning pen. There, their troubles would be ended forever.

One particularly busy afternoon, there was a sudden commotion in the yard, and my presence was demanded to inspect a cow brought in for casualty slaughter. She was a big Friesian, trying to give birth to a Hereford cross calf. The hind legs were presented, and there the calf was stuck. In these circumstances, the farmer has several options. He can put ropes on the legs and pull the calf out with a tractor. This sometimes works, but the cow can be injured, perhaps fatally. He can call in his vet who might decide on a Caesarean, an expensive operation which might leave the cow unfit for future breeding. If the calf is dead, he might decide to cut it up inside the cow and remove it piecemeal. This also can cause injuries to the cow and reduce her chances of producing calves, and therefore milk, in the future. The final option is to cut his losses and send the cow for immediate slaughter. This is often the most economic option and, from the cow's point of view, the most humane.

I inspected the big Friesian.

'The calf is still alive,' I observed. 'What a waste!' Peanuts, the slaughterman, overheard.

'Do you want the calf?' he asked.

'I could rear it,' I answered, 'but when you bleed the cow, you exsanguinate the calf, too. By the time you get him out, he'll be dead.'

Horn blaring, the abattoir lorry turned into the yard and began to back up to the lairage. The big Friesian was slapped on the rump and guided into the slaughter race. Calm and full of dignity, she walked to her death. Half an hour later, I entered the slaughter hall, having seen the cattle unloaded and penned. Peanuts was washing down the wall, whistling cheerfully.

'Hey! Inspector!' he called. 'Present for you in the straw shed.'

Puzzled, I returned to the yard and looked in the shed. Tucked behind the first row of bales was a Hereford bull calf, wet and bloody, trying to sit up. I rubbed him dry with handfuls of straw and he seized my fingers and sucked avidly. Peanuts must have removed him from the cow before she was bled. He knew as well as I did that this was forbidden, but the evidence was all cleaned away, and I had no proof. One of the men put the calf on the scales—he weighed it at eighty-one pounds—and then plonked him in the back of my car with the dogs. They all washed him.

I stopped on the way home at the farmers' shop where I bought food for the horses, and purchased a bag of milk powder. I wanted to call the calf Lazarus, but the girls preferred Hovis. He lived in the stone shed with the goats, and drank a gallon of milk a day, at first from a beer bottle with a special large teat, and later from a bucket. We weaned him on to calf mix, and he ate the ponies' hay, and thrived.

I sometimes thought I ought to make a small charge to the people who came to look at our garden at weekends. They strolled casually past, peering over the wall, to watch me weeding the onions or cutting the grass. The goats were usually tethered by the hedge, clearing the long grass from the hedge bottom and pruning the twigs within reach. Rabbits and guinea pigs frisked on the grass and nibbled the carnations. A pony or two might be grazing the lawn, or standing, eyes closed, dozing in the sun. For a time, a magpie or a squirrel could have been seen, perched on my head or shoulder. To all this, a big brown and white calf was added, blundering through the roses, or high-tailing across the grass, chasing the dogs.

I sold Hovis when he was four months old, to a local farmer who reared beef cattle in the old-fashioned way, selling them off grass at three years old, so our calf would have had a longer and less stressful life than most meat animals. He probably returned to the slaughterhouse where he was born, but by that time I had left the practice and was far away.

15

The evening surgery started quietly enough, but by six-thirty, when it should have ended, the waiting room was packed. Most of my patients seemed to be suffering from overgrown toe-nails or impacted anal glands, or needed booster vaccinations.

'No brain surgery required tonight,' said Wendy cheerfully as she wiped the consulting room table. 'Gosh! Didn't Mrs Taylor's dog smell awful? Even this strong disinfectant can't hide the smell.'

'It's not surprising,' I replied. 'She admitted the poor old thing had been worrying about his tail end all week, but they left it until his glands blew up into a great big abscess before they did anything about it. No wonder he tried to bite me.' I rinsed the soap off my hands and dried them gingerly, wincing as I rubbed my knuckles where the Poodle's dirty teeth had grazed them.

'Wheel in the next customer,' I said.

At twenty to eight, Wendy ushered the last person out into the wet autumn night, clicked the latch on the door and turned off the porch light. I put away the file cards and began to tidy the consulting room. Wendy looked through the door.

'Leave that for me,' she commanded. 'I've put a cup of tea and the biscuit tin in the prep room for you.'

'That's very kind,' I sighed, 'but I think I'll go straight home. I'm starving, and a bit tired.' This was the understatement of the week. It was a long time since breakfast, my legs felt woolly and my hands shook with weariness. Wendy's face fell.

'Sorry. Mr Leadbetter rang about ten minutes ago; one of his best cows is down with milk fever. I said you'd go when you had finished here.'

I groaned, and sat down in the chair provided for my patients' owners. Wendy fetched the tea and biscuits, putting them on the hastily wiped table.

I gulped the tea and put some biscuits in my pocket.

'I'll just ring the girls . . .' I began. Wendy beamed and adjusted an imaginary halo.

'I've already done it. Liz said she had found the chops in the fridge, and they had their supper ages ago. And they went down to the horses' field on their bikes and fed them, so you won't have to bother.'

'Oh! Gosh!' I was dismayed. 'I thought the surgery might be busy as it's Friday, so I fed them before we started. They've had double rations, so they'll be Whoops, whoa Neddy at the show tomorrow afternoon.'

'Worse than that,' grinned Wendy. 'Liz gave them extra feed because of the show. Never mind! the girls won't mind if the horses are jumping out of their skins. Now then, I tidied your car while you were operating this morning, and there's plenty of calcium in the box, so you can go straight to Leadbetter's. I'll clear up here, and switch the phone through to Liz before I leave.'

I had called at home during the afternoon and left the dogs in the warm house, much to their vociferous disapproval, and I knew Liz and Louise would feed them. Thunder rumbled overhead as I drove to Leadbetter's dairy farm, and the wipers worked overtime to keep the windscreen clear.

Parking in the farmyard, I took a deep breath and opened the car door. By the time I had squelched round to the back of the car and opened the hatch, I was soaked. I put a rubber coat over my soggy anorak and pushed reluctant wet feet into clammy wellingtons. The farmer appeared, outlined for an instant in the open farmhouse door, then vanishing in the gloom as it banged shut. I heard him splashing across the yard towards me.

'She's out in top meadow,' he shouted. 'We'll have to take the tractor. Land-Rover won't make it in this downpour.'

Resignedly, I put the flutter valve and syringe case in one pocket and a selection of bottles in the other, and followed him across the yard. He heaved himself into the tractor cab and pressed the starter. The engine fired with an ear-shattering bellow. Mr Leadbetter waved his arms at me.

'Stand on here,' he gestured behind him, 'and hang on!'

With some difficulty in my stiff coat and slippery boots, I did as he commanded and we set off. It was not far, just up a lane, across two fields and through a gateway. Sitting on his padded seat, Mr Leadbetter was quite happy, but standing behind him on the metal floor, my bones felt every jolt in the lane, and I clutched frantically at his coat as the tractor roared up and down the undulating pasture. In the gateway, he switched off the engine and produced a flashlight from his pocket.

'She's over there . . .' he pointed vaguely . . . 'just by the fence.'

I stumbled in the direction he had indicated. There was no fence that I could see, but I found a cow lying flat out on her side, groaning, grinding her teeth and shivering violently. Mr Leadbetter flashed the torch around.

'Good job she got out of the gateway before she went down,' he observed, 'it's not quite so wet on this higher ground.' He dropped a bale of straw in the mud. 'Brought this in the forage box,' he said. 'Thought we might need it.'

Together, we heaved and grunted and lifted the heavy cow into a sitting position. The gas trapped in her distended belly began to burp up.

'I'll hold her,' I gasped, 'while you wedge the bale under her shoulders to hold her up.' As he took his hands off the cow's back, she made a violent effort to get up, pushing me backwards. My feet slid from under me and I lay prone in the mud, my face against the cow's backbone. I lifted my head. There was a blue flash and I was hurled in a graceful swallow-dive straight over the cow's body, landing on all fours on the other side.

'Electric fence,' said the farmer laconically. 'Forgot to warn you it was on high. It must have touched the back of your head.'

'It feels more like a hammer touched it,' I answered, rubbing the back of my neck and turning my head carefully from side to side.

172

We sat the cow up again, propping her with the bale. Taking the metal cap off one of the bottles in my pocket, I eased the hood of the flutter valve over the top and balanced the bottle carefully beside the cow. My fist, pushed into her neck, blocked the blood flow in her jugular, and I stabbed a needle into the distended vein, then attached the tube of the flutter valve and gurgled the calcium solution into her bloodstream. She looked brighter straight away. I stepped back, tripped over the electric fence and received another jolt as I scrambled to my feet. The farmer grunted, stomped off into the darkness, and returned.

'Turned it off,' he said. 'You'll exhaust the battery, shorting it out like that.'

Suitably chastened, I put another bottleful of calcium under the skin on the cow's flank, and injected a stimulant into the muscle of her leg. She made another attempt to rise, almost succeeding this time.

'She'll do,' decided the farmer. 'I'll have another look at her before I go to bed and ring you if she's not up. Better get back now. I was halfway through my supper when you came.'

Lucky old you, I thought. I haven't even cooked mine yet.

Rather to my surprise, I survived the nightmare journey back to the farm without falling off the tractor. Mr Leadbetter headed towards the farmhouse.

'Dinner's probably cold by now,' he said reproachfully.

I drove home, parked the car and staggered damply into the kitchen. Louise was bustling about, trying to look domestic.

'Liz is having a bath,' she announced. 'She put your dinner on to cook and told me to keep an eye on it. Golly! You are wet. And look at the mud on your clothes! Good job it's washing day tomorrow. Wait there, and I'll get you some clean jeans and another jumper.'

Wearily, I peeled off the outer layer of sodden garments and dressed in the fresh clothes. Louis pattered out into the kitchen, sniffed perfunctorily at my feet and went back to his place by my chair. As I entered the sitting-room, Ceilidh opened his eyes and beat the hearthrug with his tail. Tania rolled over on her back on the settee and stretched luxuriously. They went back to sleep. Obviously, they had not forgiven me for leaving them behind. I sat with the tray on my lap, beginning to revive.

'I made an apple pie today,' offered Louise doubtfully. Liz appeared in a dressing-gown.

'I think she made the pastry with cement,' she declared. 'My back teeth are all shattered. You'd better let it soak a while in the custard.'

Before I could reply, the telephone shrieked. Anticipating my reaction, two cats removed themselves precipitately from my shoulders, digging their claws through my jumper in their haste to depart, and Louis hurriedly got away from my feet. I galloped into the oversize cupboard which did duty as my study and snatched up the receiver.

'We have a dog here which cannot open or close its mouth,' said an overbearing voice. 'He hasn't eaten anything and he has difficulty drinking. And he smells frightful.'

'How long has he been like this?' I demanded.

'I don't know,' returned the voice peevishly. 'It's my mother's dog. We are visiting her, and the smell put us off our tea.'

I wondered how long ago they had had tea.

'Can you come and see to it? I think it ought to be put to sleep.'

'Bring the dog to the surgery in fifteen minutes,' I suggested.

'It would be more convenient if you came here,' insisted the voice. 'My mother is disabled, so I would have to take the creature.'

'No,' I disagreed. 'It would be more convenient at the surgery. And cheaper for you.' This was usually a clincher, and I was not surprised when the caller capitulated. I made a note of the name and address of the owner and returned to the sitting-room.

'We heard,' cried Louise. 'I'll leave the apple pie in the larder. You can have it when you come back.'

'You'll need a hammer and chisel,' said Liz darkly. 'We are going to bed because of the show tomorrow. Will you be able to fetch us? We can hack there, but the horses will be a bit tired by the end of the show. It would be nice to have a lift home. Caroline's father will lend us their horse box.' I thought for a moment.

'I've got to do the morning surgery,' I said, 'and deal with any visits in the afternoon, but I should be finished by teatime. I was hoping to go for a ride on the beach.' Their faces fell. 'But I can take Jubi out on Sunday,' I continued. 'I'll fetch you.'

They cheered, and stamped noisily up the stairs while I carried the dishes out to the kitchen. I put on a mackintosh. The rain was easing but it was still a horrid night. The dogs gathered by the back door. Rain, hail, shine or pink snow, they had no intention of being left behind again.

At the surgery, I switched on the porch light, left the door on the latch and awaited my patient. Half an hour later, a sleek new Rover was driven into the car park and a tall, bespectacled man carried a little terrier into the consulting room and dumped him on the table with an expression of deep disgust.

'The creature stinks,' he complained. 'It's not healthy. My mother ought to have it done away with. We could do it now, while she's not here. You could say it died under the anaesthetic.'

I was horrified and very angry, but remained calm.

'I shall examine the dog,' I stated. 'If he is suffering from an incurable and painful condition, I shall recommend euthanasia, but you would have to sign a consent form. If he can be treated, I shall certainly not destroy him unless the owner asks me to.'

'What a fuss!' grumbled the objectionable man. 'Well, get on with it, then.' I switched on the Anglepoise lamp.

'Face him this way, please,' I asked, 'and hold him steady.' He reluctantly complied. I slid a loop of bandage into the terrier's mouth, lifted his head and carefully pulled down his lower jaw with my finger. He shrieked and jumped back, but not before I had had a quick glance into his mouth.

'There's something across the roof of his mouth,' I said. 'Please take a seat in the waiting room, and I shall call the nurse to help me. We'll give him an anaesthetic and remove it.'

We found a length of rib bone, probably from a chop, wedged across the dog's palate, between his largest molar teeth. It had been there for some time. The roof of the mouth was severely ulcerated and the teeth loose and infected. I cleaned up the mess and injected antibiotic. Carol carried him to a recovery cage in the hospital room, while I called the unpleasant man into the surgery and explained to him. He was still complaining.

'If we could get rid of the wretched dog, she could go into a home,' he whined. 'Then I wouldn't have all this bother every weekend, coming all this way to visit her.'

'You can collect the dog during morning surgery tomorrow,' I said, almost pushing him out of the door. He began to raise more objections, but the sudden shrilling of the telephone silenced him, and he departed. I did not explain that the call was on Carol's private line . . . the surgery phone was transferred to my house. I began to clean up the consulting room. Carol came downstairs again.

'That was Liz on my phone,' she called. 'Dog in road accident in Sandy Lane, just off Thornbury Road. Do you know it?' I nodded. 'OK. I'll finish here,' she offered.

Thornbury Road was on the other side of the town. It was eleven o'clock and the pubs were closing, so there was a lot of traffic weaving about. The flashing light on a police car guided me to the accident scene. The young constable looked sick.

'It's pretty bad,' he muttered. 'Only one thing to do.' A quick inspection of the dog's horrendous injuries proved he was right, and the merciful injection of barbiturate ended his pain forever. I eased the pathetic body into a plastic sack and stowed it in the back of the car. My dogs ignored it. The small knot of onlookers dispersed, clucking to each other about hit-and-run drivers.

'No collar,' said the constable. 'Probably a stray. We don't pay for these call-outs any more.'

'I know,' I replied. The RSPCA doesn't either. It's just one of those things we write off in the name of humanity.'

I left the plastic sack in the cold room at the surgery, then

176

went home. The lights were on downstairs but the house was quiet and peaceful. There were no messages on the pad by the telephone. I tiptoed into Louise's bedroom.

'Nothing else,' she mumbled sleepily. 'Did you go to the accident?'

'Yes,' I replied. 'All dealt with.'

'You were very quick,' she said. 'Must have put it to sleep. Poor dog.' I kissed the top of her head and patted the blanket over her shoulders.

'Go to sleep now,' I said, and went downstairs.

Unable to face the concrete apple pie in its shroud of custard, I offered it to the dogs. They ate it gratefully. 'Don't tell Louise,' I whispered as I washed up the plates. It was almost midnight, and I decided to have a hot drink and go to bed. The telephone rang as I sat down.

'Leadbetter here,' he grated. My heart sank. 'Just been up to see that cow,' he continued, 'and I'm not happy.'

'I'll come straight . . .' I began.

'That's not necessary. She's up on her feet and eating. Turned the fence off, didn't I? Because you kept falling over it and wasting the battery. Didn't put it back on, so half the herd were in my winter wheat. No damage, but it took half an hour to round them up again. Thought you ought to know.'

He obviously took a malicious glee in the idea that he had woken me up to tell me. I disillusioned him.

'Thank you for letting me know,' I said quietly. 'I've had a very busy evening, but I can go to bed now, knowing you won't call me out again.'

I put the phone down gently and went back to my chair. The dogs and cats arranged themselves on and around me. I stared at the dying fire and thought. It had been a pretty average Friday evening. Only three calls and I had actually been able to eat half my supper. I had recently celebrated —if that was the right word—a quarter of a century in general practice. Did I really want to spend the rest of my professional life like this? I recalled two conversations with my bank manager. The first had been a couple of months ago. Like most assistants in general practice, I was supplied with a house, a car, and a fairly ungenerous salary. I had

177

discovered that the bright young men who flitted through the practice, gaining experience on their way to higher things, were all paid considerably more than I was. My employers knew that I might have trouble finding another job in a rural practice, and expected me to be tolerant. So far, I had, but Liz was now working at a local riding school until she could take a place at a training stable and learn to be an instructor. Louise had no ambitions to follow an academic career, and with both girls finished with full-time education, my tax demand had doubled. The bank manager had advised me to buy something, such as my house, but Building Societies took one look at my salary and turned me down. I went to see him again.

He put the tips of his fingers together and gazed at me over the tops of his spectacles.

'Change your job, dear lady,' he said. 'Find employment elsewhere.'

Easier said than done, I thought as I descended the carpeted stairs to the main bank premises below. I had put his advice out of my mind until now.

Reaching carefully behind me to avoid disturbing prickly cats, I pulled the *Veterinary Record* from under the cushion. It fell open at the back page—Situations Vacant.

Taking up a quarter of the page was an advertisement by the Ministry of Agriculture, Fisheries and Food. 'Come and join our team,' it said. I gazed at the dying fire and went on thinking. One of my College friends had recently joined the Ministry. I was vague about what he did, but he left home at eight o'clock each morning and was always home by half-past five. He seemed to have nearly every weekend free. He admitted to spending half his time at a desk, but pointed out that in some weathers, a nice centrally heated office had much to recommend it.

I looked at the advertisement again. The salary at the bottom of the scale was nearly twice what my present employers thought I was worth. Allowing for a mortgage and the purchase of some sort of car, I should still be no worse off.

'Annual increments,' said the ad, 'and salaries under review. Send now for application forms!'

I stood up slowly, allowing cats to disperse without digging their claws in me, and padded into the study. I took a pad of writing paper from the desk.

'Dear Sirs,' I wrote. 'Please send application forms.'

*   *   *

The Ministry sent a short acknowledgement of my application, then seemed to forget me. October went out in a blaze of glory, November was cold and bright and December wet, windy and miserable. Christmas Day that year was a Saturday, which meant there were three days of holiday. To my delight, I found I was off duty Christmas Day and Sunday, and working only on Boxing Day. Liz, who had another temporary job at a stud and livery stable fifty miles away, phoned to say she had the whole weekend off—after she had fed and tended all the horses in the yard on Christmas morning. There were about twenty of them, and she reckoned it would take her until well after teatime; she was very despondent.

Louise and I discussed the problem and came up with a plan. We got up well before daylight on Christmas Day and packed the slightly surprised dogs into the car. The weather had turned much colder, and I drove carefully through the wintry darkness, arriving at the stable yard in a snowstorm, just as Liz emerged, yawning mightily, from the caravan she shared with the other girl groom.

With three of us digging over beds, trundling wheelbarrows, lugging bales and filling haynets, the work evaporated. Most of the liveries were being ridden by their owners next day and hunted on Boxing Day, and could be allowed a day off, so the only exercising necessary was the stallion, who was lunged in the covered school, and a group of young mares, who were turned out into the outside manège to trot about, neigh and toss their heads coquettishly. By half-past ten, the yard was clean and tidy, all the horses fed, groomed and exercised as necessary, and the feeds for the afternoon weighed out and left in a row of buckets in the feed room.

The dogs had had a lovely morning, playing on the muck-heap, looking for nonexistent rats in the feed shed and hunting rabbits in the paddock. We cleaned them up as best we could, but since we were nearly as mucky and odorous as they were, we didn't worry overmuch. The snow had ceased, but the sky was grey and lowering, so after tea and mince pies in the caravan, we set off for home, feeling extremely cheerful and singing tunelessly. Louise gave us a new version of 'While Shepherds Washed Their Socks By Night', and Louis and I gave our rendering—the only possible description—of 'God rest ye merry gentlemen'. Fortunately, there were very few other cars on the road. We arrived home with time to shower and change our clothes before lunch. We would be expected to eat a conventional roast turkey dinner at the family gathering at my mother's house next day, so our Christmas lunch was a glorious mixture of all our favourite foods. We had melon, avocado, smoked salmon, fried chicken with Waldorf salad, fresh pineapple, Christmas pudding and ice-cream. The dogs and cats had an extra feed of titbits.

Before collapsing in front of the fire with everybody else, I had to visit Jubi in the aeroplane field, which he was sharing with a friend's three ponies. He was the only horse still in the family, Louise having sold Ozzie some weeks previously, and Manny having joined Liz at her stables. The dogs were not interested in coming, so I drove there alone, the sugar beet, barley and grass nuts in the bucket augmented with apples, sliced carrots and a whole packet of Polos.

He gobbled greedily, putting his ears back and raising a hind foot threateningly when I adjusted his New Zealand rug. Quite confident that the threats were only for show, I smacked his bottom smartly.

'Not many owners,' I assured him, 'would stand in the snow on Christmas Day while you ate that great big bucketful of food. If you weren't such a wimp, I could leave you to get on with it and go home.' By far the biggest animal in the field, Jubi was notably lacking in courage, and would allow the ponies to chase him off and steal his food if I did not stand guard over him. He shook the snow off his mane and went on eating. There were icicles in his tail, but under the waterproof rug, his back was dry and warm.

I put the empty bucket back in the car and drove home. The girls had fed the rabbits and goats, and relieved Natty of the small amount of milk she was giving. Their treat was apples and a packet of digestive biscuits. The rabbits had a banana, but the goats preferred the skins and the brown paper bag.

We had a happy family party next day, but had to return early because Mike was putting the phones through to me before he went to bed. Nobody rang Sunday night, and the telephone sat, black and silent, all Boxing morning and afternoon. Before dark, I left the girls listening, and took the dogs to Jubi's field to feed him and check his rug. They had little interest in ploughing through the wet snow, and returned thankfully to the blankets in the back of the car.

As the wind dropped, the temperature followed suit, and ice crackled on the snow and made the roads slippery. Just as I arrived home, the telephone rang, making everybody jump. Liz answered it while I peeled off my wet coat and tugged reluctant wellies off my frozen feet.

'Sorry, Mum,' she said when she came out of the office. 'That was Mr Herbert of Lower Leaze. He's got a heifer calving and she's been trying since dinner time. He thought he ought to tell you before it gets any later. Oh! and Mrs Laker phoned a little while ago. You won't have to take me back tomorrow. She is visiting her son in Chichester and can pick me up on the way back.' Mrs Laker was the owner of the stud. I was much relieved, having forgotten to warn Harry and Sean that I would need time off to take Liz back to work.

'I told Mr Herbert you'd go straight away,' she added. 'Shall I make you a quick cup of tea first?' I decided not to sit down, because it would make going out again much harder. Pushing unwilling feet back into the cold boots, I borrowed Louise's dry coat.

'Don't wait for me if you want supper,' I said. 'There's plenty of food in the fridge, and bottles of stuff in the cupboard. Open a bottle of wine if you like.'

I drove with great caution along the icy roads. Lower Leaze was not far away and, turning into the gate at the end of the farm drive, I could see the house ablaze with lights in every window. The drive was narrow, and I judged the centre carefully, measuring the distance from the hedges and keeping well away from the deep ditch on either side.

Mr Herbert and his enormous son heard the car and rolled out of the farmhouse kitchen door to greet me, accompanied by a blast of hot air and a pounding of music from a party obviously in full swing. They weaved towards the sheds on the other side of the yard, opened a door and switched on the light. We all stood, blinking at a big Hereford heifer proudly licking a very newly-born calf.

'She's beaten me to it,' I laughed. 'I'll go home again.'

'You'll have a little drink with us first,' declared Mr Herbert, taking my arm.

'I'd better go back,' I said, 'there might be . . .'

'Got to have a little drink for Christmas,' hiccoughed the son, taking my other arm. Between them, they propelled me across the yard, opened the door and we entered the furnace heat of the kitchen. Mrs Herbert, redfaced, perspiring and cheerful, was setting out mountains of food on the table. She greeted me with delight.

'We're just going to have a bit of supper,' she declared. 'Sit down, love. Take off your coat. Here! Have some turkey and a bit of ham. The tongue's nice, and help yourself to salad. How about a cup of tea? Or something stronger?'

I found myself sitting at the table with about a dozen women. The men took heaped plates into the adjoining room, and the clink of bottles and glasses mingled with the murmured talk of fatstock prices and the progress of the lambing season. Lunch seemed a long time ago, and I attacked my plateful with a will but drank only tea. The girls knew where I was and would telephone the farm in an emergency.

Eventually, everybody had packed away as much food and drink as they could. I reluctantly stood up and prepared to face the cold, white world outside. Mr Herbert and his son came to see me off and, clad in my warm, Aga-dried coat and boots, I ploughed across the yard for another look at the heifer, the two men staggering and weaving behind me.

The calf lay on the straw, legs neatly folded, milk still

dribbling from its greedy mouth. The heifer yearned over it, making reassuring maternal hummings. Satisfied, I switched off the light, climbed into my cold car and set off. The farm collie, released from the shed for its evening run, chased after me and disappeared somewhere in front of my wheels. Unthinkingly, I stamped on the brake. The car swung gently across the drive and nosedived into the ditch.

Answering the farmer's shouts, several men poured out of the farmhouse, wavered over the yard and seized various parts of my car's anatomy. Herbert junior slid, feet first, into the ditch, put a massive shoulder under the car bumper, and heaved us back onto the drive. The merry throng returned to the house, slapping each other on the back and declaring they would need another drink to drive the cold out.

Through the open kitchen door, I heard Mrs Herbert berating her son.

'Look at you!' she scolded. 'Wet through! Take those wet trousers off!' There was a short pause, followed by squealing from the assembled ladies.

'Not in here!' she continued, aghast. 'You great lummox! Get in the scullery!' The door closed and, cautiously, stone-cold sober, I drove home, leaving the revellers carousing.

My house was very quiet. Liz lay full length on the settee, snoring gently, two torpid cats on her chest. Louise was sprawled in my chair, Louis upside-down on her lap, Ceilidh and Tania, also upside-down, abandoned on the rug. Nobody moved as I entered.

'Any messages?' I asked. Liz opened her eyes with some difficulty.

'No,' she said. 'We've had supper, and I opened a bottle of that stuff like cold custard.' She went back to sleep and I picked up an almost empty bottle of advocaat from the floor.

'Have you finished the whole bottle?' I exclaimed. 'No wonder you're drunk!'

'The dogs had some, too,' Louise protested, coming slightly to life, 'and the cats liked it.'

I heaved another chair closer to the fire. Crimpy jumped on my lap, and I tickled her ears.

'All the world's drunk,' I said sadly, 'save me and thee.' She purred, rolled over, fell on the floor and remained there, still purring.

'And I don't think thee's entirely sober!' I added severely.

16

I parked the car, switched off the engine and sat for a moment. Ceilidh and Tania yawned and stretched. Louis uncoiled himself from the back of my neck and scrabbled impatiently at the door.

'All right! All right!' I muttered peevishly. 'Just a minute!'

Letting them out, I followed them across our backyard and opened the kitchen door. All the lights were on, and pop music belted out, full blast. Obviously, Louise was home. The dogs rushed in and announced our arrival.

'Hallo, Mum!' she called from the sitting-room. 'You're jolly late. I thought you must have been caught for the evening surgery.' Blessedly, the noise subsided.

'No,' I replied, 'Harry's on tonight. It's my weekend on, though.'

'I found the chops in the fridge,' she continued proudly, 'and I've done some potatoes.' She appeared in the kitchen. 'Gosh! What's that awful smell?'

'Me,' I admitted ungrammatically. 'I pulled a couple of very dead lambs out of one of Mr Herbert's ewes. She's very sick, but she might survive. Then I had to do a post-mortem at the knacker's yard. The cow died yesterday and ponged a bit. I'll get the supper going and then have a bath.' Louise Hurriedly pushed me aside.

'You have a bath first,' she suggested. 'I'll do the cooking.'

'OK,' I agreed, 'but I mustn't use too much hot water. It's washing night.'

'Oh, leave that,' she said, 'I'll do it in the morning.'

'I thought you were going out with Brian,' I said.

'He's working,' she said. 'I'll do the washing—' she adjusted an imaginary halo—'then I'll take Jubi out on the beach.'

The food tasted better for being cooked by someone else, and she had fed the dogs and cats while I scrubbed off the odour of the knacker's yard. We washed up, and I sat down with a sigh.

'There's a couple of letters,' said Louise. 'They look like bills.'

The first one was the electricity account. I winced, and tucked it behind the clock. The second was a command from the Ministry to present myself for interview at their Headquarters in London.

'When?' demanded Louise.

'March 28th,' I replied. 'Crikey! That's in ten days' time. I wonder if I can have the day off?'

'You'll take the day off!' decided Louise firmly. 'And I'll have my day off too, and come with you. You had better wear that grey skirt, and I'll lend you my new blouse.'

The partners let me take a day off my annual holiday allowance for the interview. 'It's a waste of time,' they said. 'You are much too old to be considered.'

We had a splendid day in London. In the short time available, I had read up all I could on current Ministry work, but the solemn gentlemen sitting in a row behind a long table didn't ask me anything I had swotted up. They encouraged me to talk about calves and welfare, and my experiences in practice.

Louise pounced on me as I emerged from the interview room.

'Well?' she demanded. 'Did you get the job?'

'I don't know,' I replied. 'They'll let me know.'

'Probably in about six months' time,' she predicted darkly. 'Let's do some shopping. And watch the Changing of the Guard.'

Two weeks later, I had an offer from the Ministry, commanding me to report at their office in the west to start work on June 2nd. I had exactly six weeks to find somewhere to live in an unknown area nearly two hundred miles away, arranging a mortgage, and remove myself, my family and household effects. Louise decided to move with me, and Brian declared his intention of coming too. I bought an enormous elderly estate car and trundled back and forth on my free weekend and at every other opportunity. The houses in my price range were awful. Brian borrowed his father's car and drove Louise to Somerset to continue the search while I was working. They returned one Sunday in great excitement. They had found the perfect house at a price we could afford. Elated, I drove down on Tuesday afternoon, my half-day, arriving at the estate agents' office at teatime. The house was just sold, they told me, and, no, there was nothing else at that price.

Bitterly disappointed, I set off to retrieve my car and, passing another agent's window, glanced in. A long arm was placing a picture of a cottage in the display. I read the details without enthusiasm, and then, on the spur of the moment, went in and asked to see it.

It was nearly time to go home, and the assistant told me to come back next day. I pointed out that I lived a long way away, and he grudgingly took me to see the house. It was love at first sight. The cottage was a wing of an ancient manor house which had long ago been divided into four dwellings. It had been a holiday home for years, occupied for a month each summer, and at occasional weekends. There was a hole in the roof big enough to crawl through. Sagging iron gutters had dribbled their contents down the sandstone walls, and in a four hundred-year-old house, there was no damp course. But it was May, and all I saw were the daffodils in the garden, the generous-sized rooms in the house, with their white walls and heavily beamed ceilings, and, from the window, park-like farmland sweeping to the horizon. The sun shone, the birds sang, and I felt I was at home. My offer for the cottage was accepted, then I took a proper look at it. And then took a deep breath!

I discovered that finding the house was the easy part. Arranging a mortgage and concluding the sale would take several more weeks, and I was due to start my new job almost straight away. Fortunately, my brother and his wife had moved to a house fairly near, and offered us temporary lodging. Jubi could be accommodated in the orchard, and my furniture stored in the barn. The cats would have to go into boarding kennels, and the dogs would be allowed in the house at night, but would spend the days outside or in my car. We accepted gratefully.

At my last visit to the slaughterhouse, I went to the office to say goodbye to the manager, and remarked on the trouble and expense of moving.

'No problem!' he declared. 'If you don't mind moving on a Sunday, I'll lend you one of my lorries.' I looked at the enormous vehicles parked outside.

'I can't drive a thing that size!' I protested.

'You haven't got an HGV licence,' he agreed. 'Ask one of the men. Try Donald. His wife's just had another baby, so he needs the money. Offer him fifty pounds, and I'll just charge you for the diesel. You've been very helpful to us in the past.' He brushed aside my thanks, and I went out to speak to Donald.

In the middle of the week, the selected lorry was backed into the drive beside the house and Donald unhitched the cab and drove off, leaving the trailer parked. Louise and I, aided by Brian, spent the next evenings after work gradually loading our goods and chattels into the depths of the lorry.

Jubi spent Saturday night in the garden, and on Sunday morning, we put the beds and the remaining kitchen bits and pieces into the lorry, closed off the partition and, with great difficulty, persuaded the horse to load into the back. The goats had been lodged at a local stables and the cats ensconced at their kennels, so when Donald arrived with the tractor part of the lorry, we were all ready to go.

I spent the next few weeks wondering if I had done the right thing. Working for the Ministry required a completely different attitude, which I found difficult to adopt. Jubi demolished the orchard fence and trespassed onto the neighbouring farm. Ceilidh and Louis terrorised the resident cats, and Tania chose this time to break her crooked leg, necessitating its amputation. My sister-in-law was understandably squeamish about this, and I struggled to keep animals and people apart. She showed great tolerance and good humour, but everyone was glad when we were at last able to move to our own cottage.

I collected the cats and introduced them to their new abode. Intoxicated by freedom after weeks of living in a cage, they spent the first night jumping from my bedroom window onto the roof of the bathroom below, and scrambling down a convenient laurel bush. They then ran across the garden, back into the house through the sitting-room window, galloped upstairs into my bedroom, across my bed and out of the window again.

I started some house repairs. The hole in the roof, the sagging gutters and crumbling chimney stack were dealt with as a matter of urgency. Inside the house, the previous owners had tried to fight the damp by covering the walls with successive layers of paint and paper, and the floors with roofing felt, plastic sheet, linoleum and carpet, all of which had slowly rotted. The floor coverings had a thriving population of earthworms, beetles and centipedes, and the bottom layer of felt had to be scraped off with a knife.

I stripped the walls to the plaster and painted them with white emulsion, allowing the damp to evaporate. I found the sitting-room paved with stone tiles and the dining-room with bricks. The kitchen floor was concrete, which I covered with pale honey-coloured tiles to match the sitting-room. Apart from a few rugs, the floors were left bare to breathe out the wet.

Louise and Brian married and moved in with me until they found a home of their own. We laboured like navvies at weekends, demolished the ancient shed and crumbling garage, and painfully dismantled, removed and re-erected a two-box stable I bought at a farm sale, so that Jubi would have shelter on winter nights. We managed to rent a small paddock, and all enjoyed exploring the forest rides.

I visited Marshton from time to time, generally to fetch my mother to stay with us, and, on one such occasion, called at the surgery to collect some medicine for Ceilidh. The waiting room was packed, and Sean's surgery obviously running late. Carol was snappy and flustered, Wendy had left, and the replacement nurse seemed unhappy. Several new assistants had tried my old job, stayed a short time and departed.

I listened to the hubbub in the waiting room, and looked

at all the anxious faces. Sean saw me when he came to call the next patient.

'You look as if you haven't a care in the world,' he said enviously. 'Next, please. I'm sorry to keep you all waiting so long. We had an emergency earlier.' Some of the owners sitting round the room grumbled to each other. I thought of my peaceful cottage and ordered life, and knew I had done the right thing.

*   *   *

Before moving to Somerset I had boarded the goats with an old man who had formerly run a small riding school, and was left with several pensioner ponies and a few pet goats. He agreed to look after mine until I moved into my own house and could come and fetch them. However, when the time came, he had become so fond of them that he begged tearfully to be allowed to keep them. I made a contribution to their future board and lodging and left them with him.

It has been said that you have to be a little mad to keep goats. Our first experience had been while we were living on the Isle of Wight, when the girls were small. I had been offered a small kid as a pet and potential milk producer. Since we lived at the time in a big farmhouse with plenty of buildings and a five acre horse paddock, I thought one little kid would not be much problem. She cost ten shillings, and was barely weaned. Of uncertain breeding, she was pretty silvery fawn, and we called her Minky. She obviously missed her mother, and attached herself firmly to my two daughters, who were delighted with their new playmate.

They taught her their own version of leap frog, bending down and encouraging her to jump on their backs, where she balanced triumphantly on her sharp little hooves. Unfortunately, she continued to play this game when she grew up. A tiny kid landing on your back when you are expecting it is fun. Over half a hundredweight of full-grown nannygoat crashing into your shoulder blades every time you bend down to pull up a weed or pick something up, is not funny, as many visitors explained.

When the weather was bad, they smuggled her up to

their room where all three trampolined joyfully on the beds. When they were tired of this, they came down to the sitting-room, and Minky sat, front hooves daintily crossed, and watched television from my best armchair. She slept at night in the end stall in the calf house so that she had company, but during the day, when the girls were at school, or not available to play, her favourite place was an old armchair in the corner of the outside lavatory. Enthroned guests found it disconcerting, to put it mildly, to discover that their most intimate functions were the object of slant-eyed contemplation from the far corner of the room.

When Minky came in season in the autumn, I took her to visit a large, smelly billy. Male goats deliberately spray urine over their bellies and legs, producing a powerful aroma which the females find irresistible. Minky thought he was delightful, rubbing herself all round him. She was banned from the house on her return, and the girls gave her a bath at the weekend.

The next spring, she produced two pretty female kids. They took all her milk, leaving none for us, but we left them to suckle, giving them a good start in life. Minky had to be tethered in the garden, because goats are browsers, preferring trees, shrubs, roses, carnations and flowers generally to grass, but she had free run of the farmyard, the buildings, and the horse paddock. I decided her breeding must have been at least partly Alpine, because she loved mountaineering. Since there were no Alps available, she practised on the house. Followed by her intrepid kids, she found that from the farmyard wall she could reach the roof of the old diary, and from there a good leap took them onto the gable end of the house. They then tightroped along the roof ridge, slid down the slates at the far end, and bounced off the woodshed, landing triumphantly on the bank at the side of the garden. I became accustomed to passing motorists pounding agitatedly on my kitchen door, to tell me there were goats on the roof.

When the kids were weaned, I advertised them for sale, and two very nice ladies came and bought them. They loved Minky too, and it was fortunate I kept their telephone number, because a short time later we left the farm and returned to the mainland, where I had taken up a new job in Marshton. We lived at first in a flat over the surgery, in the middle of the town. I sold the cattle, found grazing for the two mares and old Jack a short way out of town, put all the cats into temporary and hideously expensive boarding, and squeezed all the dogs into the flat with us.

Some weeks later, we at last moved into a proper house, with a garden, a big back yard, a stone shed and, it was pointed out, no reason at all why we should not get another goat. I was reading the small ads in the local paper at the time, and my eye had been caught by one particular advertisement.

'What about a Golden Guernsey?' I suggested. 'It sounds attractive.'

'A Guernsey is a cow,' objected Louise.

'A Guernsey is a cow,' I agreed, 'and a Golden Guernsey is a breed of goat. I read about them in that book I got out of the library last week. Where did I put it?' I rummaged about in the book shelves beside my chair.

'I don't know how you get through so many library books,' muttered Liz.

'She reads on the loo and in bed,' explained Louise.

'And at lunch time and some evenings,' I added. 'Now, breeds of goat. Here we are. Golden Guernsey, beautiful golden colour—'

'Sounds logical,' interrupted Liz.

'—often called the smallholder's goat,' I continued, undeterred. 'Lives on forage rather than concentrates. Moderate milk output. I should think one of those would suit as well. The advertisement in the paper says it's a year old, so we have it served in the autumn and it would kid and start milking next spring. I'd love a golden goat. Think how pretty it would be.'

We rang the owner of the advertised Golden Guernsey, and arranged to go and see her on Sunday. She was a neat little goat, shining with health, friendly and very pretty. There was one big disappointment.

'She's black,' I said querulously. 'You said she was Golden Guernsey.'

'She is three-quarters pure,' replied the owner, 'and a quarter Anglo-Nubian. She should have golden kids if you take her to a Golden billy.'

'She's a natty little goat,' decided Liz. 'We'll call her Natty, short for Natalie.'

It seemed the decision to buy had been made, so I swallowed my disappointment, and we took her home. She travelled on the back seat of the car, surrounded by dogs, which did not seem to worry her. Before embarkation, I took the precaution of walking her a short way up the road, waiting until she had sprayed rabbit-like pellets and splashed copiously on the pavement, thus avoiding catastrophe on the journey home.

She lived in the stone shed, with several rabbits and guinea pigs. We tethered her in the garden to protect my few flowers and the vegetable patch, but she had the run of the yard, and was taken for frequent walks in the fields and along the road. She loved the local park, especially the children's adventure playground.

When the time came, I took her to a Golden billy, and she produced two beautiful golden kids. Alas, they were both male, but they were so pretty that the owner of the little zoo in the local park offered to give them a home. Suitably dehorned and castrated, they were a big attraction, and played happily with the children.

Still anxious to have a female Golden goat, I took Natty back to the same billy the next autumn. This time she had twins again, one male, one female, and both the same glossy black as their mother. I was very disappointed.

'We can sell the female when she's old enough,' I told the girls, 'but the male is no use for anything.' Unlike most people, they were well aware of farming facts of life. Many town folk do not realise that in order to give milk, a dairy animal, be it goat or cow, must first have a baby, and the baby is then removed, and the milk produced for its sustenance is taken for use by humans. Some of the female babies are needed for flock or herd replacements, but the only use for the males is for meat, since only a tiny proportion are needed for breeding. Calves are economically valuable, producing beef or veal, but a male kid is practically worthless, since few people wish to eat goat meat. Most males are therefore killed at birth.

'We can't kill Natty's baby,' Louise objected tearfully. 'It's unkind to keep Natty by herself, you keep saying so. Instead of trying to get a Golden female to keep her company, can't we keep this little black male?'

So I gave up all thoughts of my Golden goat, and operated on the little black kid. A billy kid rapidly becomes smelly, and they use their horns in play, with dangerous effect, so castration and dehorning were essential. The female was sold to a good home, and Natty and her son settled down to life together. They lived in the back yard, with frequent expeditions, and were great favourites with local children, the postman, the milkman and the dustmen. The energetic billy kid gave Natty a second childhood, and she joined in all his mountaineering escapades.

Goats like something elevated to sit on, like a chair or a box. Natty and her son, called Diamond from a little white mark on his face, took to sitting on the dustbin, perched side by side on the lid. Diamond grew bigger and heavier, and the day came when he jumped up beside his mother, and the plastic dustbin lid collapsed, precipitating them both into the rubbish in the bin. I kept several tubs in the yard, in which I hopefully planted flowers. Goats eat flowers, but I had found after much expensive experience that they don't like marigolds, so we had a brilliant golden display. After the demise of the dustbin, the goats took to sitting on the tubs, and I found that squashing was just as lethal as being eaten.

Natty produced a moderate amount of milk, but there was sometimes enough for me to try my hand at cheese making. The first efforts were pretty horrible, even the dogs scorning them. I gave a piece of the latest effort to Ceilidh one morning. He took it gingerly, and carried it carefully out into the yard. There, he dropped it, pushed it about a bit with his nose, and when it obstinately refused to disappear, lifted a derogatory leg and pee'd on it. That was his considered opinion of my cheese making.

Now, having left Natty and Diamond with the old man in

Marshton, I was once again goatless. I had become accustomed to the taste of goat's milk, and I liked to have a lot of milk available for my own use and to give to the cats and dogs, who expected it to appear each time they looked at the dish by the refrigerator. Scanning through the local paper one day, I saw the magic words, 'Golden Guernsey'. Hurriedly, I rang the number given.

'We have built up a commercial herd,' said the voice at the other end of the phone, 'and now we are selling off some of the foundation stock which are not really suitable for a full-time milking herd. One of them is a Golden Guernsey, but we have had a lot of enquiries.'

As soon as I could, I rushed out to the address given, and met a triumphant woman leading a pretty golden goat out to a van parked in the lane.

'I'm terribly sorry,' the herd owner said. 'You missed her by minutes. There are others for sale, but no more of that breed.'

I inspected the other goats on offer, but none took my fancy. In a pen on its own was a skinny white goat, her pendulous udder and long straggly beard indicating considerable age.

'That's old Sooty,' I was told in response to my enquiry. 'She won't last another winter in the herd. She's about ten years old and is going to the knacker for dog food when she is dry.'

Needles to say, I returned home with a skinny, bearded goat, who not only lasted the winter, but several winters more, and is at this moment approaching her twentieth birthday. I bought a young goat in Taunton market to keep her company, and between them they produce enough milk to supply me, and two neighbours. They are popular with local children, especially when the kids are born.

A stranger appeared one evening, a boy staying in the holiday cottage at the end of the lane. He watched me milking for a time.

'Where are the kids?' he demanded.

'You've just missed them, I'm afraid,' I replied. 'I sold them last week.'

'Sold them?' He looked puzzled.

'Yes,' I said. 'They were girls. I got fifty pounds each for them.'

'Do you always sell your kids?'

'Only the girls,' I said. 'The boys are kept until they are four months old and then I take them to the butcher.' His eyes widened.

'To the butcher? What for?'

I don't believe in lies for children. 'For meat,' I replied. 'I put it in the freezer.'

He looked absolutely horrified, and backed away from me.

'Do you eat the meat?' he demanded. I nodded and, to my surprise, he cried out in terror and ran off.

It did not occur to me until some time later that he was a Londoner, and his initial enquiry about kids probably referred to human kids, which I would call children.

He probably went back to the cottage and told his parents that the natives were cannibals.

17

'That's a pretty one,' I said, pointing to a grey filly cantering along at the front of the group.

'Too pretty to kill,' replied Geoff. 'Make me an offer!'

It was not meant seriously, but I stopped and considered. Since our move to Somerset, Jubi had lived alone. I had two stables at the end of the garden and the use of a paddock at the other end of the village, and he was very pampered, but horses are social animals and it worried me that he had no company. His solitary life did not appear to distress him but he showed great excitement when we met other horses out in the woods. I had been toying with the idea of getting him a small companion to live in the other stable and share his paddock. I could break it to harness and go trotting round the lanes as a change from riding. I was officially on Geoff's farm to inspect sheep for the Ministry, but the little herd of ponies had caught my attention. I stood considering and Geoff laughed.

'Make me an offer,' he repeated. 'You know I'd rather sell them alive.'

He owned an abattoir and bought cattle, sheep and horses for slaughter for meat. When he had spare grazing on his farm, anything which might grow or fatten was kept there for a time.

'Bought them in Wales, three months ago,' he explained. 'Mostly two-year-olds, off the mountain. Meat trade was pretty quiet so I put them out here until the autumn. They'll go soon.'

I judged the weight of the grey pony, worked out her value per pound as meat, added a bit more to make a round figure. Geoff frowned.

'Good estimate,' he admitted. 'Tempt me a bit more.'

I added another £25 and stipulated it should include

197

delivery. Geoff beamed. 'Done!' he said. 'I'll bring her over Sunday.'

On Sunday morning, I moved Jubi out into the orchard at the top of his paddock, and opened the gate into the road so that Geoff could back his enormous lorry into the field.

'Wish you luck with this one,' he grunted as he slid back the bolts and lowered the ramp. 'Wild as a hawk, she is. Took eight of us to get her in here.'

He lifted the gates back, revealing a tiny shivering figure at the far end of the lorry. Snapping a stick from the hedge, he stepped onto the ramp, but I restrained him.

'Don't chase her out,' I begged, 'she'll come in a minute.'

Jubi, greatly excited by the lorry, thundered along the hedge between the orchard and the paddock.

'Who's there? Who are you?' he bellowed.

Hesitantly, the pony, which I had decided to call Nimbus, crept towards the inviting opened back of the lorry. We stood back.

'I'm young and very small,' she squeaked.

Jubi stood on tiptoe, trying to see over the hedge.

'Well, hello there,' he neighed.

The pony made up her mind and trotted confidently out of the lorry, across the grass and straight over to the hedge, where she stood reaching up to Jubi over the top of the blackthorn. They inhaled each other's breath, whickering excitedly.

Geoff lifted the gates closed and locked them, then picked up the spring-loaded ramp and crashed it shut. I handed over a wad of notes.

'That's what we agreed,' I said. He handed back a pound note for luck and drove off, satisfied with his bargain and happy to have sold a live pony. I left Jubi and Nimbus to get acquainted and went in to have my lunch and explain to the cross dogs why they had been shut in.

After lunch, I let Jubi back into his paddock, and he and Nimbus trotted up to each other, smelt each other all over, then settled to graze side by side, as if they had known each other for ever. Next day, when I came home from work, I took two small buckets of corn into the field. The big gelding loves his stomach and did not need calling twice.

Dropping his nose into the bucket, he munched eagerly. Nimbus followed him, and watched with interest. I put the other bucket down a short way away, and the pony, copying her companion, put her nose into it, liked what she found, and ate it so fast that when Jubi, his own feed finished, came to investigate, the bucket was licked clean.

The next day, I put the buckets side by side, and stood between them while they ate, stroking Jubi's neck, and the following day I patted the pony's neck, too. She flicked an ear towards me, but did not stop eating. By the end of the week, I could run my hands all over her body, and she made no protest when I produced a brush and plastic curry comb and pulled some of the dead hair out of her coat. In the process, I found she had a thriving population of lice, so both horses were doused with evil-smelling powder.

During the weekend, I picked up her feet and rasped the overgrown horn. She would follow me if I carried a bucket, so I slipped a rope around her neck and put slight pressure on it as she walked beside me. This caused no trouble, so the next step was to slide a headcollar over her head, and lead her towards the gate. She came confidently, so I opened the gate and we went for a walk down the lane, Jubi's protesting neigh ringing loud behind us.

I saw Geoff in the market on Monday.

'How's the pony?' he asked. 'Been able to catch it yet?'

'She's halter broken,' I replied casually, 'and I've de-loused her and trimmed her feet. I'm going to get her into the stable this week.'

His jaw dropped. 'Don't believe it,' he said. 'I'll never believe it.'

'Jubi did the gentling,' I admitted. 'He's so greedy, he'll do anything for food, and she just copied him. She looks very immature, by the way. Are you sure about her age?'

He insisted she was two years old.

During the autumn and winter, she bloomed, growing and filling out. Perky and full of self-confidence, she accepted every strange thing I did. Believing it best to start young, I put a bit in her mouth and a saddle on her back, and led her about the lanes, teaching her the meaning of 'Walk ON, Trrrrot! Steady Wa-a-a-lk! and Whoa.'

199

My neighbour's seven-year-old daughter Lisa asked if she could sit on her. I explained that Nimbus was too young to be ridden properly, but decided it would do her no harm to have such a light weight on her back for short jaunts. We progressed to taking her out in the woods, led from Jubi, who marched along proudly, head and tail high, his little friend trit-trotting daintily beside him.

At two-and-a-half years old, a pony should cast its middle baby teeth and grow its first grown-up gnashers. Christmas came and went, and Nimbus showed no sign of changing her teeth. Nothing happened in January or February, and one day I opened the pony's mouth and had a proper look at her teeth, then examined her carefully all over. It was quite a shock. Not only was she only eighteen months old, a year younger than we thought, she was also definitely pregnant.

She made such a fuss when I took Jubi out that I decided it would do her less harm to continue to come for very short trips to the woods, in spite of her extreme youth, rather than leave her to gallop about in the field.

We all went for a ride one lovely June evening and, at Lisa's insistence, I let her off the lead rein on the way home. Nimbus broke into a spanking trot, Jubi pounding along behind, and Lisa apparently unable or unwilling to slow down. The two young things arrived back at the stable very pleased with themselves. That night, Nimbus gave birth to a tiny filly foal. I called her 'Serendipity, soon shortened to Dippy, which suited her well. Foaled bright chestnut, she began to change almost immediately to the same pretty dapple grey as her mother.

Nimbus, of course, being a year younger than I thought, had an extra year to grow, and eventually became big and strong enough for me to ride. She was immensely popular with visitors, especially Liz and Louise, who much preferred her to my dear Jubi. She went like a rocket in harness, flying jubilantly up the road, all tossing grey mane and kettle drum hooves. Her daughter, smaller, more delicate, and with flashing, fiery action, is a perfect harness pony, and really seems to enjoy playing with the local children, who take turns riding or leading her.

My little starveling, unhandled, unloved, destined to become expensive steak in a foreign restaurant, turned out instead to be the biggest bargain I have ever struck.

* * *

Breaking Nimbus to harness proved surprisingly easy. I knew nothing about driving horses, and she knew nothing about being driven, so we set out to teach each other. I started with a long piece of string attached either side of the head collar, and tried to persuade her to walk in front of me. Accustomed to being led from the side, she was not sure what was expected of her, and as I dropped back behind her, slowed her pace to try to keep abreast of me. We tried again the next evening, and she suddenly got the idea, marching along the lane, towing me behind her.

At enormous expense, I purchased a set of driving harness, and earnestly studied illustrations in books to work out where the different bits went. The driving pad and belly band were no problem—they felt like a saddle to Nimbus. The crupper around the root of the tail was no new sensation, because I had had to fit one to her saddle when she was very young to stop the rider sliding forward over her non-existent shoulders when they went downhill. She fidgeted at the breeching hanging round her quarters, and when I led her forward, leaped spectacularly into the air, kicking out behind in a graceful capriole. When she had settled, I took up my position behind her again, hoping she would not repeat the performance.

The next step was to put on the breast collar and attach the heavy leather traces which would actually pull the cart. I tied the ends of the traces together with rope, and slid them over my shoulders and around my waist to give her something to pull on.

'Walk on!' I commanded. She jumped forward into a brisk trot, with me pounding along behind. After a few hundred yards, I was puffing mightily.

'Steady, walk!' I called. She trotted gaily on, and I suddenly realised that two bits of string fixed to a headcollar gave me no control at all.

201

'Nimbus!' I called desperately. 'WALK!'

She walked, tossing her head and looking at me over her shoulder. 'That was a joke,' she snorted. 'Laugh!' I was too breathless.

She accepted the heavy blinkered bridle and the reins, and I finally found I had real control over her.

I bought a home-made breaking cart from the local blacksmith, a car axle with pneumatic-tyred wheels, with a bench seat for two built over it and long metal shafts. It was comfortable and free-running, and being low to the ground, was easy to enter and leave and should be difficult to overturn. I hoped.

Louise came to stay one weekend, and helped put Nimbus to the cart for the first time. We showed it to her, and rattled it past her a few times. She was unimpressed. I lined her up in front of it, and Louise picked up the shafts and slid them along her sides. Nimbus felt the constraint, looked over her shoulder, then gazed ahead, sighing deeply.

'Walk on,' I said. She stepped forward, and Louise tugged the cart along by the shafts, keeping it in position. Nimbus ignored it.

'Tomorrow,' declared Louise exultantly, 'we'll put the shafts in the tugs, and fix the traces to the cart.'

'No. We'll do it now,' I said.

We looked on the traces, buckled the breeching straps, and I held my breath, crossed my fingers, and told her to walk on. Nimbus surged on up the lane, really pulling the cart. I walked beside her holding the reins, then stepped nonchalantly into the cart and sat down. The extra weight made no difference.

'Whoa,' I called. She stopped. 'Walk on,' I commanded. She walked. 'Trrrot,' I cried. She trotted, throwing out her front legs and taking great leaps over the ground.

Louise hopped with excitement.

'Let me! Let me!' she begged. I got out of the cart reluctantly, and she took the reins and they set off up the lane. Nimbus walked, trotted, stopped, turned left and right, totally ignored a tractor, and finally pulled us both home.

'I don't believe it,' crowed Louise. 'It isn't possible to

break a pony to driving so quickly.' Nimbus crunched another Polo mint, tossing her head. 'It's easy,' she snorted.

She outgrew the little breaking cart, and I bought a high-backed gig, known soon as the Posh Cart. Perched high up behind Nimbus's bouncing bottom and floating silver mane and tail, I toured the lanes and by-ways, seeing the fields from a different perspective.

One of my friends from work came to tea one Sunday. She had recently undergone major surgery and still looked very frail. I was worried that she might find a jaunt in the Posh Cart too tiring, but it was a lovely spring day, and she insisted she felt quite strong, so we set off. Nimbus was on her very best behaviour, and we trotted through Spaxton and turned onto the old coach road, heading back towards home. The unmade road had its share of ruts and pot-holes, and we walked along it, jolting over the bumps. Primroses, violets and celandines bloomed in the banks. A mist of early bluebells scented the copse as we drove slowly past. The lime trees arching overhead were in pale early leaf and gave welcome shade. Farmer Robbins had planted the fields on both sides of the far end of the road with oilseed rape, which was just coming into eye-aching yellow bloom. Beehives clustered in the gateway, and when we stopped to breathe the heavy scent of the flowers, we heard the loud, steady hum of the busy pollinating bees. My friend, Pippa, relaxed and smiled.

'Just what I needed,' she said, sniffing the heady air.

We reached the end of the coach road, and turned onto the metalled road leading towards home. Nimbus broke into a smart trot. The shafts of the Posh Cart are very long, and the reins are not really quite long enough for comfort. I usually drive with them looped around my middle finger. Pippa noticed this.

'What happens if you drop the reins?' she asked.

'I never drop the reins,' I said, shocked. At that precise moment, Nimbus snatched at the bit and threw her head up, jerking the rein free of my hand. The long leather band whipped down and smacked the pony in the rump. Incensed at being hit when she was doing her best already, she broke into a gallop. Horrified, I had to lean forward over the dash, like a stunt man in a cowboy film, and try to catch the rein as it flipped up with her pumping feet. To my immense relief, it had tangled in her long tail, and I was able to catch the loop, sit back, and ease her back to a controlled trot. Fearfully, I glanced across at Pippa, expecting her to be clinging, whitefaced and fainting, to the side of the vehicle. She smiled happily at me, perfectly relaxed.

'I see,' she said. 'That's what happens.'

I have always regarded Nimbus as a superlative ride-and-drive pony, but she proved recently that she can also rise to an occasion. A little girl living opposite was elected Queen of the Village Carnival, and said she would like to ride in the carnival procession in the Posh Cart. Nimbus is very steady with ordinary traffic, but is not perfect, and is still very young. She sometimes shies at cattle standing in gateways, or plastic left on the road, and I had no idea how she would react to the carnival noise.

Her Majesty-elect was insistent, so I agreed, with inner feelings of trepidation. After a week of cold winds and squally showers, the Great Day dawned bright and hot. I polished the harness with black boot polish and rubbed at the brass buckles and browband until they glittered. Nimbus was brought in from the paddock, and Lisa helped groom her until her dappled body gleamed in the sun. I dunked her long tail in a bucket of warm water heavily laced with washing-up liquid, then washed her white legs in the same solution, brushing the mud from her feathered heels. Carefully hosing all the suds away, we dried her legs on an old towel, and swung her tail to throw off the water.

Then I dressed her in the polished harness, and finally oiled her black hooves. The cart had been taken to the stables at the top of the lane to be decorated, and in good time we set off to collect it. Gold lamé had been sellotaped to the back and sides, and a red velvet cloak covered the seat. An arch was fixed over it, covered with crinkled gold material and decorated with fresh flowers and leaves. The effect was delightful, and Nimbus, her mane and tail twin silver waterfalls, completed the picture.

She was very excited, and I let her trot part of the two

miles to the village, hoping the decorations were firmly fixed. We approached the car park rendezvous through the new housing estate on the edge of the village, known disparagingly to the 'real' villagers as Legoland. Some of the carnival floats were parked on the road, tractor engines panting and ear-splitting pop music pounding from loud-speakers. I led Nimbus past them, and she picked up her feet and minced along. At the car park, we had half an hour to wait, so I unharnessed her and led her back up the road to have another look at the floats. The noise hurt my ears, and must have been painful to her more sensitive hearing. Crowds of people had appeared with prams, pushchairs, small children, balloons, and paper flags. She regarded them all with equal disdain.

Returning to the car park, I asked a member of the brass band if he would bang the big drum to see how she reacted. He thumped it heavily, and she just flicked her ears at him with a pained do-you-have-to? expression. Other bands-men joined in, and standing around her, serenaded her with an enthusiastic cacophony of trumpet, kettle drum and glockenspiel. She sighed and looked bored. A by-stander laughed and asked if we were training her to be a police horse.

The procession organiser arrived and began to organise. Nimbus was put to the cart again, and the queen and her attendant hoisted up. The procession was led by the village fire engine, followed by the band, followed by the queen in her chariot. The incredibly noisy floats were immediately behind us. The organiser waved us on, and the fire engine set off.

'BOONG, BOONG, BOONG,' began the big drum.

'RATterterTATterterTAT,' snapped the kettle drums.

'RAH, RAH, RAH,' brayed the trumpets, and the glockenspiel counterpoint tinkletankled loudly.

A few feet behind this outburst, close enough to hear that the middle man in the back row had squeaky shoes, Nim-bus walked sedately, head high, and only her wildly semaphoring ears betrayed her inner turmoil. I walked beside her, bursting with pride, and speaking comfortingly close to her ear.

'Clever girl!' I told her. 'Very, very good pony!'

Several times the fire engine stopped and the band marked time to allow the slow floats to catch up. Each time, Nimbus stood stock-still until I shouted over the noise for her to walk on, then threw herself into the collar and pulled with a will.

It took nearly half an hour to parade through all the village streets, and the only thing the pony found upsetting was the clapping as we passed by. She bounced when the clapping was loud, gently jogging the little queen in her seat. We turned up the side road and back to the car park. The firemen pulled the shutters down over the sides of their engine, the band fell blissfully silent, and the lads clambered into their waiting coach. The queen and her attendant were lifted down from the cart and whisked off to present the prizes for the best float and fancy dress.

Nimbus erupted. Trotting rapidly on the spot as if the ground were red-hot, she trod on my foot and wrenched off one of my shoes. I retrieved it from under the cart, hopping clumsily, then skipped briskly up into the cart, sat down, and pointed her head towards home. We left a trail of petals, ruined flowers and leaves as she cantered along the lane, the tumult dying behind us.

Back in the field, she snatched a mouthful of grass, selected a bare, muddy patch and, sinking down, blissfully rubbed her back and shoulders on the red earth. She stood up, mud on her mane and a bramble tangled in her tail and, whinnying shrilly, raced down the field, bucking and kicking, to join Jubi and Dippy at the far end.

'Carnivals?' she snorted derisively. 'You can keep 'em.'

18

I often see deer in the forest when I ride or walk there
—generally red deer, but I get an occasional glimpse of a
shy roe. Roe deer are small, about the size of a large dog,
and live in pairs or small family groups. They are browsers,
eating the leaves of trees and shrubs, and, in small number,
do little damage. In many parts of England, they have
established themselves successfully in the little woods and
copses of cultivated land. Many farmers shoot them, some
indiscriminately, but most with a regard for conservation.
There is a ready market for venison, and some people like
the little pointy horns mounted on a wall plaque as an
ornament.

Red deer need much more space. They are bigger animals
and move around in larger groups of up to a dozen. Besides
eating trees and bushes, they also graze, and can cause
severe damage to farmed crops. They eat young green corn
down to the ground, and in a field of kale or turnips, move
along the rows biting the heart out of each plant, leaving
ruin behind them. Having therefore been chased off cultivated land, they have taken refuge in the few remaining
wilder parts, including the Quantock Hills.

Alas, there they are hunted with hounds, and frequently
disturbed by the packs of Foxhounds which also hunt
the hills. The result is that when they encounter people
or ridden horses, they flee. The usual view of them,
after the first startled upfling of the head, is of a succession of white rumps and flag tails disappearing in the
trees.

My horse, Jubi, finds deer very exciting. Being a herd
animal, the behaviour of others around him affects him
strongly. When the deer run, he wants to run, too, but is
not sure where.

One beautiful early spring day, I was riding in the forest quite early in the morning. Rain had fallen overnight, but the clouds were blowing away and gave an occasional glimpse of the sun. The Forestry people had been busy in Great Wood, and felled tree trunks lay in disarray like giant spilled matchsticks. Their unfamiliar appearance upset Jubi, who reckons that trees should stand upright, not loll about naked on the ground. He picked his way delicately along the path, feigning terror at the sight. The dogs followed close behind him; there were no animals to chase in all that shattered habitat.

We climbed steadily upwards and around the next corner reached the beginning of a long slope up to the top of the forest, where we usually had a brisk canter. Jubi began to fidget and prance. With a sudden clap of wings, a pigeon exploded out of the branches above us. It was just the excuse the horse needed, and with a buck and a squeal he grabbed the bit and took off at a gallop. Throwing what little decorum I possess to the wind singing in my ears, I crouched over his shoulders like a jockey and shrieked, 'GO, man, GO!'

He went.

His maternal grandfather won both the English Derby and the Irish Curragh, one of only three horses ever to achieve this. Occasionally I am reminded that the blood of that noble stallion courses through Jubi's veins. Neck outstretched, ears flattened against his head, he surged up the hill, his breath pumping in rhythm with the heart-lifting four-beat tattoo of his hooves.

DIDdleydum, DIDdleydum, DIDdleydum, DIDdleydum. With each stride, he flung his shoulders forward, grabbed the ground with his hooves, then swung his haunches and kicked the track contemptuously behind him. Long before we reached the hill crest, he ran out of breath and began to slow down. I urged him on for a few more strides to remind him who made the decisions, then slowed him to a head-tossing walk.

'Could have reached the top if you hadn't stopped me,' his snort seemed to say.

'Don't kid yourself, Chubbychops.' I patted his steaming

neck. 'With your great belly full of wet grass, it's a wonder you can gallop at all!'

I glanced behind me. The dogs were toiling along half-way up the hill, their tongues hanging out like pink dish-rags. We walked on gently to give them time to catch up, and turned on to the track along the top of Cockercoombe. On our right, great rhododendrons climbed the slope, and to the left, the ground fell away steeply to the track and stream far below.

After a late start, spring had finally arrived in the forest. Even the serried ranks of sombre conifers were trans-formed. The larches, which drop their old needles every autumn, were misted all over with iridescent new growth. The tip of every twig of every pine and spruce bore tufts of soft, bright new needles. The sun, suddenly shining along the length of the coombe, lit a million pale green candles.

Jubi jolted to a stop, jerking me out of my poetic reverie.

I peered along the track ahead of us. 'Nothing there,' I said.

He goggled down the slope, and I felt his back hunch up as he tensed his muscles ready to flee. Looking between his pointing ears, I saw a group of seven red deer hinds less than fifteen yards away, peacefully eating the young spring growth. They were aware of our presence. Their soft eyes were on us, and their long hare-like ears constantly flicked in our direction. Their scent wafted up, like heifers in a farmyard, but stronger and gamier.

I smoothed Jubi's mane. 'No need to fuss. Just stand quietly.' Their attention suddenly switched to the corner behind us, and I heard the panting of the dogs. Quietly but insistently I called to them. 'Ceilidh! Come here and Sit.'

Looking surprised, he came and sat beside Jubi. Tania followed.

The poodle, Louis, had seen the deer, and stood quiver-ing, glancing at the lurcher for a lead in the chase. Sud-denly, Ceilidh saw them too, and half rose, the hackles on his neck lifting.

'SIT!' I whispered fiercely. He sat, and Louis subsided beside him, disappointed and cross. The deer recom-menced feeding, still keeping us in view, their jaws chomping at the leaves. Jubi stretched his neck, asking politely, and I let the reins run through my fingers. He dropped his head and nibbled at the wiry grass.

Gently, almost casually, the deer moved down the slope away from us. With a sigh of content, I gathered up the reins and we continued on our way. The wetter parts of the track had bright orange puddles on the dark pink ground. The dogs stopped and drank the murky, iron-rich water, then rolled in the pink mud. Jubi drank from the next puddle, but when he began to paw the ground I hastily pushed him on. There is always fresh water in the stable and the paddock, but all the horses like forest puddle water. I have no objection to them drinking it, but object to them rolling in it, especially when I happen to be in the saddle.

A sudden loud crashing on the slope above startled us both. A solitary stag skittered off through the trees, the dogs storming after him in full-throated pursuit. When they are close behind their quarry, they run mute, conserving energy for the chase. If they are hopelessly outdistanced, they give vent to their frustration with furious yells. Judging by the noise, they would soon be back. I calmed my mettlesome steed, who was disturbed by all this excitement.

'No rushing about after a drink,' I told him, 'or you'll get colic.'

As we turned the next corner, the dogs reappeared from the undergrowth and fell in behind us, panting and satisfied. Rain began to fall, washing the mud off the dogs' backs. It hissed quietly through the fir trees, bringing out their strong resinous scent. Large drops fell on my head and trickled down my neck. Far in front of us, a rainbow arched through the clouds.

As we neared home, we met my neighbour hurriedly scrambling into his car. He gazed at us, wet, bedraggled and tired.

'Shocking day,' he declared.

'Oh, no,' I contradicted. 'It's been a beautiful morning.'

* * *

Keeping horses in the summertime is easy and pleasant. They spend the time at pasture, gently exercising themselves, feeding on the grass under their feet, and needing little attention. I need only look at them night and morning, check that the water barrel is topped up, and they are there to ride in the evenings if I wish.

Spring and autumn are quite easy. I put them in the paddock before I go to work in the morning, and bring them into the stable when I get home. I can ride in the evenings until the clocks go back, and the stables need only minimal attention to keep them comfortable and hygienic—just a daily topping up with straw and a proper clean-out at weekends. I enjoy the nightly feeding routine, and the horses obviously like the comfort of their stables when the weather is bad.

About three or four months in winter are hard work, with little reward. It is barely light when I go to work, and dark again long before I return home. A horse-orientated neighbour, who no longer has horses of her own, turns them out for a time each day if the weather is suitable, and brings them in at teatime. While they are out she tidies their beds, and she rides them when she likes, and when she has time. In the evening, I give them hay, and their ration of sugar-beet, barley, maize, linseed, and whatever else is on their menu. It always seems to be raining.

I enjoy looking after them—brushing some of the mud out of the ponies' shaggy coats and making sure Jubi's rugs are dry and comfortable. When the weather is really bad, they might have to stay in the stable all day, sometimes two or even three consecutive days. They are so fat and well protected with hair and New Zealand rugs that rain and snow will not harm them, but they can do great damage to their grazing paddocks when the ground is soft and wet, or frozen hard. Then the grass is slow to grow in the spring, and the grazing season is delayed. During winter weekends, when they have been confined for long periods, I exercise them whatever the weather.

Just before Christmas one year, we had had a succession of cold days of wind and snow, and the horses had not been out of the stable on Wednesday, Thursday or Friday.

Saturday dawned crisp, dry and cold. The field was wet and half-frozen. I shuddered at the thought of the damage twelve iron-shod hooves would do if suddenly liberated after their long confinement.

'There's no help for it,' I told the dogs, 'we'll have to go walkies in the woods.'

Their yells and shrieks of glee stirred the already wildly excited ponies to a frenzy. With some difficulty, I saddled Nimbus and put a leading rein on her daughter, Dippy. Followed by the dogs, we walked, then trotted up the long drive and into the forest. Nimbus saw tigers behind every tree, and shied away from every shadow. Dippy did not wish to soil her dainty hooves, and tried to skid round every puddle and patch of mud, with wrenching effects on my arms. The sun glittered on the frozen snow, a cold wind dried our sweat, and their hooves clattered loudly on the stony tracks. It was impossible to go slowly, they were too full of energy, and by the time we returned home, the dogs were panting and exhausted. The ponies, calmer after their excursion, munched their hay contentedly, but my big horse, Jubi, almost hysterical with suppressed energy, was trying to leap out over the stable door. I knew the dogs could never keep up with him in their tired state, but was equally sure they would howl, shriek and generally object if I left them in the house.

Accordingly, I bundled them into the car, where they collapsed in a heap, and were quite happy to be left. They were not too wet, and had a beanbag and several blankets to burrow into. The sky had clouded over, the temperature had dropped, and I did not intend to be long.

With a few strong words, I persuaded Jubi to stand still long enough to put on his saddle, then, making sure my crash hat was securely buckled, I swung creakingly into the saddle and headed for the woods again. He leaped, pranced, skipped, neighed, shied, slithered on the ice, neighed, bucked, reared, and neighed. After half an hour, we were both very warm. I found a green track where the going was not too hard, and after an initial eruption, kept him at a steady canter all the way to the top, which effectively took the tickle out of his toes.

It began to snow, and I thought longingly of fires and armchairs and cups of tea. Jubi was very fat and unfit, and I decided that a final brisk walk home would be enough. The snow fell in large, cold, melting flakes, and we turned onto a narrow, little-used trail which was a short cut home. It was a mistake. Young spruce and tall rhododendrons grew on either side, their branches, weighed down with snow, almost meeting across the middle of the path. As we brushed past, each branch bowed politely, depositing its icy burden on my lap, into my boots, and down my neck. In a few minutes I was soaked and shivering. Jubi, also very wet, was making his discontent obvious.

We reached the wider track leading past the farm and out of the forest. On our left, mature trees grew dense and dark. On the other side, one of the many forest streams, rimmed with ice, sang and gurgled, the brilliant sparkles on the banks of snow beyond it dappled with patches of violet shadow. The road was partly flooded and Jubi splashed mud and melting snow as he began to trot, anxious to get back to his stable and hay.

'Can't get any wetter,' I told him. 'You might as well trot on a bit.'

As I said it, I had a confused impression of tree trunks rushing past, and the world rapidly rotated. When it stopped, I found Jubi was facing back the way we had come, eyes popping, ears back, feet skittering on the snow. Behind us, the deer which had caused the excitement melted into the trees. I turned him round, and felt the saddle slip under me. Unthinking, I lifted one knee, stuck my leg forward, and felt under the saddle flap for the girth buckle, intending to tighten it. At this moment a second deer, which I should have anticipated, poked its head out of the wood, barely ten yards ahead.

Trees, tossing black mane, mud-splattered shoulder and leg, sliding hoof, stones and snow, all slid past my face in apparent slow motion. My back was against the far bank of the stream, my legs in the air, and my hips pressed painfully on the rim of the ice. My body acted as a dam and the water built up on one side, then overflowed into my lap, soaking into my clothes. It was paralysingly cold. I tried to

213

move, and felt the bitter stream flow behind me between my shoulders.

Jubi stood on the path above me, gazing down in astonishment. I still clutched the reins, and he had braced himself to stop his front hooves sliding down into the stream with me. It is said horses have little intelligence and cannot have a sense of humour, but he definitely laughed. I dropped the reins, hoping he would not immediately go home without me, and with an enormous effort, turned over onto my knees and crawled out. Jubi snorted warmly into the back of my neck, tossed his head, and neighed earshatteringly. With another enormous effort, I heaved myself into the saddle, remembering to tighten the girths first.

Squish-squelch, squish-squelch, we set off home. In the depths of my frozen, teeth-chattering misery, it suddenly struck me how weird I must look, and I laughed so much I nearly fell off. Almost hysterical, I pushed Jubi into a trot, and we reached home in record time, fortunately without meeting anyone. I led him into his stable, removed the soaked saddle and bridle, and rubbed him down with handfuls of dry straw. By the time he was dry and clean, I felt much warmer. I put on his stable rug, gave him some more hay, and took the dripping tack into the house.

Beginning to shiver uncontrollably, I retired to the bathroom and peeled off my saturated clothes, dropping them numbly onto the floor. My skin was wrinkled, clammy and a pale shade of blue. Rubbing with a towel had little effect, so I stood under the shower and gradually increased the temperature from tepid to scalding. It took several minutes for my skin to regain a fairly normal appearance, then I pulled some fresh clothes out of the airing cupboard, dressed, and trotted to the kitchen to put the kettle on. The sitting-room fire needed a log to cheer it up, and I pushed my chair closer to the heat. The kettle boiled, and I carried a loaded tray into the peaceful and curiously empty room. Empty! Good Heavens! I had left the dogs in the car!

Hastily depositing the tray on the television, I hurried down the garden path, ruining my new slippers, and let them out. They ran ahead of me into the house, and crowded round the fire, shivering ostentatiously. Their expressions were eloquent.

'Left us in the car while she sat in here in the warm, drinking hot brown stuff and eating biscuits.' They glared at me. 'Eating biscuits,' they repeated.

Taking the hint, I offered them a biscuit each. Silently, each dog took a biscuit, and dropped it on the carpet. They all looked at me reproachfully.

'I got wet, too,' I assured them, 'and I haven't—please eat your biscuits. I'm sorry if I forgot you.'

Grudgingly, Ceilidh picked up his custard cream and ate it messily. Tania crunched her ginger biscuit and hoovered up Ceilidh's crumbs. Louis held his Digestive in his paws like a bone and gnawed it. Sighing, they all settled down to sleep, and I poured myself another cup of tea.

'It's fun, isn't it?' I said. 'Exercising horses?'

19

The postman hunts, and the baker, and the man who drives the grocery van. Local people follow the hounds on foot, on horses, in Land-Rovers, and on scramble bikes. Many farmers and their wives regard the summer as a dull interval between hunting seasons; I find their obsession totally incomprehensible and they are equally nonplussed by my abhorrence of their activities. At least three days a week, staghounds or foxhounds hunt the forest behind the village where I live.

On Saturdays, I try to go out early and get home by eleven to avoid meeting the hunt. Sometimes we are delayed, and I watch Jubi's ears as we trot along the paths. If they flick sideways or back towards me, I can relax. If they suddenly point forwards, and his muscles tense under the saddle, I know he has heard hounds or the shrieks of the followers. Such sounds, or the sight of horses galloping about or hounds bustling through the undergrowth, cause him to take leave of his senses.

He does handstands, and performs impossible dance steps. If we see or hear anything, it is safer to go straight home. But sometimes we come upon them unawares. Riding in the forest one bright, quiet October evening, with the dogs trotting along behind me, we came across a group of riders and several hounds waiting soundlessly in a clearing. Before Jubi had realised they were there, there was a sudden flurry of activity, and with a crash of hound voices they thundered off into the trees. It took several minutes to collect Jubi's scattered wits, and I realised, to my intense dismay, that Tania and Louis were missing.

Finding it impossible to search for them and control my wild-eyed steed as well, I decided to take him home. It was not very far, and I found Tania sitting waiting for me on the lawn.

I shut the two dogs in the house, put Jubi's sweat rug over his back, and gave him a net of hay to distract him. Followed by protesting wails from Ceilidh, I returned to the forest, clutching a torch. The dogs heard me depart, and were furious. Didn't I realise, they demanded, that it was Feeding Time? They were hungry. And they wanted to come with me.

By the time I reached the place where Louis had disappeared, it was getting dark. For an hour I searched, in increasing despair. In spite of the torch, I became entangled in brambles, tripped over fallen branches and tree stumps, and fell headlong down a steep bank. It was obviously dangerous, and doing little good to carry on looking there, so, hoping against hope he might have returned, I went back to apologise to Ceilidh and Tania, and give them their belated supper.

Louis had not appeared. I telephoned the staghound kennels and spoke to the kennel-huntsman.

'Was he a funny little black dog?' he asked. 'Oh, yes, I saw him. Tagged on behind the pack and hunted with us all through Ramscombe and up to Dead Woman's Ditch.'

'Then where did you go?' I asked anxiously.

'We boxed the hounds and came back. I don't know where your dog went.'

Dead Woman's Ditch was miles away, the other side of a tract of forestry land and a stretch of ploughed farm land. I got out a pile of ironing, a job I hate, and attacked it ferociously, my tears sizzling on the hot iron. At eleven o'clock, the heavy velvet curtains stirred. I looked up, expecting to see one of the cats coming in through the window. Louis appeared, jumping down on to the window seat, then to the floor.

'Hello,' he said offhandedly. 'Phew! I'm jolly tired.'

He sat down, picked some mud from between his toes and spat it out. He had a sudden thought, and went to the door.

'What about dinner?' he asked. 'Is there anything to eat?'

He followed me out to the kitchen, and had a long drink

while I cut up some meat and mixed in the biscuit, then he ate hungrily. Suddenly very tired, I had a shower and went to bed, leaving all the dogs lying together by the fire. Hardly had I turned the light out, when all three decided to desert the fire and join me.

They crashed and scrambled up the stairs, and Tania heaved herself onto her old chair on the landing. Ceilidh thudded onto his bed beside mine, and Louis rattled across the bare wooden floor, his nails clicking loudly, and made a half-hearted effort to jump up on the bed. With a grunt, he fell, scrambled up, and tried again. I sat and groped down beside the bed, slid a hand under his chest and lifted him up. He staggered to his usual place at the bottom of the bed, snuggled between my feet, and sighed deeply and contentedly.

We saw hounds a few times during the winter, but Louis did not seem to be interested, and I usually made my way rapidly homewards. In early summer, right at the end of the hunting season, history repeated itself. Walking gently along a mossy path, the dogs padding behind, we came out into the sunshine of an open ride, and found a group of riders and many hounds. Jubi erupted, Tania fled homewards, and Ceilidh sat down to await developments. Louis wandered off towards the hounds. I called him, and he glanced back at me impatiently but did not stop.

Jubi plunged under the trees, almost decapitating me on a low branch. I slid off, and pulled the reins over his head, and turned to look for Louis. At that moment, a blast on the horn and a sudden bellowing of hound voices brought all the riders to attention, and they galloped off down the ride. Wrestling with my frantic horse, I thought I heard a thin, desperate scream in the clamour. The last rider disappeared, and Jubi kept still for a moment, listening intently. Ceilidh stood up and yawned. Louis was—where was Louis? With a lurch of the heart, I remembered that scream, dropped Jubi's reins and ran to the middle of the ride.

Louis lay trampled in the mud, his mouth open, his tongue blue. He gasped his last breath as I picked him up. The shocking suddenness was shattering. Cradling him in my arms, I walked home unseeing, sobbing my protests to the indifferent trees. Jubi and Ceilidh followed unbidden.

Savagely, I dug a grave in the rose bed. I used to despise people who hunted down deer and killed them for fun. From then on, I hated them, too.

*　　*　　*

During his five short years, Louis was quite convinced he was top dog. Outside the house, he recognised Ceilidh's superior size and experience, but indoors, he regarded himself as boss. Although he rarely sat on my lap, he objected strongly to other animals doing so, and forcibly ejected cats when he found them sitting on me. Whenever Ceilidh approached me, Louis attacked him with great noise and ferocity, hanging on to the mane of long hair on the lurcher's shoulders. The bigger dog was remarkably tolerant, usually ignoring his small tormentor, occasionally snarling horrendously, but never hurting him. I always took Ceilidh's part, holding the hysterically furious Poodle until Ceilidh had climbed onto my lap or settled on the settee beside me, or laboriously clambered up on my bed in the morning. Once he was settled, they ignored each other and peace was restored.

After Louis was killed, Ceilidh no longer had to compete against him, and he suddenly and visibly aged. He had never shown the affection for Louis that he had for Oscar, but obviously missed him sadly. Tania missed him, too. As I had feared, Ceilidh developed severe arthritic changes in his joints as he grew older, and his speed and mobility decreased. Louis tormented Tania into chasing him, and the Greyhound became so excited by the chase I sometimes feared for Louis' life, but he was far too speedy and agile to be in danger.

She only came in season at long intervals, and it had happened twice in Louis' short lifetime. Ceilidh took little notice, except to discourage fraternising with other dogs, but Louis always knew before anyone else, and appointed himself her shadow and personal attendant. As she became sexually receptive towards the end of her season, he

219

developed a one-track mind, trying to mate her hind leg as she walked along, squeaking and whimpering with frustration day and night. I had had to put her in kennels for the last week or so. Both dogs mourned during this time, sleeping in Tania's chair at night and quarrelling over her blankets. When she returned from purdah, a brief investigation showed she was no longer interesting and everything settled back to normal.

While Louis was with us, taking the three dogs out was fairly noisy. If they followed the horses, they told the whole neighbourhood about it. When we went anywhere in the car, and I let them out for exercise, they fell out in a heap, yelling with excitement. Louis always seized Ceilidh's tail and swung on it, Ceilidh always objected vociferously, and Tania snapped at the air over Louis' back and barked hysterically.

Without Louis, their life became quieter and duller. For a time, they continued to follow Jubi to the woods, but without a strong competitive urge to push him along, Ceilidh lagged behind and was easily tired. When I let them out of the car, they stretched, yawned, shook themselves, and waited for me to tell them which way to go. At home, they behaved like an old married couple. They shared their days companionably, sometimes quarrelling briefly, rarely getting excited. When Tania came in season, he was mildly interested. She snapped at him—'Go away! I've got a headache!' He shrugged his shoulders and left her alone. I think Ceilidh enjoyed the lack of competition, and I remained poodle-less for nearly two years. Then one day, the friend who had operated on Tania's leg telephoned.

'Do you want another Poodle?' she asked.

'No!' I said firmly. 'Thank you, but Ceilidh likes being the only dog, with no Poodle to boss him about.'

There was a short silence, then a sigh.

'Oh dear! You were my only hope. He's quite old and not very pretty, so nobody else will want him. All right, I'll put him to sleep.'

'Wait,' I cried. 'I'll see how Ceilidh reacts, and whether they get on with each other, but he's getting old, and I don't want him upset or worried.'

We went to the kennels to fetch the Poodle. His previous owners, deeply disappointed in him, had never really liked him much. On their retirement, they had decided he would inconvenience their future life-style, and took the opportunity to be rid of him.

He was small, stout and self-contained. His sparse, off-white fur gave glimpses of mottled pink and grey skin. He had lost several teeth, and the remaining top fangs gave him a faintly Draculean expression. His name was entirely inappropriate, and he ignored it anyway, so I called him Diddy, to which he soon learned to answer. At times, he was also called Smelly, Small Scruff and—when I was feeling unkind—Baldy. He was neither pleased nor sorry to come with us. He had his own cushion, and a plastic shopping bag with collar and lead, hairbrush, and a shrunken, felted knitted coat. He sat on the seat beside me on his cushion. Ceilidh and Tania sniffed him with little interest.

He took no notice of them. When we arrived home, he investigated every room, downstairs and upstairs. He pounced on the first two cats he found, but after receiving indignant swipes across his face, left the rest of them alone. He explored the garden and the stables, and was about to roll in the effluent from the manure heap but I caught him just in time. We all walked across the pony paddock at the end of the garden. He trotted busily along the path to the gate at the far end, ducked underneath it, and marched off up the lane. Racing after him, I turned him round, and he obediently followed me home.

Over the next two or three weeks, I wondered if I had been wrong to adopt him. He was clean in the house, ate everything I gave him, with evident relish, and enjoyed walking in the woods and on the beach, but he seemed a sad little dog. If I went out, he never seemed particularly pleased to see me when I returned. He rarely barked or became excited. If I went towards him suddenly, he flinched away, and was obviously worried when I scolded Tania for foraging in the kitchen rubbish bin. My cries of 'Bad dog!' sent him scuttling into a corner, and it was impossible to convince him I was not cross with him.

His skimpy coat was dry and scruffy and he had a strange mousy smell, but I bathed him only when he waded through deep, malodorous mud in the woods or rolled on something stinking he found in a field. He accepted the showering and drying stoically. Ceilidh and Tania never minded being bathed or getting wet in the rain, because they loved to be dried. They enjoyed being wrapped and rubbed with an old towel, and the expression of sensuous delight on their faces when I switched on the hair-dryer was almost ludicrous. Diddy just tolerated the attention. He hated to be groomed, until I threw away his spiteful hard brush, and substituted a soft clothes brush.

He took himself off down the lane at every opportunity and was twice picked up over a mile away. I wired in the whole garden and mended the fence to make it poodle-proof. I could no longer open the back door in the mornings and let dogs out to do what dogs have to do in the morning. Instead, I took everybody for a walk down the lane, along the road, and back across the paddock, watching Diddy all the time.

One morning, we turned into the road, and a car came round the corner behind us, much too fast and too close to the side of the hedge. For one horror-struck moment, I thought Diddy had been killed, but the rear tyre had trapped his leg and badly bruised it. He screamed piteously, and I picked him up, trying to console him and rage at the driver at the same time. I carried him home, murmuring inanities about poor, brave little poodles, and he suddenly realised I really cared. He limped for a week, but was a different, far happier dog. He found that if he approached people in a friendly way, they stroked him and talked to him. He boldly went up to the neighbour's children. They picked him up and cuddled him, and he was delighted. Visitors to the house were sat on and beamed at and followed about. He loved the whole world and evidently thought the whole world loved him.

This increase in self-confidence made him more aggress-ive. He had to be fed separately in the dining-room, or he would leave his own meal to growl at the other two dogs, spitting biscuit all over the floor. He sat on my lap or close beside me, and began growling at Ceilidh when he approached, but the lurcher good-naturedly ignored him, sometimes almost squashing the Poodle as he climbed onto my lap himself. In fact, both Ceilidh and Tania ignored him most of the time and I was disappointed that they had apparently not accepted him.

Our favourite beach for walking dogs was reached by driving along a rutted track through a farmyard, up a steep hill and down the other side. At the bottom of the slope, we had to park the car, then toil up another hill, down the other side across a field, sharp right along the top of the cliff, then scramble down a path to the shingle below. Crossing the pebbles, we reached the wide, sandy beach, interspersed with tumbled rocks and small secret pools. A few people went there at weekends, but, not surprisingly, it was generally deserted.

We went there one evening when Diddy had recovered from his accident and was walking comfortably again. Picking my way across the shingle, I was concentrating on keeping my feet and did not look up until I landed safely on the sand. Gazing around, I saw a solitary figure a hundred yards away with a dog on a lead. To my intense dismay, I recognised Mrs McCloud, and her pit bull terrier. The bitch had been rescued from a gang in the Midlands, who arranged matches between the fighting dogs. When her wounds had healed, she had been adopted by Major McCloud and his wife, and they brought her with them when they retired to Somerset. Generations of careful breeding, coupled with savage early training, had instilled into the bull terrier the determination to kill every living thing she encountered, or die herself in the attempt.

She was said to be safe with adult humans, and the McClouds claimed she was affectionate, but could not be trusted with any other creature—dogs, cats, farm live-stock, even the McClouds' young grandchildren. Diddy, bursting with new-found confidence, was trotting across the sand to introduce himself, straight into the waiting jaws. It was like one of those awful dreams where you try to run, and your feet stick to the ground. The wet sand sucked at my shoes as I tried desperately to catch him up, the horrible choking snarls of the bull terrier drowning Mrs McCloud's agitated cries.

Suddenly, Ceilidh shot past me, barking in a strange, high-pitched voice. Reaching the killer just before Diddy, he lunged and darted at the tethered dog, snapping, and jumping back out of reach. Apoplectic with rage, the bitch dragged her owner along the sand, but Ceilidh kept himself just out of danger, and the contest gave me time to reach Diddy and snatch him up.

'Leave, Ceilidh!' I gasped, and he stood back, panting and wagging his tail.

After mutual apologies and protestations that all was well, Mrs McCloud and I walked off in opposite directions. I was not sure whether Ceilidh had deliberately rescued Diddy, or whether, as top dog of my group, he had responded angrily to the bull terrier's threats. When I thought we were a safe distance apart, I put Diddy down on the sand. He trotted ahead of me for a few yards, then I saw a thought cross his mind.

'Never asked her name,' he said, did a rapid U-turn and began to run back the way we had come. Panting after him, I saw that Mrs McCloud had let her bitch off the lead, and she was running free.

Once again, Ceilidh ran past me, overtook Diddy, and stopped just in front of him to sniff a rock with great concentration. Diddy also stopped, sniffed, decided there was nothing interesting, and was about to continue on his way when I flung myself on him and held him down while I fished a length of string out of my pocket for a lead.

Breathless, heart banging uncomfortably, I led him back to where Tania waited for us, reflecting that all this violent exercise was not good for my constitution. Ceilidh lolloped along beside me.

'You're a very clever lurcher,' I assured him, 'rescuing Diddy like that.'

He swished his tail, pleased with my approving tone.

'Somebody's got to look after the silly ass,' he seemed to say. 'He's family, isn't he?'